Shared Society or Benign Apartheid?

Also by John Nagle

MULTICULTURALISM'S DOUBLE BIND

Also by Mary-Alice C. Clancy

PEACE WITHOUT CONSENSUS

Shared Society or Benign Apartheid?

Understanding Peace-Building in Divided Societies

John Nagle
*Visiting Research Fellow, EXCEPS, University of Exeter, UK,
and Lecturer, University of East London*

and

Mary-Alice C. Clancy
Research Fellow, EXCEPS, University of Exeter, UK

First published 2010 by
PALGRAVE MACMILLAN

Palgrave Macmillan in the UK is an imprint of Macmillan Publishers Limited, registered in England, company number 785998, of Houndmills, Basingstoke, Hampshire RG21 6XS.

Palgrave Macmillan in the US is a division of St Martin's Press LLC, 175 Fifth Avenue, New York, NY 10010.

Palgrave Macmillan is the global academic imprint of the above companies and has companies and representatives throughout the world.

Palgrave® and Macmillan® are registered trademarks in the United States, the United Kingdom, Europe and other countries.

ISBN: 978–0–230–24004–9 hardback

This book is printed on paper suitable for recycling and made from fully managed and sustained forest sources. Logging, pulping and manufacturing processes are expected to conform to the environmental regulations of the country of origin.

A catalogue record for this book is available from the British Library.

Library of Congress Cataloging-in-Publication Data

Nagle, John, 1971–
    Shared society or benign apartheid? : understanding peace-building in divided societies / John Nagle, Mary-Alice C. Clancy.
        p. cm.
    ISBN 978–0–230–24004–9 (hardback)
      1. Peace-building. 2. Conflict management. 3. Ethnic conflict – Political aspects. I. Clancy, Mary-Alice C. II. Title.

JZ5538.N34 2010
303.6'6—dc22   2010027545

10   9   8   7   6   5   4   3   2   1
19   18   17   16   15   14   13   12   11   10

Printed and bound in Great Britain by
CPI Antony Rowe, Chippenham and Eastbourne

Contents

Tables and Figures

Tables

Figures

Abbreviations

AV	Alternative Vote
BBC	British Broadcasting Corporation
BNP	British National Party
CHLR	Campaign for Homosexual Law Reform
CND	Campaign for Nuclear Disarmament
CPA	Coalition Provisional Authority
CRM	Civil Rights Movement
DUP	Democratic Unionist Party
ECHR	European Court of Human Rights
EU	European Union
FDI	Foreign Direct Investment
G7	Group of 7
GAA	Gaelic Athletic Association
GFA	Good Friday Agreement
IFI	International Fund for Ireland
ILO	International Labour Organization
IRA	Irish Republican Army
LGBT	Lesbian Gay Bisexual Transgender
MLA	Members of the Legislative Assembly
MP	Member of Parliament
NATO	North Atlantic Treaty Organization
NICITU	Northern Ireland Committee for the Irish Congress of Trade Unions
NIGRA	Northern Ireland Gay Rights Association
NIO	Northern Ireland Office
NIVTA	Northern Ireland Victims of Terrorism Association
OAS	Organization of American States
OFMDFM	Office of the First Minister and Deputy First Minister
OSCE	Organization for Security and Co-operation in Europe
PFI	Private Finance Initiative
PPP	Public-Private Partnership
PSNI	Police Service of Northern Ireland
PUP	Progressive Unionist Party
RRI	Reinvestment and Reform Initiative
SDLP	Social Democratic Labour Party

SIB	Strategic Investment Board
STP	Stop the Parade Coalition
STV	Single Transferable Vote
UDA	Ulster Defence Association
UFF	Ulster Freedom Fighters
UK	United Kingdom
UN	United Nations
UNESCO	United Nations Educational Scientific and Cultural Organization
US	United States
UUP	Ulster Unionist Party
UVF	Ulster Volunteer Force
TNC	Transnational Corporation
WTO	World Trade Organization

Acknowledgements

John Nagle would like to acknowledge that some of the research for this book was conducted at the Institute of Irish Studies, Queen's University of Belfast, as part of an ESRC funded (RES-148–25–0054) project entitled 'Imagining Belfast'. He thanks Dominic Bryan and Liam Kelly at the Institute for their valuable assistance. We acknowledge Audra Mitchell for reading a complete draft of the book and providing many invaluable insights. We also thank the anonymous referee for making a number of constructive comments to improve the manuscript. All errors are the responsibility of the authors, however. Parts of the book were originally published in the journals *Antipode*, *Political Geography* and *Ethnopolitics*, and the authors thank the editors of these publications. The authors would like to extend their appreciation to the Asia-Europe Foundation, which provided us with the funding to examine some of the issues in this book. Mary-Alice thanks Gareth Stansfield at the University of Exeter and all of the staff at EXCEPS. She also extends her gratitude to her mentor, Paul Bew. We express sincere thanks to Alexandra Webster and Renée Takken at Palgrave for their enthusiasm and assistance in getting this project kick-started and completed. Both authors humbly submit their love to their families.

Introduction

What is a deeply divided society? Deeply divided societies are defined in this book as those in which ascriptive ethnic ties have generated an 'antagonistic segmentation of society, based on terminal identities with high political salience, sustained over a substantial period of time and a wide variety of issues' (Lustick 1979: 325). The main fissure in divided societies is not just the presence of multiple ethnic group interests; a deep conflict over the legitimacy of the state itself provides the basis for violent division. In divided societies, social identities are often constrained by communal allegiances, which provide little room for multiple and fluid encapsulations cross-cutting the divisions. For this reason, civic and social life tends to occur within, rather than across, ethnic cleavages. The groups forge separate political parties, which advance 'catch-us' rather than 'catch-all' policies (Mitchell and Evans 2009), and they often possess distinct media outlets, places of worship, schools, cultural activities and even trade unions. This division is reinforced by historically embedded patterns of social segregation and endogamy meaning that levels of intergroup distrust and hostility are high, economic growth is low and group boundaries are sharp enough so that 'membership is clear and, with few exceptions, unchangeable' (Lustick 1979: 325). As the various social and political cleavages buttress rather than cross-cut ethnicity, democratic stability is very difficult to achieve in such societies given the structural incentive for political élites to ethnically outbid each other (Lijphart 1969). Examples of violently divided societies include Northern Ireland, Bosnia, Cyprus, Kosovo, Iraq, Sri Lanka and Lebanon.

What might a shared society look like to replace one which has been historically divided in a violent manner? A normative answer might conclude that a shared society is simply the opposite of a divided one.

Although a shared society may be ethnically and/or nationally diverse, political parties are based on promoting policies which appeal to all sections of society rather than to a distinct ethnic segment. Despite citizens of such societies possessing different ethnic identities, a superordinate civic and/or national belonging prevails and the public sphere is a place where conflict can be peacefully negotiated. There is, hence, a single, shared public identity to which all can claim allegiance and which facilitates the distribution of public goods. In a shared society, the complex determinants of social identity are not constrained by a single communal narrative; individual identities are numerous and they cross-cut multiple cleavages. Moreover, citizens are autonomous subjects free to decide their affiliations and have the right of exit from any group they deem as a threat to their freedom. Finally, levels of residential segregation and endogamy are low and do not underpin ethnic cleavages.

In order to ensure that violent conflict ends and is replaced by sustainable peace it would seem that there should be a correlative transformation from a divided to a shared society. In divided societies, such as Northern Ireland, there often appears to be a degree of public and political support for policies which encourage greater integration and sharing between the groups. It is common to read, for example, pundits claiming that 'if Northern Ireland's children would all attend the same schools, the divisions would be over in a generation' (Needham 1998: 230). Similar sentiments are advanced that segregated housing should be ended, and that political parties should forge policies for the common good rather than those which benefit their particular community.

The virtues of sharing are extolled by a range of actors. The European Union (EU 2007) fund programmes in Northern Ireland which they identify as 'reconciling communities…and contributing towards a shared society'. State agencies too actively 'encourage and promote a shared society' (OFMDFM 2003 np). Even the political parities which represent the various communal interests in a divided society are frequently supportive of the abstract notion of a shared society. In Northern Ireland, rhetorical support can be seen from Sinn Féin (2009: 3), currently the largest nationalist party, which calls for a 'shared society based on equality for all', and from the Democratic Unionist Party (DUP 2009), the largest unionist party, which argues that 'If we are…to remove the divisions in our society, we need a shared strategy to achieve this'. Undercutting such apparent cross-cleavage consensus is a high degree of interpretation and acrimony over the exact form a shared society may take. Sinn Féin criticizes the DUP's plans to implement a shared society and vice versa. While, some other commentators question the commitment of both Sinn Féin and DUP to the merits of a shared society because they have supposedly 'thrived for decades on communal division' (Wilson 2009a).

A survey of the various approaches conducted by interested groups points to the fact that there is little consensus to practically define 'sharing' in divided societies: the concept is profoundly contested or even rendered nugatory by some. Debates continue to rage. Specific initiatives aimed at sharing are condemned for institutionalizing sectarianism by creating a vocabulary for antagonistic expressions of difference. Other projects are cited as shining examples of peace-building. Alternatively, is sharing always the desired outcome in a milieu in which commonalities between groups, rather than being a source of social cohesion, can instead provide the basis for the most destructive antagonism? Can sharing, therefore, be defined in terms of how we respect and equally accommodate group differences within a polity?

This book seeks to provide not only a comprehensive overview and analysis of the bitter debates and numerous projects designed to promote a shared society, but also provides suggestions regarding why some initiatives seem to flounder or are counterproductive, engendering fresh conflict, while others accomplish positive results. Understanding in greater depth what seems to work and fail in terms of creating sustainable peace can help with the search to formulate a consistent model of best practices, public policies and democratic accountability for divided societies. The book also has a strong international interest for those who wish to understand peace-building projects in divided societies.

Shared identity?

One of the main questions we explore in this book is to what extent is it possible to transform identity differences between groups in divided societies so that a new shared encapsulation can flourish. Can ethnic and/or national identities be transformed to engender sharing? If so, what processes are instrumental in transforming ethno-national identities in divided societies so that a shared identity can be fashioned? We illuminate, for instance, the impact that the forces of globalism and economic liberalism may have in challenging the seemingly particularistic basis of exclusively imagined notions of ethno-national belonging. Correspondingly, we track whether supranational institutions, such as the European Union, can construct new shared cosmopolitan identities less tied to ethnicity or nationalism. Or can a shared regional culture and identity be fostered in divided societies which can claim the allegiance of all groups? Furthermore, we explore some of the policies, initiatives and groups which are central to the debate about what is a shared society and how it can be delivered in a divided one scarred by a recent history of violence. What are the role of shared public spaces, political power sharing institutions, civil society groups, shared ways to 'deal with the past' and shared cultural forms, symbols and rituals contributing towards conflict management and even sustainable peacebuilding? Is sharing achieved through the recognition of the differences between the competing identities? Or should sharing be aimed at forming cross-community identities which seek to deconstruct and reformulate ethnic cleavages? Do group-differentiated rights facilitate or hinder the construction of a shared society, and can public goods be distributed effectively in lieu of a shared identity?

In this book, however, we critically examine the idea of a shared identity as a panacea for the problems of a divided society. Although a shared identity appears normatively attractive, it may not always be the most practical immediate goal to deal with the violence and conflict which arise from deeply embedded cleavages. The idea that groups can be encouraged to abandon their ethnic identities so that they forge a shared society, in short, may be unrealistic and impractical and could have unfortunate consequences which expedites further conflict and violence. As Varshney (2002: 25) reminds us: 'the world might well be a happier place if we could eliminate ethnic … conflicts from our midst, but a post-ethnic, postnational era does not seem to be in the offing … our short-to-medium-run expectations should be better aligned with our realities'.

The task of conflict management, we argue, is not always to neutralize ethnicity as an object of political mobilization or to try and transform differences so that a new shared identity emerges instead. A more realistic settlement of ethnic disputes accepts that ethnic divisions between groups will remain; but the significant issue is how to ensure that differences do not become the focus for politically destabilizing claims and violence. Crucially, ethnicity, while a marker of difference between groups does not have to be a cause of violent conflict and animosity. Conflict can be successfully managed via democratic forms which allow for cooperation between groups to take root, even if ethnic modes of political mobilization remain important.

For some, this may seem a bleak view of humanity, which appears to legitimate ethnic differences and even promote *de facto* apartheid social structures. This is not so. We argue that strong support should be given for individuals and groups which enshrine plural and non-sectarian identities. These people and groups, under certain conditions, can provide an important bulwark against further violence by fostering positive social relations between groups (see Varshney 2002). It is also reasonable to suggest that liberal values encompassing tolerance, human rights and social equality should be allowed to flourish in a milieu underpinned by nonviolent principles (Kymlicka 2007). Moreover, although we argue in this book that it is unlikely in divided societies that ethnic differences can be transformed into a shared identity, it is possible to reframe the antagonistic ways in which such identities are expressed in opposition to rival groups. In other words, ethnic forms of identification do not axiomatically have to be expressed in ethnocentric terms which are measured positively against an out-group which is stereotyped as both inferior and threatening. When initiatives are designed to ameliorate the aggressive and provocative content of ethnic identities in divided societies, this can provide a supporting scaffold for the task of conflict management (see Ross 2007). Peace-building begins by 'changing perceptions of the conflict and softening out-group boundaries by redefining collective identities in ways that are empowering and yet less polarizing' (Smithey 2009: 85).

Examining a shared society

On what basis can we question those, who as we will see, advance in different ways the virtues of a shared society and identity? One fundamental assertion is that since ethnic identities are constructed, often at the behest of extremist ethnic leaders seeking to further their own interests, they can, if the correct context and pressure is applied, be reconstructed and remade into a new shared form. While this is not an unreasonable aspiration, it is an improbable one. In situations where sustained intergroup violence has occurred, ethnic identities tend to become hardened, uncompromising, staunchly held in opposition to the despised rival group, and unlikely to undergo change for the short term, at least. As Varshney (2002: 34) notes, the fact that identities are 'constructed does not mean that they are not *deeply* constructed. Often identities do not change even if interests do' [emphasis original].

We are not arguing that ethnic identities are primordial attachments which are firmly rooted in ethno-biological modes of existence. Clearly, ethnic identities can go through profound change, even disappearing in some cases; individuals often have multiple overlapping identities, they can choose to leave ethnic groups and, in some circumstances, attain new encapsulations (Smith 1991, Baumann 1996). At the same time, it needs to be appreciated that once formed some group-based identities provide a high degree of resilience against change, especially when they are continually iterated through narrative forms, symbols, rituals, social and political activities. Just because ethnic identities are socially constructed does not correlate to the idea that they can be easily reconstructed. Perhaps, paradoxically, the immediate aftermath of intense ethnic violence, even when a peace process has taken root, may not represent an opportune time to try and transform divisive identities to allow a shared identity to prosper. Practitioners of conflict management and peace-building, we argue, have to take seriously the proposition that their task may not be to try and convert ethnic identities into seemingly more superior shared forms. A more reasonable approach is one which aims to house ethnicity in a secure environment so that it is afforded every chance to eventually defuse.

Such a perspective bears some resemblance to Mouffe's (2000) conception of 'agonism'. Mouffe argues that the task of democrats is to transform antagonism into agonism, deadly enemies into peaceful adversaries, violence into critical engagement and reflection (see Dryzek 2005: 220). For Mouffe, conflict between groups in society is simply unavoidable and cannot be eliminated through the operation of abstract reason; instead, a vibrant clash of democratic political positions can be channelled into progressive political institutions. Although the point is not to achieve consensus between groups on the issues which fundamentally divide them, it is possible nonetheless to combine contestation with a space for social differences to be heard and recognized by parties, so that adversaries possess a shared adherence to the ethico-liberal principles of liberty and equality. This form of engagement does not necessarily end conflict between groups, nor can it be expected to always lead to positive outcomes.

Post-agreement Northern Ireland

Although in this book we examine a number of different examples from various divided societies, we mostly concentrate on Northern Ireland. Northern Ireland is largely, though not exclusively, divided between British unionists/loyalists and Irish nationalists/republicans. There is also a strong overlap between religious ascription and national identity in the region with a high percentage of Catholics identifying as Irish nationalists and a roughly equal number of Protestants who are British unionists (Hayes et al. 2007: 455). The main basis for conflict, though, is the existence of competing national claims over the question of sovereignty with unionists wishing for Northern Ireland to remain British, while Irish nationalists desire the north to be unified with the Irish Republic (McGarry and O'Leary 1995). The dominant tendency within both national traditions is to deny legitimacy to the aspiration of the other.

Similar to many divided societies, there is much shared between the two groups. As Dryzek and Dunleavy (2009: 188) note, the two groups 'look alike, wear the same sort of clothes, speak English in the same accents…eat equally bad food, and often have trouble telling which side a person is from when meeting them for the first time.' Despite this, as we shall illuminate, Northern Ireland contains many of the key markers of difference characteristic of a divided society: most political parties mobilize along ethno-national lines, the groups often claim cultural distinctiveness and descent, there are separate domains for living, socializing, schooling, separate sporting affiliations, some examples of separate forms of employment and even shopping, and levels of residential segregation and endogamy are high. For instance, only 5 per cent of Northern Ireland's children attend integrated schooling, only one-in-ten marriages is mixed, and 98 per cent of Belfast's public housing estates are highly segregated to the extent of belonging almost wholly to either Catholics or Protestants (McGarry and O'Leary 1995, Breen and Hayes 1996, Breen and Devine 1999, McKittrick 2004, Hayes et al. 2007).

Even though divisions are historically long-standing, they intensified during the phase of violent conflict which broadly began in 1969, often euphemistically titled the 'Troubles'. During the period 1969–1998 circa 3500 people lost their lives as a result of the conflict and 40,000 were seriously injured (Morrissey and Smyth 2002: 3). In a Nobel lecture, the poet Seamus Heaney (1995) summed up the impact of the conflict as a quarter-century of 'life-waste and spirit-waste, of hardening attitudes and narrowing possibilities that were the natural result of political solidarity, traumatic suffering and sheer emotional self-protectiveness'.

It was hoped by many commentators that the peace agreement signed by unionist and nationalist parties in 1998 would create an auspicious environment for the people of Northern Ireland to 'forge a new shared identity, transcending the insular-looking group identities of the past' (Byrne 2000: 8). For one politician, the power sharing institutions brought about by the Agreement were specifically meant to augur 'the transformation of rigid political identities and the fusion of Planter and

Gael [unionist and nationalist] into a new political unity that retains the good in both and abandons the bad in both' (Maginness 2009). While violence has not been completely eradicated, it is certainly of a vastly reduced level compared to the height of the Troubles. Despite a slowly consolidating peace, however, a number of commentators claim there has not been a correlative weakening of divisions (see Wilford and Wilson 2003, 2006, Graham and Nash 2006, Finlay 2006, Shirlow and Murtagh 2006, Taylor 2006, Tonge 2009, Wilson 2009a). In fact, they claim that levels of social segregation and political polarization even appear to be intensifying. The cause for this paradox, they explain, is the terms of the peace agreement and the political institutions created to sustain peace. These forms, they argue, do little to deal with the root causes of conflict and instead institutionalize and encourage conflicting ethnic interests, thereby providing a disincentive for the emergence of a shared vision of society. It is thus common to read some commentators arguing that 'the lack of shared identity is a key aspect of Northern Ireland's problems' (Barton 2005).

As we shall argue in Chapter 2, however, it has been more a matter of assumption rather than fact that the institutions of the agreement have aggravated social divisions. In fact, it is highly debateable to what extent, if at all, Northern Ireland is becoming increasingly polarized. Another way to look at the Agreement is that by accommodating the saliency of ethnicity, it has provided a context for peaceful democratic and nonviolent politics to mature. It may even, in time, provide a context in which ethnic identities can be transformed. The logic here is that as ethnic groups increasingly feel ontologically secure through the provision of equality in the public sphere, the more likely a situation will occur in which the antagonistic and virulently oppositional basis of ethnic identities can be ameliorated to allow intercommunal trust and cooperation to prosper.

Book structure

Chapter 1 provides an overview of the main theoretical issues of the book. In particular, we address how ethnic groups come about, and how and why ethnic conflict occurs. By looking at Northern Ireland, the chapter then begins to critically examine the many different – often contested – ways in which commentators suggest a shared society could be constituted. Chapter 2 examines how consociational power sharing has become the default mode of conflict regulation in Northern Ireland and many other divided societies. We also illuminate many of the main critiques of consociationalism, especially those which accuse it of institutionalizing differences and maintaining intergroup conflict. Chapter 3 looks at the concept of shared public spaces in divided societies. The chapter outlines a longitudinal study of struggles to control the public space of Belfast City Centre, the capital of Northern Ireland and a 'sacred space' for nationalists and unionists. Chapter 4 considers a range of social movements which have tried to formulate alternative, often global, identities from that of ethno-nationalism. Chapter 5 investigates the role of shared symbols and ritual in both generating conflict as well as providing an opportunity for conflict management. Chapter 6 focuses on attempts to formulate various shared mechanisms in violently divided societies for dealing with the recent violent past as a means of creating a society and for providing both a healing and restorative dimension. Chapter 7 examines whether patterns of capitalist consumption and the introduction of neoliberal forms of state restructuring in Northern Ireland are contributing to the formation of shared consumerist values which have the potential to weaken ethno-nationalism.

1
Nostrums and Palliatives: Exploring a Shared Society

Outsiders, encountering for the first time a society characterized by ethno-national division and conflict are often at a loss to clearly distinguish members of one ethnic group from another. These outsiders have yet to acquire the insiders' skill of 'telling': the syndrome of signs (dress, name and place of residence) that people use to stereotype strangers as belonging to a particular ethnic group (Burton 1978: 4). Without the proficiency of 'telling', outsiders are confronted with people who often share the same skin colour, language, values, and many other common cultural accoutrements. For instance, in his analysis of the conflict in the Balkans, as part of his 'journey into the new nationalisms', Ignatieff (1993: 22) observed: 'An outsider is struck, not by the differences between Serbs and Croats, but by how similar they are. They both speak the same language…and have shared the same village way of life for centuries'. Commenting on Northern Ireland, an English politician claimed that its citizens 'are so similar in outlook, humour, language, attitude…that for an outsider to understand their bitter, ancient differences is well-nigh impossible' (Needham 1998: 165). Likewise, considering Rwanda, Volkan (1997: 14) notes that 'the physical distinction between many Tutsi and Hutu has gradually lessened, to the degree that most foreigners cannot distinguish between members of the two groups'.

Why, the outsider might ask, are these groups embroiled in ethnic conflict when they ostensibly seem to share so much? Even when the outsider eventually becomes *au fait* with the prerequisite skill of 'telling', they might discover that ethnic differences between groups are minute rather than the result of wide cleavages or clashes of opposing civilizations. They might also note that ethnicity is 'constructed', rather than rooted in biology, and that antagonistic expressions of difference have been inflamed by so-called ethnic entrepreneurs as means to secure their own political powerbase. If ethnic differences are really small, is it possible to emphasize an alternative narrative which tells of the commonality between groups so that a shared society can be constituted based on reconciliation and sustainable peace?

In the detritus of societies breaking down into violent conflict, rather than seeking to piece back the fragments into a shared identity, peace agreements often institutionalize the existence of ethnic differences. For instance, the Good Friday Agreement (GFA) of 1998 (NIO 1998) in Northern Ireland is predicated on equally recognizing and validating UK unionists and Irish nationalists' divergent political aspirations and cultural identities. For the supporters of the Agreement, it is necessary that we do so, because the groups are unlikely 'to assimilate, fuse, or dissolve into one common identity at any foreseeable point' (McGarry and O'Leary 2009: 26).

In Northern Ireland, the idea that ethnic distinctions should be afforded any degree of institutional legitimacy has been critiqued by some for supposedly freezing groups and their cultures in mutually exclusive communities so that they face each other in perpetual conflict. According to one critic, 'the Agreement…does not envisage "a shared, united society". The ideal it envisages is of two communities living not as one but separately' (McCann 2009a). The task of politicians is to alternatively promote the 'concept of an already existing non-threatening common heritage or to generate a new sense of tradition' (Nic Craith 2002: 5).

If the alternative to a divided society is to create a shared one, what exactly does this involve and what forces are instrumental in its delivery? Is it important to try and transform ethno-national identities by constructing a larger, shared one based on either regional or supranational allegiance to Europe or even a humanist notion of a 'one world humanity'? Can ethno-national identities become sublimated into more 'worthy' shared class based encapsulations? Perhaps the task is to create a shared civic identity, where ethnic affiliations are demoted to the private realm? Or, alternatively, is sharing best achieved by recognizing the diversity of political identities and allowing them to be treated with equal esteem? Beyond these questions, it is important to identify what relevant social processes and forms, if any, can engender a shared society and sustainable peace. In short, what are the roles of electoral and government institutions, public spaces and festivals, civil society organizations, mechanisms that seek to 'deal with the past' through remembrance and truth recovery procedures, and processes of economic prosperity? Is it possible to identify one or more approaches that contribute towards a harmonious shared society based on common values that are perhaps conducive to long-term peace?

To begin addressing these questions, it is essential to provide an analysis of what causes conflict in divided societies. By identifying the cause of conflict in ethnically diverse societies it is possible to begin proffering some suggestions regarding what a 'shared society' may mean and whether it can be initiated.

Ethnic conflict

All societies are riven by conflict regardless of whether they appear to be ethnically homogeneous or extremely plural. These conflicts can be over economic, health and gender inequalities, between faith groups, over the role of religion and secular values in public life and over various political and cultural identities. Not all conflict is destructive and violent; conflict can engender peaceful, positive change, such as delivering forms of social equality (Mouffe 2000). Conflict thus 'is neither good nor bad, but intrinsic in every social relationship…the real issue is not the existence of conflict but how it is handled…rather than solved' (Darby 1993: 4). Despite conflict being a constant in society, ethnic differences do not automatically lead to the unleashing of atavistic ancient hatred and vicious resource competition. In fact, 'ethnic differences are not inevitably, or even commonly, linked to violence on a grand scale' (Habyarimana et al. 2008).

Although Winston Churchill believed that the 'mixture of populations [will] cause endless trouble' (cited in Muller 2008), there is absolutely no evidence that societies containing numerous ethnic groups display a recidivist pattern characterized by perennial bouts of violent confrontation (Wolff 2006, Laitin 2007, Habyarimana et al. 2008). Most societies are ethnically plural and every few are ever ravaged by violence with peaceful coexistence and cooperation being the norm (Laitin 2007: 11). For instance, in their research in Africa, Fearon and Laitin (1996) noted across the continent tens of thousands of ethnic pairs who could have been in conflict. For every 1000 such ethnic pairs, they found fewer than five incidents of violent conflict. Even in places where ethnic violence erupts, it is incorrect to assume that it is due to any powerful ancient hatred. During the late 1980s in Yugoslavia it was recorded that there were very high levels of positive coexistence between ethnic groups, and little evidence of resentments or suppressed violence (Gagnon 2004: 34).[1]

Why then does ethnic conflict occur? This question may initially be addressed by questioning whether ethnicity is the cause of division between groups. As we have argued, it would be wrong to say that ethnicity *per se* expedites conflictual relationships between groups. Such an argument would only essentialize differences between groups, rendering them fixed nodal points in time, without any hope of conflict ever being transformed. Relationships between groups, as we shall see, are interactive, and changing depending on political circumstances, which are constantly in flux and stress. The relationships within groups are also important as well as the impact of other exogenous factors, such as 'third party' neighbouring groups and institutions. In order to better understand when ethnic differences generate violent conflict – and identifying the methods required to respond to them when they do – requires a deeper understanding of how ethnicity works (Habyarimana et al. 2008).

What is ethnicity?

The question of what are 'ethnic' groups and how they come about is an issue that is often addressed in terms of either 'primoridialism' or 'constructivism/instrumentalism'. As Fearon and Laitin (2000) note, social constructivists assume that ethnic groups are social categories distinguished by two main features: (1) rules of membership that decide who is and is not a member of the category; and (2) content – characteristics thought to be typical of members of the category. Ethnicity is thus socially constructed because it is said that membership rules and content 'are the products of human action and speech, and that as a result they can and do change over time' (Fearon and Laitin 2000: 848). This perspective may also exalt the power of leaders in constructing ethnicity for their own political ends by mobilizing a group (Brass 1991). Ethnic identities, hence, 'are not stamped in our genes' (Van Evera 2001: 20), but individuals have multiple identities, and their mode of ethnic identification is malleable depending on external forces; as individuals' identities change, so do ethnic groups.

The primordialist approach, at its narrowest definition, sees ethnic groups as a fact of nature, sometimes enmeshed in human biology and embedded in social structure; they are therefore static entities which inextricably shape who we are as members of such groups (Isaacs 1977, Van den Berghe 1981). The aetiology utilized by primordialists leads them to believe that immutable ethnic differences will propagate unavoidable and unending violent conflict between groups in close contact (Muller 2008).

It would be fair to say that in the field of contemporary social science the constructivist approach holds sway and 'primordialism has become the straw man of ethnic studies' for constructivists to argue against (Horowitz 2002: 72, see also Fearon and Laitin 2000: 849). However, as a number of theorists have noted (Smith 1991: 25, Varshney 2002: 28, Horowitz 2002, Wolff 2006: 36), in some respects the gap between constructivism and primordialism may not be as great as it is often assumed. Many so-called primordialists agree that ethnic groups are often constructed for various purposes. What they argue, in contrary to the constructivists, is that ethnic groups are experienced by group members as 'primordial attachments' which they attribute 'to the tie of blood' and from a 'natural affinity' (Shills 1957: 142, Geertz 1973: 259). Fearon and Laitin (2000: 848) have also termed 'everyday primordialism' to describe how many people take for granted the naturalness and unchanging essence of their ethnicity. Such beliefs in the primordial quality of identity make ethnicity extraordinarily resilient once formed and less prone to reinvention for any political exigency.

In this book we take not only a broadly constructivist approach, but also recognize its limits (see also Smith 1991, Horowitz 2002). We note how ethnic identities, in specific circumstances, can become 'inflexible, resilient, crystallized, durable, and hard' (McGarry and O'Leary 2009: 17). Unlike many instrumentalists, we do not believe ethnicity is something that can be conjured *ex nihilo* (Van den Berghe 1981), as if by process of political alchemy by leaders for their own machinations. Mobilizing groups into ethnic units is not just a Pavlovian act of leaders pressing buttons and eliciting responses from the masses (Gagnon 2004: 8). Nor is the construction of ethnic identity a matter of making something brand new in the image of a nascent political project guided by élites; it is more a process of patching together various pieces, old and new, as if a mosaic, to make it appear that a whole group exists with a definable ethnic identity.

To elaborate further, it could be said that diverse linguistic groups replete with distinctive kinship systems, political structures, religious practices, symbols, myths and other cultural forms have always existed. However, because a group of people share a stock of common traits does not mean that they represent a cohesive ethnic group. As we shall see, groups who share a fairly consistent repertoire of cultural signifiers can view each other as distinctively different ethnic formations (Harrison 2002). Cultural similarity does not signify ethnic collectivity (Smith 1991: 21). Neither is ethnicity always the most significant way that groups organize themselves in any given society – class, religion and/or gender may trump ethnic affiliation amongst members (Gagnon 2004: 13). Within these groups social identity is often fluid, multiple, overlapping and contextual. For a group to become primarily mobilized as an ethnicity requires changes in the way individuals identify themselves as a group; it means transforming what is already there into something slightly different.

Returning to the analogy that ethnicity is constructed like a mosaic, pieced together through existing and contemporary fragments, provides something of an answer regarding how groups come about. Most of the required pieces already exist; it requires powerful actors to first interpret in a specific way what the fragments mean before they are reconstructed to create a definite image of an *ethnie*. These fragments can be thought of as religious practices, ideas of descent, political institutions and cultural forms. However, once the mosaic is completed, it is hard to disassemble as the glue of collective identity acts as a powerful cohesive. Notably, 'ethnic identities, while constructed, are hard to reconstruct once they form … the conditions needed for reconstruction are quite rare, especially in modern times, and especially among ethnic groups in conflict' (Van Evera 2001: 20). Conflict hardens identities by enhancing ethnic memories, myths and a sense of common victimhood for future generations; it creates a shared sense of purpose within the group, thus reinforcing positive in-group and negative out-group narratives (Smith 1991: 27).

The idea that ethnicity is constructed, as Brubaker (2002: 13) notes, may be helpful, but authors rarely 'specify how "groupness" can "crystallize" in some situations while remaining latent and merely potential in others'. Applying the mosaic idea may be of use here. In some instances, ethnic differences were forged to suit *divide et imperia*. In the Great Lakes region of Africa, although patterns of intermarriage, a cross-cutting clan system, desegregated living and shared customs had weakened ethnic differences (Wolff 2006: 25–26), the clan system contained existing hierarchical relations with Tutsi dominating Hutu. Belgian and German colonialists fixed these differences by introducing identity cards which reinforced Tutsi dominated political and economic structures (Wolff 2006: 26). As we can see, ethnic identities are thus constructed through existing pieces rather than arbitrary processes of invention.

Ethnic groups are not just a process of top-down imperial or statist machinations. It is often the case that members of the same group choose to work with each other because it is efficient: 'they speak the same language, have access to the same types of information, and share social networks' (Habyarimana et al. 2008). In situations where they are faced with limited resources, they may even choose to work together against other groups (Habyarimana et al. 2008). Deep cleavages, consequently, begin to develop, often at the behest of ethnic activists, as social life centres on the activities of one's own kin group (Wolff 2006: 83), quickly expanding to the economic and political sphere.

In order for the group to cooperate together it still requires interaction within the group, for leaders to show that the best interests of the collective are ensured by cohesive action as an ethnic group rather than as a socioeconomic group or any other form of encapsulation. Again, this fits in with the 'mosaic' approach: the group is pieced together through cultural fragments which come to stand for a whole. It is down to leaders to interpret what pieces are salient and are likely to engender group togetherness. That ethnic groups are put together by collating existing fragments does not mean ethnic differences will be the source of conflict between groups. The crucial issue is how groups interact with each other. To help understand how ethnic differences can facilitate a sense of separateness and conflict it is useful to explore the notion of the 'boundary'.

The idea of the boundary as an explanation of ethnicity is that the emphasis is not placed on a fixed inventory of cultural forms which mark distinctive groups for eternity, but on how groups use cultural forms to draw boundaries between themselves and selected others. The boundary is drawn not from any objective differences in cultural features, but only from those the actors themselves regard as significant; while some features and emblems are used as signals of differences, others are ignored and in some relationships radical differences are played down or denied (Barth 1969). The boundary in ethnic group maintenance is important because it shows how cultural attributes are endowed with different degrees of significance depending on wider political relations within the group and between groups. This is particularly pertinent in circumstances proceeding and during conflict. For instance, in the former Yugoslavia before the beginning of the conflict in the 1990s, when Serbs still hoped to keep Bosnia in Yugoslavia, the media frequently highlighted similarities with Muslims. Croats, alternatively stressed that Bosnia had been part of historical Croatia and that most Bosnian Muslims were originally of Croatian descent (Banac 1994). When the war began, minor differences between the groups were turned 'into a monstrous fable according to which their own side appeared as blameless victims, the other side as genocidal killers' (Ignatieff 1993: 22).[2]

It is important to note that in defining boundaries, groups are not working from an infinite repertoire; it is unlikely, but not impossible, that ethnic groups can simply invent a whole new culture. Ethnic groups operate from an inventory of cultural forms, which can be added to, as well as readapted and modelled for contemporary circumstances. In short, the forms typically have to be historically significant and have emotional appeal. Smith (1991) notes that constructivist accounts over-emphasize the modern, invented aspect of ethnicity while ignoring the symbolic aspects of identities (including cultural values and traditions) that have been carried over from premodern times (Olzak 2006). The issue, thus, is not merely whether ethnic differences exist, but also the salience and esteem which the differences are accorded. On the whole, ethnic differences between groups are not that particularly relevant, groups may live together without too much hostility and there may even be relatively high levels of peaceful coexistence. Even though the notion of distinct ethnic groups can exist over long periods of time, replete with identifiable forms, what can change quickly is how the differences between the groups are valued. When differences go beyond a particular threshold, relationships between groups and members can fundamentally breakdown leading to hostility and violence.

Ethno-nationalism

This leads us to ask what creates these breakdowns. Conflict occurs when one or more group mobilizes to achieve political goals on the basis of their ethnicity, which, in turn, is resisted by another group who sees it as adversely impacting upon its own social and/or political position. Largely, however, conflict occurs depending on the nature of the claims of one group and how it is perceived by other interested groups – 'what is at stake is the relationship itself and how the relationship is defined' (Lulofs and Cahn 2000: 4). The source of conflict, notes Deng (1995:1), 'lays not so much in the mere fact of differences as in the degree to which the interacting identities and their overriding goals are mutually accommodating or incompatible'. Conflict can involve *zero-sum* and *variable-sum* outcomes. The former relates to where a gain for one group is experienced as an equal loss for another. The latter refers to conflicts over goods which are not in short supply – like cultural recognition– and so do not mean that one group must lose for another to gain (Jacoby 2008: 20).

One of the most destructive forms of zero-sum conflict occurs when incompatible political claims for a particular territory are made by rival ethnic and national groups. This occurs when ethnic groups require a particular territory or homeland to fulfil their national ambitions. Ethnic groups at this juncture become ethno-nationalist movements: a 'collective action designed to render the boundaries of a nation congruent with those of its governance unit' (Hechter 2000: 7). Ethnicity merges with nationalism when it makes specific historical claims and attempts to administer the group as a political community. This change from ethnicity to ethno-nationalism, as mentioned earlier, necessitates a change in how a group views itself. While members of ethnic groups paradoxically may not be aware of their membership – they are peoples not yet belonging to a larger ethnic element – 'a nation must be self defined' (Connor 1994: 102–03).

Importantly, not all ethnic groups are forms of nationalism and not all nationalist groups are purely ethnic. A key distinction between ethnic and nationalist movements is that the latter reflect claims to authority over territory and self-determination that are currently unsatisfied (Hechter 2000). Nationalist movements need a territory so that they can realize their dream of being an independent, self-ruling sovereign nation state. A particular territory may represent the ethnic group's cradle of civilization; it is naturally resource rich allowing for economic reorganization, it has natural borders and access to the sea thus representing group security and a defensible space (Smith 1991: 22–23, Wolff 2006: 43).

Many indigenous ethnic groups believe that in the past they were a self-defined nation located in a particular territory before the colonial powers took their land (Kymlicka 1995). In other instances, in the wake of empires and federations dissolving, and national borders being redrawn, ethnic groups may find themselves minorities on the wrong side of the border and cut-off from their kin state. These 'orphans of secession' (McGarry 1998: 215) may wish to unify with their kin state. In some instances an irredentist kin state will seek to enlarge its own territory by laying claim to territories in neighbouring states, which often contain kin group members (Wolff 2006: 45). These ethno-national movements demand 'formal withdrawal from a central political authority by a member unit or units on the basis of a claim to independent or sovereign status' (Hechter 1992: 267).

Where groups have clearly formed ethnic identities that are in part based on claims to the same stretch of territory, and where there is an irredentist kin state, violent escalation is more likely (Laitin 2007: 5). For instance, in Bosnia, Croats, Serbs and Bosniaks staked claim to the same territory to fulfil their ethno-national desires. Ethnicity, here, becomes a tool to be utilized to express immutable and intractable differences between the groups. For ethno-national groups it is a grave problem that within the boundaries of their desired state there are other ethnic groups and individuals holding multiple overlapping identities. Such diversity of social space can be problematic, because formal politics requires a level of homogeneity that diverges from the socially heterogeneous realities. The point is to make social space homogeneous. As Gagnon (2004: 8) notes of conflict in the former Yugoslavia, the task of ethno-national groups is to utilize extreme violence to destroy existing identifications and relationships that were fluid and overlapping. The result was to construct 'ethnicity as a hard category, and ethnic groups as clearly bounded, monolithic, ambiguous units whose members are linked through ineffable bonds of blood and history' (2004: 8).

It is important to reaffirm that the existence of numerous ethnic groups in one state does not automatically lead for competition over national sovereignty. As Wolff (2006. 55) argues, '[d]ifferent ethnic identities can, and in many cases do, peacefully coexist in the same state; different nationalisms cannot'. Although ethnic identities are often politically mobilized, this is not to say its direction is necessarily geared towards constituting national sovereignty or unifying with its kin state. In many cases, forms of federalism and autonomy have been given to the ethnic group, which include land rights, political powers and tax raising powers (Kymlicka 2007). In some cases, the form of the ethnic mobilization is to challenge the group's unequal position within a state dominated by a larger ethnic group. In this situation, the minority may demand a uniform system of equal citizenship, including voting rights, access to jobs and housing. They may also paradoxically reject cultural assimilation and wish to have their distinct cultural identities endowed with equal recognition and validated by the host nation. However, it is too simple to argue that grievances are the cause for ethnic mobilization or violence. Grievances are constant in society; it is only when a group's threshold for grievances are breached that serious conflict can erupt. Even then it requires agents to frame issues as worthy of mobilization and confrontation.

The obverse of this is that ethnic conflict can be produced by the way majority groups frame the intentions of minority groups. Minority groups may not be demanding secession or independence, but by calling for equal rights the majority grouping may unwittingly or purposely misread their intentions and claim the minority represents a threat to the very survival of the state. In this case the minority group is 'securitized'. By doing so, the state often legitimates the use of extraordinary measures to contain a minority 'threat' by limiting normal democratic processes. Under conditions of securitization the capacity of the minority group to politically mobilize is severely limited, its political parties may be banned, minority leaders may be placed under secret police surveillance or even arrested without trial, and the raising of minority demands in public fora may be proscribed (Kymlicka 2007: 119–20). If securitization is sustained by state violence, this will probably ignite minority grievances and secessionist tendencies thus, paradoxically, appearing to justify the state's use of excessive force in the first place.

In this book, we are primarily concerned with conflict in divided societies in which rival ethno-national groupings possess irreconcilable claims over the same territory. This has been the central matrix for conflict. We are also particularly interested in divided societies where violent conflict has more or less ended with the arrival of a peace agreement and institutional arrangements have been set up to ensure power sharing between the contending ethno-national groups. Despite the absence of war, peace agreements do not necessarily represent an end to conflict. The groups continue to pursue their nationalist goals through cultural and political strategies. In such cases, though violence has ended, ethno-national differences continue to be negatively valued thus hindering constructive, functional relationships between groups. Although it may be the case that rival nationalist projects have not ended, it may still be possible to alter the esteem which the respective identities of the groups are held. Indeed, trying to eradicate ethnic and political differences may actually end in disaster, as it evokes ontological insecurity and fresh conflict. A shared society, therefore, is probably not going to arrive though the obliteration of ethno-national differences, but through the regulation and control of ethno-national animus.

From management to transformation

Now that we have explored the nature of ethnic groups and ethno-national conflict, it is time to address how a 'shared society' has been imagined by some to contribute to sustainable peace. In assessing peace-building processes, we distinguish between *conflict management, conflict transformation* and *conflict resolution. Conflict management* can be defined as 'the attempt to contain, limit, or direct the effects of an ongoing ethnic conflict' (Wolff 2006: 134). A transformation in actors' perceptions of their interests (that they are better off pursuing their interests through political, as opposed to violent, means) may lead to their participation in *conflict management* structures. *Conflict management* may, however, lead to *conflict transformation*, which occurs when a conflict's root causes are altered. *Transformation* of a conflict's root causes in turn allows for a 'redefinition of the interests and identities of the parties' (Noutcheva et al. 2004) thus paving the way for *conflict resolution* (Noutcheva et al. 2004).

What might a discussion of sharing and a 'shared society' contribute to our understanding of conflict management, transformation and resolution in divided societies? To start, the term sharing encompasses a range of meanings, many of which are incongruent. Sharing can be interpreted as the coming together, the suturing of hitherto oppositional identities. As such, it can signify groups exploring their commonality. The importance of sharing is that we begin to see our common humanity and social needs rather than limiting our horizons to the particularistic and divisive politics of ethno-nationalism. To assist with sharing, in this analysis, it is eminently important 'to invest in creating impartial and credible state institutions that facilitate cooperation across ethnic lines' (Habyarimana et al. 2008). In another interpretation, sharing is about respecting what makes us different, recognizing the myriad ways cultural forms express our various ways of being human and expressing the good life. Indeed, it could be said that attempts to push ethnic groups too close together inevitably ends in antagonism as the groups wish to have their putative distinctions maintained (Blok 1998). In this instance, political institutions work best when they accommodate the distinctive needs of groups.

As we have already argued, we do not think it is possible to create a shared society by simply mobilizing to eradicate ethnic differences. The question is how can group based differences be accommodated without a correlative process of ethnic reification, almost total segregation, destructive resource competition, and other separatist agendas which adversely impact upon the life prospects of group members. How can non-members, those who refuse to be corralled into binary either/or demarcations of ethno-national identity, be encouraged to participate in social decision making processes? To address these issues, we introduce below three heuristic categories – transformationist, assimiliationist and multicutltturalist – which have been broadly utilized to argue for a shared and peaceful society in Northern Ireland, our main area of interest in this book. We tease open each category, illuminate where they overlap, and explore their potential and limits regarding managing and transforming ethno-national conflict.[3]

Transformationist

The transformationist perspective is driven by a constructivist analysis of ethnicity. The logic here is that since ethnic identities are constructed by ethno-national entrepreneurs, they can just as easily be disassembled and rearranged into a more progressive identity that cross-cuts cleavages. For example, Farry (2009: 170–71) argues that since 'identity has been constructed and divisions further entrenched during different periods of history of Northern Ireland ... this construction of identity holds out the prospect that communal identities can be reconstructed ... as identities have been shaped by various influences in the past, they can be reshaped in the future'. The task for those proposing transformationist remedies is to identify the stimuli which can expedite the reconstruction of ethnicity. Of these, we include *class*, *globalism*, *Europeanization* and *regionalism*.

Class

This analysis stresses that ethno-national division is the product of class forces. Simply put, the capitalist bosses are responsible for stirring up ethno-national separation in order to keep the workers at variance, wages deflated and trade union mobilization across the cleavage limited. A shared workers' identity, hence, calls for all workers to see their common interests in terms of their position within the mode of production rather than as divided ethnicities. Trade union activity in the north of Ireland has historically been envisaged as an activity to challenge divisiveness. In 1893, for instance, a leading Belfast trade unionist addressed the point of trade unionism: 'trade unionism is the ism ... whose mission it shall be to free our unhappy land from the incubus of religious bigotry and political intolerance' (cited in Cradden 1994: 69).

Paradoxically, however, attempts at fostering class unity between Catholics and Protestants have often exacerbated division. One reason for this is because Irish republicans, in particular, have often assumed that the struggle for a united Ireland is coterminous with class struggle. The analyses of 'green Marxists' attributes the conflict's genesis to imperialism as a form of capitalist colonialism. In short, British imperialism in Ireland was framed by green Marxists as a capitalist venture which created and aggravated divisions between Catholic and Protestant peasants and workers for the purposes of *divide et imperia* (see McGarry and O'Leary 1995: 64). The removal of British rule, according to Irish republicans, would expedite an independent socialist Irish state.

Problematically, for this analysis, Protestant unionists refused to submit to the desire for Irish unification. According to republicans, the reason for working-class unionists' obstinacy was due to false-consciousness: unionists in Northern Ireland were accused of being a 'labour aristocracy', endowed with the best possible jobs (Farrell 1976). The task for republicans was to convince Protestants that they were really Irish and that shared class interests might overcome sectarian division.

Rather than facilitating class action across the cleavage, the use of violence by republicans to achieve a socialist united Ireland was interpreted by Protestants as sectarian and thus solidifying their unionist identity. Similarly, unionists have also utilized class politics to mobilize working-class Protestants, such as, for instance, the Loyalist Association of Workers, which operated in the early 1970s to promote sectarian politics instead of class unity. In divided societies, class identities may be important, but rather than automatically cross-cutting cleavages, they can equally work to reinforce them (Smith 1991).

Globalism

The idea here is that globalization is eroding the power of nation states and the particularity of ethnicity thus expediting new cosmopolitan identities unfettered by ethno-nationalism. Globalization, in this sense, refers to global political institutions, multinational corporations, planetary politics and a 'state of mind'.

To begin with, there has been much speculation about the capacity of transnational or supranational organizations to replace a nation-state system which is on the wane. For Held (1995), the relationship between the nation state and the political community is gradually being subverted. These global political institutions include, for example NATO, the UN, World Trade Organization (WTO) and to a lesser extent the EU, organizations which, it is argued, removed some nation state political powers and weakened sovereignty. Another challenge to state authority derives from what could be called global capitalism. Here, nation states are tightly integrated in transnational finance networks and markets. Political decisions are primarily responses to the demands of the international economy: 'States no longer have the capacity and policy instruments they require to contest the imperatives of global economic change' (Held 2002: 53). The role of the state as the 'protector and representative of the territorial community [is] in decline' (Held 2002:54).

In their most utopic analyses, commentators argue that the withering away of nation-state political authority allows for citizenship to become re-orientated away from the nation as the predominant community.

The logic is that if the struggle for the control of territory is the root of zero-sum intractable conflicts, then the unbundling of territoriality associated with globalization could be the *deus ex machina* that resolves them (cf. Ben-Porat 2006: 2). Commentators see opportunities for new forms global citizenship to emerge, which are no longer tied to the petty chauvinisms of ethnic and national politics. Sassen (2001), for example, sees the 'unbundling of the exclusive authority over territory and people we have long associated with the nation-state'. This provides 'operational and conceptual openings' for radical global social movements to emerge proclaiming a planetary-minded politics, including universal human rights. Local issues are only germane as far as they relate to the global. Common global risks, like climate change and nuclear proliferation, fosters 'a sense of a globally shared collective future' (Vertovec and Cohen 2002: 1).

Another sense in which it is hoped globalization is eradicating the salience of ethnic identities is that we are all increasingly living in a 'global ecumene': we have a 'consciousness of the world as a single place' (Robertson 1992: 132). The proliferation of new technologies and the mobility of goods, capital, people and symbols wrought by global processes means that 'we are drawing on the traces and residues of many cultural systems' (Hall 2002: 26). As such, actors no longer, if they ever did, possess singular identities circumscribed by ethnic groupness; instead, they are equipped with overlapping interests and belong to heterogeneous or hybrid publics which challenge conventional notions of belonging, identity and citizenship. We are not encumbered by the groups into to which we were born into. As Day (2006: 203) notes: more and more, 'people take up their identities and social meanings from groupings which they have elected to join, thereby implicitly reserving the right to leave again if circumstances change'. The purest manifestation of this anti-essentialism is the notion of a cosmopolitan identity. Here, identity is conceptualized as 'allegiance to the world community of humankind and almost always defined in contrast to nationalism, because national boundaries remain the chief mechanism for separating "us" from "them"' (Lamont and Aksartova 2002: 2). Cosmopolitanism, Anderson-Gold (2001) argues, 'stands opposed to various forms of communitarianism that assert a universal moral priority of obligations to members of local associations over obligations to non-members'.

Perhaps unsurprisingly, globalism and cosmopolitanism have been suggested as prescriptive for ethno-nationalism in divided societies. For example, Taylor (2008: 191) asks why the constitutional status of Northern Ireland is posed as an either/or issue 'when increasing global interconnectedness...has resulted in a declining significance of national sovereignty and national borders'. Wilson, furthermore, calls for cosmopolitan thinking to be applied to Northern Ireland in contrary to a society where people are 'pigeonholed into the categories of ethno-nationalist division'. The horizon of this cosmopolitanism, claims Wilson (2009b. 230–31), 'does not end at the boundary of the nation state'.

The argument that global cosmopolitan values are eradicating ethno-national differences and politics is unconvincing thus far. Although in strictly economic terms the power of most states organized at the national scale is eroding, national and ethnic identities are incredibly robust entities (Smith 2002). As one of the leading proponents of cosmopolitanism recognizes, although relatively discrete national economic systems have become enmeshed in global processes, 'there are few grounds for thinking that a concomitant widespread pluralisation of political identities has taken place' (Held 2002: 56). Globalism, while it offers the opportunity for identity to be a palimpsest upon which any number of associations can be penned, is also a profoundly disorientating process. Many ethnic conflicts are inspired by a backlash against globalism, especially 'the disruptive effects of global integration, and the failure of markets to self-regulate in a way that protects the interests of the people' in the poorer regions of the world (Kilcullen 2009: 8). This can lead to attacks against global migrants, like violence against Javanese migrant workers in Aceh, who are seen as competing for jobs with the local population.[4] Moreover, when globalism is seen to threaten the integrity of local religious, economic and cultural systems, reflexive displays of ethnic particularism can ensue.

A further flaw in the globalism thesis concerns the role of international organizations. Rather than actively formulating policies aimed at eliminating ethno-national differences, or creating 'citizens of the world', a consensus has been developed in recent decades to recognize ethno-national minorities as a means to manage conflict. Supranational and interstate organizations – as diverse as the UN, UNESCO, the Organization for Security and Co-Operation in Europe (OSCE), EU, NATO, the World Bank, the International Labour Organization (ILO), the Organization of American States (OAS) – have, in different ways, asserted that the accommodation of ethnic diversity is not only consistent with but also in fact a precondition for the maintenance of a legitimate international order (Kymlicka 2007: 45). However, there is a debate whether these strong global trends towards minority rights have reduced the incidence of violent ethno-national politics (Gurr 2000: 11), or if it is a causal variable of ethnic mobilization by providing an international rostrum for group concerns, as well as standardized international human rights to which groups can demand access to (Olzak 2006). The point remains: globalization is seen as conducive to the accommodation of ethnic difference rather than its eradication. Despite the hope that global forces could contribute towards a shared cosmopolitan identity in divided societies, it appears more reasonable to suggest that it will either exacerbate or peacefully accommodate ethnic mobilization.

Europeanization

There has been optimism expressed by some commentators that European integration can bring about a shared identity by eroding ethnonational divisions and even the power of nation states. Richard Kearney (1997: 15), for example, claims that 'in the new European dispensation, nation-states will...become increasingly anachronistic...future identities may...be less nation-statist and more local and cosmopolitan'. Kearney continues to ask whether a semi-autonomous Northern Ireland, within a federal Europe, might 'enable both nationalist and unionist communities to put their sovereignty-quarrel behind them and work for the common good of their region under a broad European roof?' (1997: 17) One commentator (Ramsay 2009: 317–20) has recently called for the people of Northern Ireland to change how they define their 'ethnicity' by labelling themselves as one of the 'European peoples' within the EU – like the Basques, Catalans and those from South Tyrol. From this, it is opined, 'a new identity will emerge, embracing both communities and superseding the former divisions' (Ramsay 2009: 319).

There is some basis for confidence regarding the so-called European project to diminish ethno-national conflict by replacing divisive identities with a broader encapsulation. When the architects of the Common Market, Jean Monnet and Robert Schuman, originally formulated pan-Europeanism their intention was to provide a model that would negate national rivalries, particularly those between Germany and France (Nic Craith 2002: 187, McGarry and O'Leary 2004: 296). EU integration has also been seen as conducive to the amelioration of tensions between Spain and Gibraltar, and it has allowed minority groups, such as the German minority in South Tyrol, some regional autonomy. The fact that since the Second World War there has not been any violent conflict between member states of the EU demonstrates its success in this particular sphere of conflict regulation.

When it comes to the issue of intra-state conflict, however, the EU's approach has been one of accommodating ethnic differences rather than striving for their eradication (McGarry and O'Leary 2004). Like many international and transnational organizations mentioned above, the EU's position since the 1980s has been to develop legislation which formally recognizes and nourishes the distinctiveness of an area's ethnic groups as part of efforts to stymie violent conflict. Similarly, another pan-European organization, the Council of Europe (1995), makes provisions so that a 'pluralist and genuinely democratic society should not only respect the ethnic, cultural, linguistic and religious identity of each person belonging to a national minority, but also create appropriate conditions enabling them to express, preserve and develop this identity'.

Despite, as noted in the Introduction Chapter, the EU funding initiatives identified as fostering a 'shared identity', in dealing with the conflict in Northern Ireland the EU has promoted the recognition of the two groups' distinct identities as a potential solution (Adshead and Tonge 2009: 219). For instance, the Haagerup Report (1984: 7), produced by the European Parliament, argued for power sharing between nationalists and unionists, contending that 'the conflict, deeply rooted in British-Irish history, is…of conflicting national identities in Northern Ireland'. Since then, as Hayward (2006: 261) notes, 'the EU's self-ascribed role towards a settlement in Northern Ireland…has followed this vein by supporting the peaceful expression of British and Irish identities rather than reconstructing them or creating alternatives'.

Equally problematic for the thesis that Europeanization is contributing to a shared identity in Northern Ireland concerns the divergent level of support given by nationalists and unionists for the project. Many unionists have displayed scant enthusiasm for the EU, viewing it as a bureaucratic, undemocratic institution which weakens Westminster's sovereignty. For some, especially Protestant evangelicals such as Ian Paisley, the EU is even seen as a covert Popish plot designed to extend the political control of the Vatican. This can be seen in the EU's origins, especially the Treaty of Rome (1957), and the power of some Catholic states and political parties in the decision making process (Adshead and Tonge 2009). Unionist scepticism of the EU project has been augmented by the fact that the Social Democratic Labour Party (SDLP), an Irish nationalist party, has articulated the most consistent level of support for Europeanization because it believes it will lead to a united Ireland (Nic Craith 2002, McGarry and O'Leary 2004: 306). Thus we can sum up by concurring with McGarry and O'Leary (2004: 321) that 'in Northern Ireland…European integration has not strengthened loyalties to Europe, or contributed to multiple, overlapping, or nested identities'.

Regionalism

This transformationist viewpoint calls for the constitution of a shared Northern Irish or regional Ulster identity. Compared to a supranational cosmopolitan global or European encapsulation, the scale of this identity goes down to the regional and local. The broad idea underlying this is that the two groups – nationalists and unionists – have 'shared values rooted in a common regional culture' (Finlay 2006: 6) which could be utilized as a fertile soil from which a shared political identity could spring.

In line with devolved regional power sharing established in Northern Ireland, research has uncovered growing popularity for a localized Northern Irish identity which transcends the fixed binary of a British/ Irish affiliation. As many as 29 per cent of respondents in one survey identified themselves as being 'Northern Irish', as opposed to British or Irish. The authors of a report claimed the research shows (See Figure 1.1) that people are abandoning 'the national and religious labels that are often purported to underpin the Troubles' (Muldoon et al. 2008). Such research holds the hope that ethno-national identities may be malleable in some cases and could help expedite wider political changes. Indeed, some commentators argue that it 'is impossible to share a cohesive and integrated Northern Ireland without endorsing a Northern Ireland identity' (Emerson 2009).

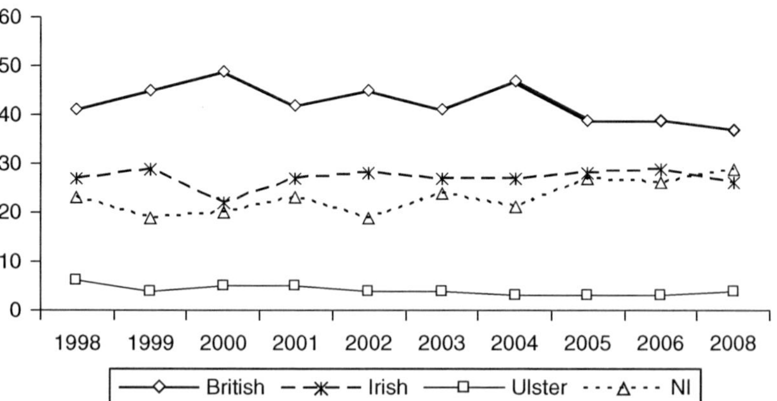

Figure 1.1   Identity in Northern Ireland (%)

Source: Northern Ireland Life and Times Survey 1998–2008, Module: Community Relations, Variable: NINATID.

There is a rich intellectual underpinning in Northern Ireland, especially within the arts, for the notion of a shared regional identity. Two of Northern Ireland's most celebrated poets – John Hewitt and Seamus Heaney – evoked through their verse the image of a common Northern Irish or Ulster identity. In 1949, Hewitt wrote: 'Ulster considered as a Region and not as the symbol of any particular creed, can command the loyalty of every one of its inhabitants' (cited in Kearney 1997: 106). This regionalism can also link with Europeanization insofar as an independent Northern Ireland could take its place as a region of Europe (Nic Craith 2002: 193, Ramsay 2009). Another related strand to the shared regional identity argues that the peoples of Ulster have always shared the same culture which clearly distinguishes them from both the rest of Ireland and the UK (Hall 2007: 13). For Evans (2005: 74), 'the communities in the north … share an outlook on life which is different from that prevailing in the south and which bears the stamp of a common heritage'. The theory here is that rather than two groups of people – 'natives' and 'settlers' – history recounts a long narrative of sharing, mixing and cross-cultural fertilization. For one subscriber to this belief: 'I have never thought of the two main communities within Northern Ireland as being anything other than *one* community … because I could never *see* any difference' [emphasis original] (Hall 2007: 4). An additional aspect is the binding agent of violence as a shared experience: 'this sense of regional fellowship has been strengthened by the horrors the Northerners have been sharing even while they have been inflicting them on each other's communities' (Murphy 1978).

A shared regional identity has also been adopted by separatist ethno-national groups. Some elements within Ulster loyalism have long promoted the idea of a separate 'Ulster nation'. This desire for separateness reflects the belief among some loyalists that the rest of the UK has practically abandoned them and the Irish Republic would prove an unresponsive and tyrannical 'cold house' for Protestants. The Ulster nation thus provides a 'third way' option. This faction claims that in the context of Northern Ireland: 'our divided people have been prisoners of their traditional loyalties for far too long … We want to encourage the reawakening of Ulster's national identity'. There is little sign that, as envisaged by its supporters, the Ulster Nation will be a civic state; its proponents display greater appetite for constituting '[a] bold, self-confident civilisation based in large part on its cultural and ethnic Ulster-Scots roots' (Ulster Nation 2007).[5]

A more inclusive alternative derives from the Alliance Party, a purposely non-sectarian political grouping, which promotes 'a common regional identity for Northern Ireland' (Neeson 1999). They call for policies to help foster this 'sense of shared destiny among our people', which surpasses the either/or binary of extreme nationalism and unionism by mobilizing the political middle ground. Problematically, though, there is no serious political support for parties that espouse a shared Northern Irish identity or any symbolic dimension to imagine it. Indeed, as we can see from Figure 1.2, survey evidence makes it clear that, in line with a growing Northern Irish identity, there is not a correlative rise in numbers of those who desire an independent Northern Ireland. The vast majority of those polled desire for Northern Ireland to remain part of the UK or to unify with the Republic of Ireland. Some other surveys have also indicated a relatively small figure of 18 per cent of those who describe their nationality as Northern Irish, 'a setback for those who hope to see a new cross-community Northern Ireland identity emerging' (Gordon 2010).

Despite some support for a Northern Ireland identity, there is no evidence that these people share any sense of common political encapsulation. In fact, it is reasonable to suggest that a 'Northern Irish' identity may mean something completely different for a Catholic and a Protestant, as it could be seen as coterminous with their national

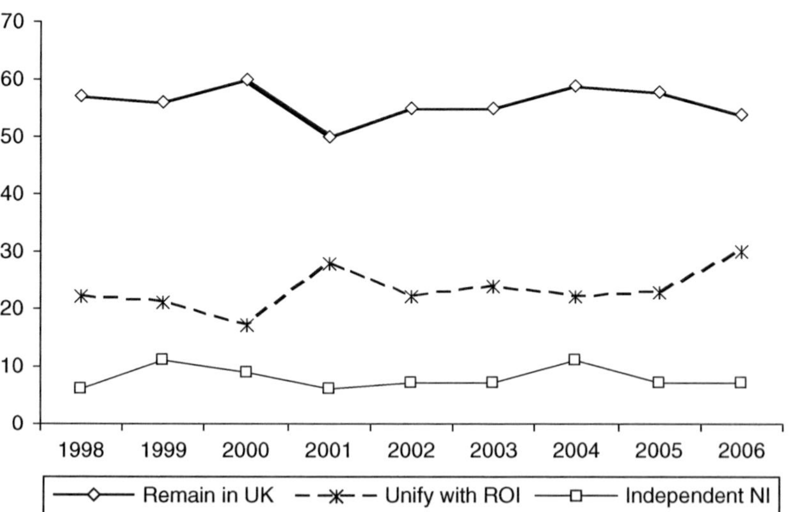

Figure 1.2   Long-term policy for Northern Ireland (%)

Source: Northern Ireland Life and Times Survey 1998–2006, Module: Political Attitudes, Variable: NIRELAND.

preferences. For unionists, support for a Northern Irish identity can be seen as compatible with the idea of a regional identity within the context of UK, thereby legitimating the idea of partition and the separateness of the north from the rest of the island of Ireland (see Nic Craith 2002: 193–94) For nationalists, the same identity can be read as a declaration of regional affiliation within a united Ireland.

Assimilationist

Unlike transformationsists, assimilationists do not ostensibly claim to want the transformation of ethnic identities; instead, they recognize the existence of ethnic identities but desire to depoliticize them by relegating them to the private sphere. The public sphere of formal politics is a place where a common civic, non-ethnic realm is developed. A common sense of citizenship is nurtured by uniform, singular and equal rights, formal social equality and justice (Barry 2001: 72–76). The public sphere is also a place where citizens debate in a rational manner issues concerning the common good rather than subordinating them to particularistic ethnic demands. In democratic politics, consequently, it is important that all perspectives should be represented in the public arena, 'but in reaching policy decisions citizens should set aside their personal commitments and affiliations and try to assess competing proposals in terms of shared justice and common interest' (Miller 1999: 106).

Assimilationists claim to have developed the magic formula to deal with ethnic conflict which would also create a shared society. This impulse is particularly strong within some forms of liberalism, which 'take as their starting point the existence of a plurality of interests – often competing, if not in actual conflict – and ask how or by what principles of political order might adjudicate between or accommodate competing claims' (Kukathas 1995: 233). The strength of the left-liberal assimilationst approach to ameliorating conflict, contend proponents, is its promotion of individual rights over group rights.

Some liberals argue that an undifferentiated and singular concept of citizenship facilitates peaceful coexistence between potentially conflicting groups. This is engendered by the maintenance of a 'neutral public sphere', in which the 'state should be neutral between competing conceptions of the good life' (Rawls 1971). In a differentiated society there are a multitude of cultures and religions, which in different ways embody diverse and sometimes incompatible ways of envisioning the meaning of the good, the just and the right moral order of society. It is not unreasonable that groups can clash by fostering 'zero-sum ideas about the way in which a polity and a society should be organized', especially when 'one group seeks to impose its ideas on a territory containing other groups' (Barry 2001: 24). The solution to this is not for the state to impose a singular concept of the 'good life', but to remain intrinsically neutral and leave citizens free as individuals to lead their chosen lives in the private sphere.

The liberal assimilationist outlook has been broadly applied as a solution to the divided society of Northern Ireland. Affiliated commentators call for voting structures which encourage cross-cutting political interests rather than ethnic-based concerns, universal individual rather than group-differentiated rights, and a public sphere characterized by a vibrant civil society of dialogue (Wilford and Wilson 2006, Taylor 2008, Wilson 2009b). A leading proponent argues that if Northern Irish society is to foster reconciliation, the task of intellectuals is to work 'towards an integrated society conforming to the democratic norm that the individual citizen, rather than the "community comprises the social unit, in line with the Universal Declaration of Human Rights' (Wilson 2009b: 221). Wilson (2009b: 230) also demands 'a neutral state – not a "binational" one'; a 'single moral realm predicated on human rights, rather than … ghettoization'; and 'recognizes the key role of the associational sphere of civic society where … intercultural dialogue can resolve the problems of daily life' (Wilson 2009b: 231).

The assmiliationist standpoint has a strong resonance with the forms of cosmopolitanism discussed above, especially the humanist belief in the commonality of all people and the importance of relieving them from the burden of group allegiances. According to Wilson (2005), if the British government had applied a cosmopolitan remedy, 'Northern Ireland's problems would have been on the way to a solution'. Thus, despite the assimilationists' claim to merely desire the depoliticization of ethnicity, they really want to transform it into something they believe is more universal and progressive: the individual rational actor emancipated from the ethical ties of ethnicity. The idea is that once ethnicity is neutralized as a political force, individuals can alleviate the dead weight of irrational tradition and make political decisions based on universal logic for the common good.

A major problem with the assimilative logic is that, as Little (2004: 3) notes, it relies 'too heavily on the ideal-type of the rational individual and the capacity of individuals to separate the methods of politics from their substantive private or non-public beliefs'. It is more reasonable instead to assume that in divided societies 'interpretations of the political and liberal concepts of justice are closely bound up with "private" concerns of culture, nationality, religion and so on' (Little 2004: 3).

Another problem with assimilationism is not so much that it is really a transformationist logic; the real predicament is conceptual elasticity. The assimiliationist stance on conflict resolution, purely conceived, was originally developed to counter religious conflict in society, especially the wars of religion which ravaged Europe in the sixteenth and seventeenth centuries. European states had been wracked by competing religious groups demanding political control; the solution to this was to banish religion to the private realm, thus marking a strict division between church and state and the formation of a neutral public sphere (Barry 2001: 24). The conflict in Northern Ireland, regardless of how it has sometimes framed as a throwback to the wars of religion, is not religious; to recap: the conflict stems from incompatible ethno-national claims to the same territory (see Chapter 2). Ethno-national identities can't merely be consigned to the private sphere; they require public recognition.

Moreover, while a nation state can feasibly be religiously neutral, no state is ethnically neutral. Although the notion of a neutral liberal state is important – enshrining religious toleration, free speech, the rule of law, formal equality, procedural legality and a universal franchise – it is argued that this neutrality only works when it is assumed that there is a broad cultural homogeneity among the governed (Hall 2000: 228). However, rather than the liberal state managing to slough off its ethno-particularistic skin to emerge in its culturally cleansed, universalistic form, it is argued that the pretense of the neutral liberal state was in fact achieved through the formation of a dominant *ethnos*. Kymlicka (1995: 108), argues that neutrality is not only an impossible goal, but also because the 'state unavoidably promotes certain cultural identities' it 'thereby disadvantages others'. The formal promotion of a state language, symbols and rituals reflects the hegemonic dominance of one ethno-national group over any number of other minority groups.

Assimilationism, hence, is often a project of nation-building. By assimilation we mean the process by which a majority ethno-national group prises the minority group from its ethnic identity (Kymlicka 2007). Assimilation thus requires one group to accept 'a set of normative standards that reflect disproportionately the interests of the dominant group' (O'Neill 2007: 422). Even if all groups are treated identically in the nation-building project, this is not necessarily fair treatment, and for Tully (1995: 64), unitary citizenship is an 'empire of uniformity'. The limits of the assimilative approach is seen by how sections of unionism and nationalism in Ireland have contained a civic element which desire a neutral state to which all individuals are endowed equal rights; below the surface, however, lies a logic which desires to de-ethnicize the other group.

For instance, in recent decades there has been a vociferous debate to formulate a non-ethnic, non-sectarian civic brand of unionism as a means to satisfactorily incorporate Catholics into the state. This vision, as Porter (1996: 128) notes, emphasizes 'a modern concept of the state, claims cultural blindness in political affairs, celebrates plurality, and thus appeals across the sectarian divide'. In line with the classic assimiliation-ist viewpoint, proponents of civic unionism call for an equal conception of citizenship to be constituted for all of the people of Northern Ireland. One proponent of this civic unionism claims that the UK 'is a state which, being multi-national and multi-ethnic, can be understood in terms of cit-izenship…all are equal citizenships under one government…it is to this intelligent unionism, which embraces both Protestants and Catholics, owes allegiance' (Aughey 1989: 19). The logic here is that equal citizen-ship rights would remove nationalists' grievances thus facilitating their easy assimilation into the state.[6] The problem with this analysis is that it assumes that a singular concept of citizenship ameliorates conflict. This is not so. The desire of minority ethno-national groups is not only to be treated as equal citizens, but also to have their national differences for-mally recognized. This paradoxical situation entails groups having their national identities validated as a measure of equality rather than being forced into assimilatory measures as part of nation-building projects.

Multiculturalist

The multiculturalist perspective, in one sense, can mean that shar-ing is achieved paradoxically by recognizing that differences between groups exist and rather than trying to transform or depoliticize them we should try to ensure that they are treated in an equal and impartial manner. Good relations, therefore, are fostered by groups learning to tolerate and respect each other's identities. An example of this thinking comes from David Trimble (1989: 45), a former unionist political leader, who argued that it is 'inappropriate…to integrate existing diversity. One should not try to blend together traditions that are essentially dif-ferent…Our object is to discuss how diverse traditions can be affirmed and enjoyed'.

A more formal multiculturalist project in 'divided societies' looks to initiating group-differentiated rights so that the national identities of the groups are endowed with public recognition. If transformationists, and some assimilationists, are hopeful that ethno-national identities can be reconstructed into some new shared form, some advocates of group rights are less confident. Such group rights can include political power sharing, 'parity of esteem' for the groups' cultural forms, representation in public media, legal exemptions, and even some instances of 'positive discrimination' in regards to public housing and employment hiring practices.[7] The idea here is that groups should be given rights to enable them to express and maintain their identities without it adversely affecting their status in society (Kymlicka 2007).

The securing of group based rights, in contrast to individual rights, reflects the notion that our identities cannot be easily detached from the groups to which we belong. There is no such thing as the 'unecumbered self'; 'we are all, to some extent, *situated* within wider communities which shape and influence who we are' [emphasis original] (May 1999:18). Human beings are thus 'culturally embedded', meaning that 'they grow up and live within a culturally structured world, organise their lives and social relations in terms of its system of meaning and significance' (Parekh 2006: 336). The absence or misrecognition of our cultural identities by others can therefore inflict great harm on our sense of self worth (Taylor 1994: 25).When antagonistic groups make the effort to 'recognize' the identities of the 'other', reinforced by institutional state support, this helps nourish peace-building by fostering mutual tolerance (O'Neill 2007).

The issue of autonomy is also related to the preservation of cultural identities. Kymlicka (1995) argues that the notion of autonomy is inherently bound with our capacity to live the 'good life' in opposition to the 'enforcement of morals'. We should be endowed with freedom to question beliefs, to 'examine them in light of whatever information, examples, and arguments our culture can provide' (Kymlicka 1995: 81). Crucially, to assist with this struggle for autonomy, Kymlicka (1989: 165) calls for the protection of cultural community: it 'is only through having a rich and secure cultural structure that people can become aware, in a vivid way, of the options available to them, and intelligently examine their value'. It is from this point we can engage in cross-community dialogue and, for some proponents of multiculturalism, this can transform identities: it elaborates 'a vision of commonalities, of what is shared across difference, and through remaking citizenship and national identity' (Modood 2007: 64–65).

Despite the optimism of proponents regarding multiculturalism's capacity to ameliorate ethno-national conflict, critics counter that it provides no shared vision for society; in fact, by recognizing the separateness of groups, the project legitimates the 'Balkanization' of society leading groups into 'ethnic fiefdoms' (Kundnani 2002). Multiculturalism, moreover, is seen as engendering conflict between groups rather than intercultural harmony. Opponents often claim that there is a 'distorted multiculturalism' wherein increasingly differentiated groups each pursue their own case for attention and resources, while jealously protecting their right not to be criticized by others (Alibhai-Brown 2000). By promoting cultural recognition over economic redistribution, multiculturalism is further seen as a form of 'divide and rule' which heads off the 'nightmare of unified political action by the economically disadvantaged' (Barry 2001: 235–326, see Nagle 2008a, 2009a).

Shared future

In the lengthy review of debates concerning a shared society to replace a divided one, the most we can say is that there are a number of theories, which often overlap or stand in opposition to rival theories, about what it should look like and which social processes will deliver it. The concept, without being too platitudinous, is heavily debated and contested regarding Northern Ireland. More pessimistically, we agree with Kerr's (2006: 16) assessment that 'it has proved impossible to build a syncretistic intercommunal or national identity in Northern Ireland, an identity that could overarch and supersede ethno-national allegiance'. Before elaborating some ideas to help move the debate forward, we first provide an analysis of the most detailed consultations on what a shared society may resemble and how it could be achieved for Northern Ireland. Such a vision was outlined in the UK government sponsored 'Shared Future' document published in 2005.

'Shared Future'

In early 2003, the UK government encouraged a broad consultation process concerning developing public policies to engender, *inter alia*, shared/integrated communities and to foster 'respect, encouragement and celebration of different cultures, faiths and traditions' (OFMDFM 2003: 6). It was requested that the delivery of these aims would require a joined-up approach by government departments. The consultative process, which ended on 30 September 2003, engaged more than 10,000 people and generated over 500 written responses from across Northern Ireland.

The upshot of the initial consultative process was the release in 2005 of the document *Shared Future*. Totalling 68 pages, *Shared Future* is a wide-ranging deliberation on the mechanisms that were identified during the consultative process to deliver a 'shared society', which is defined as:

> The establishment over time of a normal, civic society, in which all individuals are considered as equals, where differences are resolved through dialogue in the public sphere, and where all people are treated impartially. A society where there is equity, respect for diversity and a recognition of our interdependence. (OFMDFM 2005: 7)

In a display of optimism, *Shared Future* (OFMDFM 2005: 11) noted that the consultative process had revealed 'overwhelming support for a shared society', although there was a clear debate over what specific form it should take.

Notably, though, *Shared Future* provided little analysis of why ethnonational conflict occurs and why some societies are deeply divided. Although *Shared Future* underscores our earlier argument that ethnic difference in itself is not the cause of conflict, and that peaceful coexistence is the norm in most societies, its identification of why some societies do become mired in ethno-national conflict and some do not is weak. *Shared Future* argues that ethnically diverse societies which remain 'integrated' are those that 'have viable democratic structures, which put a premium on dialogue' (OFMDFM 2005: 7). Notably, *Shared Future* fails to specify which societies conform to these strictures. In antithesis, 'multi-ethnic societies that don't work follow a different logic' (OFMDFM 2005: 7). In these societies, argues *Shared Future*, 'individuals are reduced to simple group stereotypes, which easily turn into enemy images. Those who exploit difference can then widen communal divisions' (OFMDFM 2005: 7). 'The underlying difficulty' with Northern Ireland, *Shared Future* opines, 'is a culture of intolerance' (OFMDFM 2005: 7).

By reducing conflict to the power of 'intolerance', *Shared Future* fails to adequately examine why particular types of multiethnic societies are characterized by intercultural dialogue and why other societies display pervasive mistrust and animosity. In short, it doesn't differentiate between different categories of multiethnic societies. It doesn't highlight the fact that societies torn between rival nationalisms are more likely to generate violence than a society where multiple ethnic groups are satisfied to be contained within the same nation state. Moreover, it's not even clear to what extent intergroup intolerance is the variable which explains why some societies are blighted by sustained ethnic conflict and why some remain peaceful. Laitin's (2007: 15–18) research on post-Soviet states with significant minority populations demonstrates that the existence of ethnic hatreds is a poor predictor for the emergence of division and violence. In fact, prior to the arrival of violence between groups, the minorities in Moldova and Azerbaijan scored highly in indices related to 'openness to assimilation' and marriage outside the group compared to those societies which stayed peaceful despite prognostications to the contrary. Laitin (2007) argues that the key explanatory variable for ethnic violence is the existence of weak states who handle their minorities in an unsatisfactory way, thereby sustaining minority grievances and/or by dealing inadequately with separatist extremists. By seeking to deal with the symptoms, rather than the cause of the disease, so to speak, *Shared Future* is unable to deal with the root problem of conflict in divided societies.

The identification of 'a culture of intolerance' as the source of conflict in Northern Ireland leads *Shared Future* to seek out solutions which highlight 'interculturalism' as the activating feature of a shared and peaceful society based on mutual respect, communication and tolerance. *Shared Future* (OFMDFM 2005: 9) identifies 'three clear' principles to engender interculturalism and a shared society:

- Everyone in Northern Ireland deserves to be treated as an individual, equal with every other – not a mere cypher for a 'community'.
- Each of us must mutually recognize our common humanity ('achievement of reconciliation, tolerance, and mutual trust') – rather than engaging in a perpetual and sterile battle for ethnic power.
- The state must be neutral between competing cultural claims ('promotion of a culture of tolerance at every level').

These three core principles of a 'shared society' based on intercultural values stand in opposition to a divided one, where 'segregation and periodic violence are the norm and democratic institutions are inherently unstable, corroded by mistrust of "the other side"' (OFMDFM 2005: 7). The document also makes clear that 'benign apartheid' is not an option: groups cannot simply demand to be left in their autonomous living zones.

Crucially, then, the emphasis of *Shared Future* is on fostering 'good relations' between groups in Northern Ireland. In public policy terms, a shared society based on good relations is envisaged in the document as including, *inter alia*:

- Elimination of sectarianism, racism and other forms of prejudice to enable people to live and work together without fear of intimidation.

- The promotion of civic-mindedness through citizenship education.
- Support cultural projects which highlight the complexity and over-lapping nature of identities and their wider global connections.

A *Shared Future* can broadly be seen as advocating a transformationist approach to a 'divided society'. As explored earlier, the transformationist approach refuses to accept that identities in divided society can be reduced to communities; where encapsulations are tied to mutually exclusive ethnic underpinnings they can be emancipated through dialogue in the public sphere. Contrary to the notion that 'good relations' are achieved by promoting respect for unitary and static cultural groups, *Shared Future* wishes to emphasize that tolerance and reconciliation are gained by seeing a person as an individual and not an appendage of community (OFMDFM 2005: 8). The intercultural emphasis of *Shared Future* is placed on promoting hybrid and overlapping identities rather than accepting the existence of quite firm ethno-national encapsulations which often exist in Northern Ireland. A shared society, so conceived, is wrought by overcoming group differences so that a common civic society can be forged.

Although *Shared Future* was sponsored by the UK government, and a number of government departments made a pledge to implement policies covered by the document, to date it has been shelved. One reason for this is a high degree of political debate in Northern Ireland over defining 'good relations', especially how it is conceived in different ways by different groups. The document, in short, failed to adequately provide working definitions of key concepts like sectarianism, racism, conflict, reconciliation and integration, thereby leaving its remit to diverse interpretations and sectarian interests.

Palliatives?

So far in this chapter, we have reviewed many of the major ideas that have been elaborated on what a shared society may mean in a divided one. It is now time to synthesize some suggestions regarding lines of enquiry and analysis, which we shall explore throughout the book. We believe these points to be important in the context of ethno-nationally divided societies:

- Although ethno-national groups and identities are often constructed, this does not mean they can easily, if at all, be reconstructed, at least in the short term. Once groups are politically mobilized, identities become highly resilient and averse to change, especially when they have been embroiled in conflict. For this reason, it is not advisable to try and transform ethno-national identities. Nevertheless, ethno-national identities can be changed from a malignant character into something more benign (Ross 2007). As Van Evera (2001) notes: 'redirecting identities is usually a Quixotic project but reflavoring identities shows great promise as a palliative to ethnic conflict'. This process works best when ethno-national identities are granted public recognition, equality and validation. When ethno-national identities feel secure, they are in a better position to be less antagonistic. Although ethno-national identities persist, the esteem to which differences are accorded can change. Collective identities can be subtly reworked in ways which are ontologically constant for groups, still bearing the imprimatur of the community, yet able to open that group's orientation to allow new nuanced views of rivals (Smithey 2009: 93). Paradoxically, ethnic identities are more likely to go through transformation and modernization when they appear to be most protected. Theorists have long noted that ethno-nationalism is a Janus-faced phenomenon: it invokes the glories of the past to mobilize people for projects concerned with social change. Seemingly, ancient symbols are used to help engender modernization (Smith 1991). Group leaders, nevertheless, can use such symbols innovatively to open up their constituency to new possibilities which can help with peace-building (Smithey 2009).

- Conflict and fragmentation arise most often 'not when compromises are made between ethnic groups or when formal ethnic, linguistic and/or religious rights are accorded some degree of recognition, *but when these have been historically avoided, suppressed or ignored*' [emphasis original] (May 1999: 20–21). In a society fraught by competing nationalisms, the political aspirations of the groups must be accommodated in political institutions, especially those which engender political power sharing. The eradication of political violence is also vitally important in helping to stabilizing institutions. The emergence of strong state-building institutions, such as the legislature, policing and judiciary are key generators of societal transformation.
- Ethno-national groups cannot be simply assimilated into a common civic identity by merely guaranteeing individual social equality for their members; ethno-national groups also desire to have their differences – their national identities – formally recognized in the public sphere. Despite the fact that group members do often have overlapping and multiple identities, this does not mean their ethno-national encapsulations are not of paramount importance. People

can be members of cross-cutting civil society groups based on gender and class interests; this does not mean such affiliations override people's desire to be primarily recognized as members of ethno-national groups. Nevertheless, it is important that such cross-cleavage associational groups are encouraged, as they are undoubtedly important facilitators of trust-building and fostering good relations between and within groups. A public sphere is also of vital importance, as it allows members of society to debate issues and where differences can be managed in a peaceful way. It needs to be stated, though, it is not always possible to disentangle individuals from their group identities when they debate pressing questions concerned with social justice.

- A simple multiculturalist celebration of difference is undesirable. Difference for difference's sake can lead to a highly fragmented society ripe for exploitation by ethnic extremists. Neither is it the case that all differences can be accorded respect by opposing groups. In a divided society, while the cultural demands and expressions of one group can be seen as legitimate, for another it is seen as threatening. Group rights can clash. A perfect example of this is Orange Order marches in Northern Ireland which demand to go through nationalist areas. While for the Orange Order the right to march represents an expression of their civil liberties, to nationalist residents the march is framed as anti-Catholic and thus a denial of their human rights. A mere uncritical promotion of diversity and pluralism does not work in these instances. It is possible that antagonistic narratives evoked in ethno-national cultural practices can be reframed to allow a de-escalation of conflict and even forms of reconciliation. The goal is not to create a consensus around a shared narrative, or to eliminate differences; the task is to foster common ground so that group differences are not perceived as threatening (Ross 2007: 47).
- Group-differentiated rights should be tempered by liberal values. As Kymlicka agues (2007: 92), ethnic groups are required to advance their claims in a very specific language: human rights, civil rights liberalism, and democratic constitutionalism, with their guarantees of gender equality, religious freedom, racial non-discrimination, gay rights and due process. Neither should group rights be used to justify material inequalities which might exist between groups. Group rights should not deter the need for society-wide economic redistribution.

We have only briefly sketched out in a fairly abstract way some principles which we believe to be conducive to peace-building. We pull short from offering any complete normative and prescriptive design for a shared society, recognizing that the concept is profoundly contested. Even so, in the following chapters we shall endeavour to provide a more holistic analysis of the different facets to sharing. The point being is that authors have hitherto examined the notion of a shared society in a silo. For instance, depending on an author's methodological and disciplinary preferences s/he might examine the idea of shared spaces or shared approaches to dealing with the past or power sharing institutions or shared festivals. While much of the work carried out has been valuable, it has not adequately demonstrated the links and overlap between these different spheres. In the rest of this book we will begin to examine the connections between these key areas. In so doing, we can better comprehend a way forward which could contribute to sustainable peace-building.

2
Consociational Power Sharing: Conflict Regulation or Exacerbation?

In the space of nine days in late October 1993, 25 people were killed in sectarian and paramilitary violence across Northern Ireland. A procession of politicians lined up to warn that if Northern Irish society was not peering down a dark abyss, it was on a civil war footing. Less than five years later, in 1998, a peace accord called the Good Friday Agreement (GFA) was signed in Belfast, which it was hoped, would herald a new shared peaceful future for the people of Northern Ireland.[8] Today it is common to read that the Northern Irish peace process and the power sharing forms which underpin it provide a successful model for violently divided societies to emulate (cf. Mac Ginty 2009). World leaders, seeking to purchase some of the kudos, indulge in hyperbole. Bill Clinton, for instance, has called Northern Ireland a lesson in how intractable disputes can be resolved, and as such should be 'studied' across the globe by those interested in securing peace (RTE 2009). If the ethno-national conflict in Northern Ireland had once appeared totally impervious to any solution (Whyte 1981), it is now commonly framed as an archetypal success story of conflict management.

Much of the success of the Northern Irish peace process has been attributed to a type of political power sharing inaugurated by the Agreement in 1998 and then subsequently modified in 2006. This power sharing model is commonly called consociationalism: a 'government by elite cartel designed to turn a democracy with a fragmented political culture into a stable democracy' (Lijphart 1969: 216). Consociationalism is based upon the idea that conflict resolution in divided societies is best achieved through the accommodation of the political élites representing the salient segments of society and institutionally anchored by inclusive coalitions and proportionality in public appointments (Andeweg 2000: 512). This all-encompassing approach to governance eschews as ill-advised and even 'despotic' in nature those majoritarian political systems which operate a *de facto* permanent exclusion of minorities from sharing political power. By seeking to equally accommodate dual or multiple public identities, consociationalism stands in contrast to those approaches which aim to forge a single all-embracing public identity through integration (McGarry and O'Leary 2009).

For leading advocates of consociationalism there is a direct causal relation between this model of power sharing and sustainable peace in Northern Ireland. According to McGarry and O'Leary (2006: 264), there is 'hard evidence that the peace process has brought greater security and stability because it was attached to an inclusive consociational settlement'. Even vehement critics of consociationalism admit that consociationalism has become 'hegemonic' as a system of governance in deeply divided societies and that the apparently successful case of Northern Ireland 'shines as the brightest star in the new consociational universe' (Taylor 2009a: 7). Such is the prevailing orthodoxy amongst the international community regarding the potential of consociationalism to build peace and democracy in divided societies, that it has been used or suggested as fit for Bosnia, Lebanon, Burundi, Sri Lanka, Cyprus, Afghanistan, Kashmir and Iraq, amongst numerous other divided societies (Rothchild and Roeder 2005a: 5).

In this chapter we examine pertinent issues concerning power sharing structures between Irish nationalists and British unionists in Northern Ireland since 1998. Two broad but conflicting perspectives have been articulated to debate the significance of consociational power sharing. The first perspective is articulated by proponents of consociationalism, who claim that it represents the best *modus operandi* to ensure that unionists and nationalists are endowed with equal recognition in all spheres of public life while also providing a range of institutions which allow for a number of issues to be peacefully and democratically addressed. Proponents state that though the system is by no means perfect, as with Occam's Razor, when all propositions are equally evaluated, consociationalism is left as the best opportunity for advancing democratic stability and peace. In fact, they state that power sharing is the most realistic option, as it takes at face value the profoundly embedded salience of ethno-national identities in deeply divided societies and the fact that ethno-national groups are not likely to melt or fuse at any point in the foreseeable future. Power sharing in deeply divided societies is therefore portrayed as the only form of democracy which works and it is better to implement it immediately rather than in the violent wake of other failed attempts to manage division. For this reason, proponents claim consociationalism has become the prescribed method of conflict regulation of the international community and the local conflict parties.

The second perspective is espoused by critics who argue that consociationalism has entrenched and exacerbated sectarian division across all domains of public and even private life, thereby ensuring that group based hostilities remain at the expense of any chance of a shared and reconciled society. Opponents argue that consociationalism is an inapt and undemocratic model for deeply divided societies. They argue that consociationalism represents an unremittingly bleak view of humanity which provides little or no scope for cooperation or the sharing of resources across ethno-national groups; it reifies and freezes groups when all encouragement should be given to individuals to emancipate themselves from antagonistic ethno-national communal identities by forging multiple, hybrid and fluid social encapsulations within the framework of a common civic identity.

The debate on consociationalism has become both highly normative and acrimonious regarding whether it can be seen as a model of governance in deeply divided societies which is successful in peacefully managing social divisions or conducive to further strengthening them. We argue that although consociationalism undoubtedly has some flaws – especially a lack of clarity from its adherents as to how it helps society move from conflict management to transformation – it is the best of all available options to bring about stability in regions which are violently divided. As such, we believe that critics of consociationalism operate from a misreading of social identity – especially ethno-national identity – and its capacity to undergo profound transformation so that new shared forms emerge. It is this misconception which leads critics to seek out alternative methods to consociationalism which aim to socially engineer shared identities. As we shall see, these alternative models are unlikely to engender non-sectarian politics and may even intensify ethnic cleavages. We will begin by exploring how consociationalism became the dominant mode of power sharing for Northern Ireland. Before doing so it is first necessary to illuminate how the conflict in Northern Ireland was diagnosed in a specific way so that consociational power sharing became the preferred prescription.

Why the conflict is ethno-national

The first step to prescribing a solution to a long-standing conflict is to correctly diagnose its cause in the first place. Conversely, proffering a wrong analysis of a conflict's roots will probably lead to the adoption of inappropriate management frameworks, which run the risk of exacerbating a conflict (M.L.R. Smith 1999: 96). For Northern Ireland to require a consociational remedy, a specific diagnosis of the conflict's causes was required. The analysis which underscored the appropriateness of a consociational management framework was one which framed Northern Ireland as ethno-national in nature. This particular analysis had been developed by Wright (1988), who had viewed Northern Ireland as an 'ethnic frontier' inhabited by two communities belonging to nations outside the conflict zone. It was subsequently refined by McGarry and O'Leary (1995), who explained the conflict in terms of an intersection of endogenous (internal) and exogenous (external) factors.

Endogenously speaking, the settlers who arrived on the island of Ireland in the sixteenth- and seventeenth-centuries Ireland possessed ethnic heritages which were distinct from those who already inhabited the island. In terms of ethnicity, the bulk of the settlers were drawn from various Protestant denominations and came from either Scotland or England; thus to a certain degree these individuals had a shared religion, historical experience and common culture. On the other hand, the bulk of the native population was largely Catholic and Gaelic in orientation.

Exogenously, the dual failure of British and Irish nation- and state-building projects on the island of Ireland meant that these separate ethnic heritages would eventually become fused with discordant national identities (Lustick 1993). The settler population easily assimilated into British administrative structures, thus displacing local political élites. Moreover, the integration of settlers into British administrative apparatuses on the island prevented the passage of conciliatory measures which possessed the potential to legitimate British rule and allow a wider sense of loyalty to the UK to take root (for example, granting Catholic emancipation with the passage of the Act of Union in 1801) (Lustick 1993: 5; McGarry and O'Leary 1995: 332; Bew 2007: 63). Thus the Catholic population's calls for reform were rarely aligned with a positive identification with the British state or nation. Catholic calls for reform eventually gave way to Irish nationalism, and its key cultural features, Gaelic identity and Catholicism, were an anathema to most of the settler population's ancestors, the bulk of whom were now settled in the northeast corner of the island. The concentration of industrial development in this area rendered Ulster – and much of what would later become Northern Ireland – all the more dissimilar from the rest of the island (Bew and Patterson 1985: 3–4). Therefore, Irish nationalist leaders' calls for agrarian mobilization only served to further alienate many northern Protestants from the Irish national project. Irish nationalism's inability to absorb the bulk of the settler population's descendants meant that both calls for Home Rule (a devolved parliament for Ireland) and later an independent Ireland were met with resistance by these individuals, who instead wished to retain the union with Britain. This clash of competing claims led to the partition of Ireland in 1921, but the resulting UK province of Northern Ireland would contain a significant minority of Irish nationalists. As nationalism is a doctrine which asserts that political and national boundaries should be coterminous, the bulk of the dispute between Irish nationalists and British unionists would centre upon divergent interpretations of these boundaries. Thus, despite the fact that there has been numerous instances of interaction and cultural overlap between the two groups (see Nic Craith 2002), the idea of two distinct *national* identities has persisted.

While the above analysis does not deny that ethnicity rests upon 'assumed givens' (Geertz 1973: 259–60) or that nations are modern constructs, it does deny that, once mobilized, ethno-national identities are either readily or infinitely malleable. Ethnic ties are assumed givens because individuals consider them to be so, and such assumptions underscore the powerful sense of self and belonging which such ties provide. Moreover, nationalist élites' ability to draw upon these pre-existing ethnic ties imbues the 'nation' with similar affective power. Therefore, one must refrain from mistakenly assuming that because ethno-national identities are constructed they can also be easily deconstructed.

Although the British government has not always recognized the ethno-national nature of the conflict in Northern Ireland (see Clancy 2010), the frameworks that the British and Irish government have implemented, or attempted to implement, in Northern Ireland since the early 1970s broadly reflect the conflict's ethno-national provenances. Indeed, until the arrival of the Good Friday Agreement in 1998, seven separate attempts to institute power sharing were tried. Nevertheless, the onset of the conflict in Northern Ireland also engendered a 'meta-conflict' regarding the conflict's origins (McGarry and O'Leary 1995: 1). Alternative explanations, however, do not withstand scrutiny.[9]

Economic

Although the above analysis underlined the importance of industrialization in further alienating northern Protestants from the Irish national project, economic analyses of the conflict cannot explain the continued persistence of the ethno-national divide in Northern Ireland. The erroneous assumption regarding the ameliorative effects which economic modernization would have on the nationalist/unionist divide demonstrates that the conflict is not fundamentally economic in nature, as the conflict emerged during a period of relative prosperity. Furthermore, periods of economic downturn have not been directly related to increased violence in Northern Ireland (Thompson 1989). Survey evidence from the period immediately preceding the Troubles in 1969 also shows that although Catholic respondents felt that Northern Ireland was improving, this did not translate into a diminished desire for a united Ireland (Rose 1971). Arguments that the conflict is a product of deprivation and/or discrimination are similarly unconvincing. Such arguments ignore that individuals respond to grievances or perceived grievances differently, and Alonso (2007) has demonstrated that personal experiences of discrimination did not play a significant role in individuals' decision to join the Irish Republican Army (IRA). Deprivation and discrimination accounts also fail to explain why the conflict has persisted in the face of numerous instances of fair employment and equality legislation and why 'the vast majority of Catholics vote overwhelmingly for parties whose *raison d'être* is Irish nationalism, and not mere individual equality within the UK' (McGarry and O'Leary 2004: 189).

Religion

Although it has been argued that religion is more than a mere ethno-national marker in Northern Ireland (Aughey 1989: 4), it remains the case that it is not a key driver of the conflict. The conflict began during a period of increased secularization and ecumenism, and greater religiosity does not translate into increased support for nationalism/republicanism and unionism/loyalism (McGarry and O'Leary 2004: 184). For example, although some evangelical Protestants did move towards Ian Paisley's hard-line Democratic Unionist Party (DUP) in the 1990s, they did so largely because of the party's moral conservatism, not because of its stance on the union *per se* (Mitchell and Tilley 2004). Similarly, Irish nationalist redoubts are often located in working-class neighbourhoods where mass attendance rates are low (Whyte 1990: 27).

Colonialism

Colonial explanations for the conflict in Northern Ireland are unsatisfying, as their reductionism is patronizing to both the colonized and the colonizer. To argue that Northern Ireland's divisions are the product of wholly exogenous factors suggests that the colonized are *tabulae rasae* and completely without agency; colonization processes are rarely that complete, and individuals are seldom that malleable. It is also distorting to view the history of British-Irish relations solely through the lens of colonialism, as issues of propinquity and administration have limited its explanatory value (Howe 2000).

Élites

While perhaps unintended by their proponents, arguments that blame the conflict on the machinations of Northern Ireland's political élites have similar patronizing undercurrents. Although Northern Ireland has had, as one commentator wittily commented, its fair share of 'rabble-rousing politicians threatening to fight to the last drop of everyone else's blood', this is not to argue that citizens are infinitely malleable and without agency. As the above analysis of the conflict origins argued, while not 'givens', ethno-national differences often predate the élites who utilize them as bases for mobilization (Connor 1994) and '[a] unilateral cross-communal move is all too often the last that a politician gets to make' (Mitchell 2001: 29). As such, political élites' stances are a reflection of the electorate's predilections (McGarry and O'Leary 2004: 22), and they do not possess the inherent power to shape their constituency. Leaders who go too far in 'jettisoning the cultural trappings of their community often find themselves with diminished influence in the community' (Smithey 2009: 93). For this reason, Northern Ireland's divisions are not merely the product of élite *legerdemain*. The deeply rooted nature of Northern Ireland's divisions also exposes why nationalist and unionist integrationist analyses of the conflict – which advocate Northern Ireland's wholesale absorption into either the Republic of Ireland or the United Kingdom – are incorrect and unworkable, as they deny the embedded character of unionists and nationalists' identities.

To reiterate, Northern Ireland's divisions are best described as ethno-national in nature. Since the sixteenth and seventeenth century, the settler and native populations of the northern part of Ireland have had separate ethnic heritages, and dual nation- and state-building failures on the island of Ireland meant that these heritages became merged with national identities which were also distinct. The Northern Ireland conflict's ethno-national basis explains why it persisted for nearly thirty years despite numerous instances of equality and fair employment legislation, and why it began during a period of relative economic prosperity and increasing ecumenism. The resiliency of ethno-national identities means that 'they are not amenable to any orthodox democratic resolution tied to notions of individualistic liberal (or class-based) justice' (L. O'Dowd 2009: 310). Ethno-national identities are, however, open to frameworks which seek to recognize them and defuse their most destructive and violent aspects (Van Evera 2001).

Thus, in similarly determining the conflict in Northern Ireland is primarily ethno-national in character, McGarry and O'Leary began to conclude in the early 1990s that the only system to successfully regulate and manage the violent conflict was consociational power sharing. However, McGarry and O'Leary faced a substantive normative and empirical problem. As it stood, for consociationalism to be applied to Northern Ireland it needed to be critically revised and made bespoke for the exigencies of the divided region. Since consociationalism was designed for countries with linguistic or religious cleavages, it was seen as impracticable for societies which were violently divided by contending ethno-national groups and where political élites did not possess a history or appetite for power sharing. It is worthwhile briefly tracing the development of consociational theory and McGarry and O'Leary's revisions so that it could be accommodated for Northern Ireland.

Consociational theory

The scholar associated with consociationalism's formalization, Arend Lijphart, began to consolidate the theory in order to fashion a rejoinder to Gabriel Almond's (1956) typology of democracies, which precluded the idea that stability could be obtained in culturally heterogeneous societies which lacked significant cross pressures. In the Netherlands – one of Lijphart's case studies – political stability existed despite the lack of cross-cutting cleavages. Lijphart theorized that stability in divided societies could be achieved through coalescent behaviour of its élites, and that élites engage in this type of behaviour when they become cognizant of the potential dangers emanating from the high levels of intersubcultural hostility within their borders (Lijphart 1975a: 182–3). Consociationalism is usually characterized as consisting of four key elements: a grand coalition representing the *main* (not all) segments of society (see O'Leary 2005: 13); proportionality in representation, public employment and expenditure; community autonomy on issues deemed to be vital; and constitutional vetoes for minorities (Lijphart 1977). Later on, Lijphart outlined several other features which were conducive to the onset of consociationalism in a divided society.[10]

Lijphart had originally restricted his analysis of consociationalism to 'segmented' rather than pluri-national societies. By using the term segmented Lijphart was primarily referring to the religious, linguistic or ideological portions of a society which represented the distinct cleavages. Examples of such segmented societies included the Netherlands, Austria, Belgium and Switzerland. Although Lijphart viewed these societies as 'divided' into relatively discrete segments, crucially they were united by sharing the same overarching national identity. This pattern of national identification, according to Lijphart, provided one key variable to allow consociational power sharing to flourish. Lijphart (1975b: 100) argued that 'the centrifugal tendencies of subcultural cleavages are counterbalanced to at least a certain degree by an overarching consensus'.

For pluri-national societies like Northern Ireland, in which the existing segments were ethno-national in character, there was a clear absence of overarching loyalty unifying the two groups, thus precluding, according to Lijphart (1977), its suitability for consociational influence. Moreover, in ethno-nationally divided societies like Northern Ireland the experience of intense intercommunal violence presented difficult challenges for élites willing to contemplate compromise (McGarry and O'Leary 1995: 343). Lijphart (1977) set further ideal-type conditions which were not particularly suitable for the context of Northern Ireland. In particular, Lijphart favoured a multi-cleavage society, fearing that in dual cleavage societies like Northern Ireland, competitive, zero-sum game politics might remain as each side would try to win a decisive majority (Tonge 2004: 37). In this way, Lijphart was also sceptical of consociationalism's prospects in those divided societies where one cleavage represented a dominant majority, such as unionists in Northern Ireland. Lijphart assumed that the élites of such majorities would have no incentive to enter into power sharing if they could already dominate the polity through existing electoral mechanisms.

Lijphart's pessimism that consociationalism would find fallow ground in a divided society like Northern Ireland appeared to have been confirmed when an agreement for power sharing between nationalists and unionists in the region collapsed in 1974. Lijphart was to conclude that if the appropriate conditions could not be engineered, Northern Ireland was best suited to partition as a terminal form of conflict management, a threat which he believed might paradoxically coerce Northern Ireland's political élites into accepting power sharing (Lijphart 1975b: 105–6). It was clear that if consociationalism was not to be discarded as a workable solution for Northern Ireland, it would have to be critically refashioned to suit the needs of the region. If classic consociational prescriptions – *a lá* Lijphart – had become stuck on resolving linguistic or religious disputes, then a revised model was required to deal with self-determination conflicts (McGarry and O'Leary 2006: 249).

Undertaking such a task, the academic partnership of McGarry and O'Leary began to formulate revisions of Lijphart's model so that it could be made more amenable to the pluri-national and violent context of Northern Ireland. Subsequently labelling their revisions 'consociationalism plus' and 'liberal consociationalism', McGarry and O'Leary retained Lijphart's four core variables – a grand coalition, proportionality, autonomy and vetoes – while supplementing the model. Recognizing that Northern Ireland's polity and society are bi-national, they sought to include mechanisms which would officially recognize the national identities of the main groups both institutionally and symbolically, especially their right to claim self-determination (McGarry and O'Leary 2009: 34). To assist with the transition from war to peace in Northern Ireland, they identified military and policing reform, demilititarization, human rights reform, and specific legislation for prisoners and victims. Lastly, while the classical consociationalism of Lijphart had 'been overly fixated on the traditional sovereign and internationally recognized state' (McGarry and O'Leary 2006: 249), consociationalism plus made provisions for the role of exogenous parties in facilitating and implementing agreements, including the UK, Republic of Ireland, the US and the EU. Taken together, it was hoped that the provisions of liberal consociationalism would have the appropriate balance of carrots and sticks to enable political élites to embrace power sharing.

The Good Friday Agreement of 1998 embodied many of the features of consociationalism plus. In terms of the grand coalition, political devolution entailed some executive powers being granted to a parliament, the Northern Ireland Assembly, made up of 108 elected representatives from across the region. Contained within the Assembly is a power sharing executive, headed by a premiership dyarchy (First Minister and Deputy First Minister possessing equal powers), and a number of cabinet ministers encompassing the main political parties based on their share of the vote. Proportionality in representation, public employment and expenditure is included in terms of the allocation of ministerial positions in the Executive, as well as the use of proportional representation to ensure that the respective groups are represented in the Assembly in proportion to their numbers in the population. Proportionality was also included in areas such as the recruitment of officers to the police service and appointments to the civil service. Constitutional vetoes were given to unionists and nationalists in the Northern Ireland Assembly for all key votes. Not all powers, however, have been devolved, with the NI Assembly remaining subservient to the UK government in policies concerning defence, immigration, international relations, taxation, borrowing and Europe. The idea of community autonomy – the idea that unionists and nationalists should be granted autonomy in the domains of separate schools, universities, places of worship and trade unions was not clearly featured, although there was a call for an Irish Language Act. The extra features of consociationalism plus manifested themselves in how the Agreement recognized the equal standing of unionist and nationalist identities and their right to pursue self-determination, a right which had to be mutually recognized by the two groups as well as the governments of the UK and Ireland. In recognition of the role of exogenous actors – particularly the UK and the Republic of Ireland – institutions were set up which recognized the links between these states and their kin groups in Northern Ireland.[11] Further to this, the Agreement addresses other issues relevant to the conflict: the release of paramilitary prisoners, the reform and devolution of policing, paramilitary weapons decommissioning, demilitarization and equality legislation.

Critiques of consociationalism

The establishment of consociational power sharing arrangements in Northern Ireland has not been met with universal praise or acceptance. Consociational power sharing has been subject to numerous critiques, at both an empirical and normative level. These overlapping critiques, broadly speaking, can be categorized as accusing consociationalism of (1) lacking empirical conviction; (2) entrenching and exacerbating sectarianism; (3) being illiberal; (4) hindering a politics of economic redistribution; (5) providing weak and undemocratic government; (6) an inability to contribute to long-term peace-building. Taken together, these critiques have sought to undermine the underpinnings of consociationalism so that it will collapse under its numerous inconsistencies and flaws (Wilson 2009a) to allow an alternative model to flourish will promote greater cooperation and the amelioration of ethno-national antagonism. These critiques require further illumination and debate.

Lacking empirical conviction

The first critique concerns empirical weakness and/or inconsistency regarding those theorists who advance consociationalism. A host of empirical criticisms have been levied against Lijphart's work (for example Nordlinger 1972, Halpern 1986, Lustick 1997). Similarly, the Good

Friday Agreement in Northern Ireland has been accused of not being consociational at all, but an altogether different kettle of fish. Dixon (2005), for example, argues that the Good Friday Agreement bears only a minor resemblance to consociationalism. These empirical concerns shall not delay us too long. Although, as we have seen, Lijphart's model of consociationalism has been adapted for the specifics of bi-national societies like Northern Ireland, this does not mean the baby should be thrown out with the bathwater. As Coakley (2009a: 125) surmises: 'it would be both unscholarly and deeply unflattering to Lijphart to treat his writings as sacred scripture, frozen in time and an appropriate objective of exegesis by true believers'. The modifications enshrined by liberal consociationalism should be clearly seen as consociational.

Entrenching sectarianism and primordialism

The second and most common critique is that consociational arrangements axiomatically entrench and exacerbate sectarianism. It is said that consociationalists institutionalize ethno-national divisions because they work from a skewed primordialist reading of ethnicity which assumes that ethno-national identities are pre-given and even biologically determined rather than inherently constructed and transformable. Thus it is common to read that the Agreement 'endorses social segregation' (Wilford 2001: 60–61); is a form of 'benign apartheid' (Graham and Nash 2006); 'the vicissitudes of the Agreement' have contributed to the 'deepening of communal divisions in Belfast and elsewhere' (Finlay 2006: 6); 'the Agreement encouraged ethno-sectarian separation' (Shirlow and Murtagh 2006: 41); the Agreement 'reinforces and perpetuates sectarian division' (Taylor 2009b: 320); consociationalism 'assumes that identities are primordial and exclusive rather than malleable and relational' (Wilford and Wilson 2003: 6); for consociationalists 'individual identity is conceived as being dependent on an inherited, primordial, communal culture' (Finlay 2006: 6). We could go on, but space simply precludes us from doing so.

Are consociationalists arch-proponents of primordialism? The grievous accusation is that consociationalists accept at face value the unchanging primacy of ethnic encapsulations in 'divided societies' and, in response, build institutional structures that do not allow for such identities to grow and transform into new non-antagonistic shared forms. As we noted in Chapter 1, most of the academic literature on primordialism does not claim that ethnic identities are undoubtedly resistant to change; what matters is that the identity bearers sincerely *believe* that their identities are non-negotiable expressions of their selves, and this 'may be decisive for political attitudes and behaviour' (McGarry and O'Leary 2009: 26). Crucially, even though ethnic identities are clearly constructed, they are incredibly hard, though not impossible to reconstruct when they have become crystallized. This is particularly apposite for violently divided societies in which identities have been mobilized and hardened through their inscription in narrative forms.

It is clearly the case that in many examples, under certain conditions, groups have undergone identity transformations. One of the most notable cases concerns the vanishing of a German-American identity during the second decade of the twentieth century. This is not particularly surprising since the disappearance of this identity occurred in the context of the First World War when the US was fighting against Germany. German-Americans deliberately abandoned their ethnic identity because it was increasingly seen to not work for members in an extremely hostile milieu: it prohibited the group from gaining collective goals for its betterment (Cornell and Hartmann 1998). The ethnographic canon is also replete with examples of how ethnic groups have become transformed or incorporated into other groups (see Barth 1969, Smith 1991: 32–33, Baumann 1996: 18, Jenkins 2004). It is important to bear in mind that such instances are occasioned through assimilation, and this is rarely a benign process achieved on a basis of equality between groups.

Does consociationalism encourage the reification and exacerbation of identities and divisiveness? Critics argue that some of the key institutional apparatuses of consociationalism not only recognize but also fundamentally conspire to categorize people into discrete ethno-national categories, thereby limiting their capacity to seek out alternative political identities. The institutions inaugurated by the Agreement, state Coulter and Murray (2009: 15), 'presuppose that people in Northern Ireland can mobilise politically only as unionists and nationalists respectively and insist that they can compete for resources accordingly'.

Two key features of power sharing in Northern Ireland are accused by critics of 'entrenching division' (Wilford and Wilson 2003: 5). The first concerns the Single Transferable Vote (STV) electoral system used to return Members of the Legislative Assembly (MLA) for the power sharing assembly. In this system, successful candidates need only to surpass a relatively small quota of votes in order to be elected. According to Wilford and Wilson (2003) the STV system dissuades candidates from pursuing moderate and conciliatory policies which would appeal to votes from rival ethnic blocs. Due to STV, they continue, 'elections have become entirely communalized affairs, rewarding intra-ethnic outbidding' (2003: 5). The second aspect to consociational power sharing which critics claim has 'legitimised sectarian division' (Tonge 2009: 49) is the system of designation for MLAs in the Northern Ireland Assembly. Assembly rules, as they currently stand, require the 108 elected MLAs to register as either 'nationalist', 'unionist' or 'other' (non unionist or nationalist). The point of the designation system is to ensure that when policy votes are taken in the Assembly, nationalists and unionists possess a mutual veto to act against majority ethnic lock-in where minority groups are excluded from the decision making process. For motions to pass there needs to be a weighted majority – 40 per cent support of each group and 60 per cent overall – or 'parallel consent', a concurrent majority of both nationalists and unionists as well as a majority in the assembly. Critics have accused the designation system as acting to 'entrench communalist politics' (Wilford and Wilson 2006: 39). According to critics, consociationalists promote group vetoes, because they assume that Northern Ireland will remain 'forever divided, requiring continual and skilful management, rather than becoming a united, through diverse, community with common goals and shared interests' (Farry 2009: 175). Specifically, the system is seen as according more weight to nationalist and unionist votes than those members who do not wish to be 'pigeonholed' in communal terms, thereby providing a deterrent for cross-community parties and politics to emerge. For once critic, the system 'locks members into sectarian groupthink and restricts freedom of association' (Taylor 2009b: 320).

Rather than institutionalizing sectarianism, advocates of consociationalism argue that they are merely legislating for what is already there and that any successful accommodation of competing ethno-nationalisms in Northern Ireland has to begin by accepting the saliency and relative historical fixity of ethno-national identities. Consociationalists take as their departure 'that communal or ethnic divisions are resilient rather than rapidly biodegradable, and that they must be recognized rather than wished away' (McGarry and O'Leary 1995: 338). Accordingly, consociationalists are apt to portray their clique as 'pragmatists who, in accepting existing divisions within ethnically divided societies, strive to regulate them through complex constitutional engineering' (Kerr 2009: 209). Consociationalists can claim such expediency on the basis that in Northern Ireland the link between religious affiliation and political preference remains the strongest in Western Europe. The supporters of each of the principal parties continue to be drawn almost exclusively from the rival ethno-national blocs. The young are more likely to vote for so-called hard-line rather than moderate parties. There does not seem to be an imminent electoral breakthrough for any of the smaller parties who advocate policies which cross-cut cleavages or promote a shared 'non-sectarian' identity (Tonge 2009: 65).

Critics of consociationalism counter that modes of ethno-national identification are becoming increasingly fragile in the everyday lives of people in Northern Ireland. The task is one of social engineering, to encourage a further weakening of antagonistic ethno-nationalisms by constructing institutions which promote, rather than prohibit, new shared encapsulations. Accordingly, critics of consociationalism deploy an array of statistics from various surveys to claim that 'a substantial proportion of the people of Northern Ireland are willing to drop communal differences' (Wilson 2009b: 222); 'traditional notions of identity are breaking down' (Farry 2009: 173); and there is 'a desire to transcend the unionist-nationalist antagonism' (Wilford and Wilson 2006: 8). As Figure 2.1 demonstrates, research points to the steady growth since 1998 of people in Northern Ireland who do not identify as being either unionist or nationalist. In fact, since 2006 the 'non-identifiers' has become the largest group consistently polling over 40 per cent.

Problematically for this perspective, there is a tendency in surveys for respondents to portray themselves as 'liberal-minded, non-sectarian pluralist, whatever their private prejudices' (Tonge 2009: 65). Such expressions of non-sectarianism rarely seem to translate into any substantial support for cross-community political parties. As we can see from Table 2.1, electoral support for nationalist and unionist parties/ candidates consistently approximates to around 90 per cent of the vote

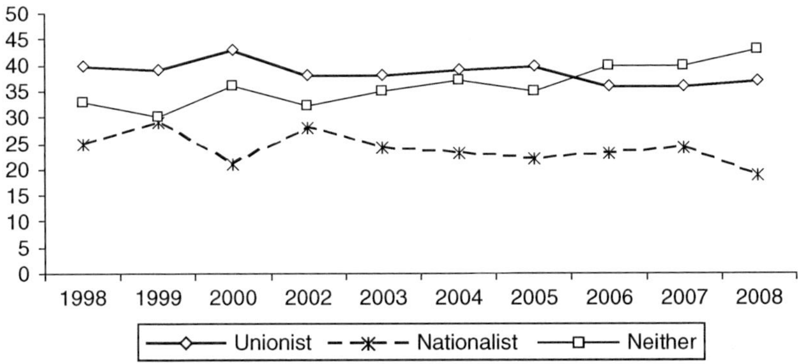

Figure 2.1   Political identities in Northern Ireland 1998–2008 (%)

Source: Northern Ireland Life and Times Survey 1998–2008, Module: Political Attitudes, Variable: UNINATID.

Table 2.1   Voting preferences in General and Assembly Elections: 1998–2007 (%)

	1997	1998	2001	2003	2005	2007
Unionist	50.5	50.37	52.9	51.87	51.8	47.3
Nationalist	40.5	40.5	43	40.8	42	41.5
Neither	9	10	4.1	7.33	6.2	11.2

Source: ARK: Northern Ireland Elections 1997–2007.

at both general and assembly elections. Support for cross-community parties and candidates remains extremely small.

Being illiberal

This brings us to the third main critique of consociationalism: it is 'illiberal'. According to Taylor (2008: 183), consociationalism 'rests on and promotes an ethno-national group-based understanding of politics that is inherently illiberal'. Liberal political theory:

> is *individualist* in asserting or assuming the moral primacy of the person against the claims of any social collectivity; second, it is *egalitarian* because it confers on all such individuals 'the same moral status and denies the relevance to legal or political order of differences in moral worth among human beings'; and third, it is *universalist* because it affirms the moral unity of the human species and accords 'a secondary importance to specific historic associations and cultural forms'. [emphasis original] (Kukathas 1995: 231)

Consociational power sharing is construed by critics as illiberal because it is seen to advocate the primacy of group-differentiated rights over those which accrue to the individual, such as those enshrined in the Universal Declaration of Human Rights. For Shirlow and Murtagh (2006: 41) the 'Agreement's fundamental flaw was that it placed traditions and group equality before the higher and more dignified principle of individual rights'. Liberal opponents of group rights reject that 'the conception of equal citizenship embodied in equal rights needs to be replaced by a set of culturally differentiated rights' (Barry 2001: 9). In contrast, they argue their model of unitary and equal citizenship rights is best placed to accommodate issues of cultural difference. If all are treated with an equal set of rights and opportunities, this should obviate racial and ethnic injustice.

The model of unitary and equal citizenship is also defended by many liberals for protecting the freedom and autonomy of the individual. The notion of individual autonomy considers that it is correct an individual is able to choose and live the life they deem fit unconstrained by distorting external forces or group allegiances. A fundamental principle of autonomy is that members of a society devote a great deal of effort 'questioning their basic beliefs and probing the rationale of the institutions and practices within which they live' (Barry 2001: 120). As such, autonomy allows agents to be free of groups and traditions they believe to be erroneous or illiberal.

Consociationalism is therefore illiberal if it is proven to promote group rights in such a way as to make the rights of the individual obsolete. Consociationalism is illiberal if it acts to pre-determine groups rather than allow them to be self-determined; if it regulates individuals as mere appendages of communal constructs rather than as autonomous agents free to select group affiliation. Certainly, in places like Lebanon, Burundi, Cyprus and Bosnia, where consociational power sharing has been implemented at various junctures, the critique has some traction. Power sharing here is based on corporate rather than liberal principles, ensuring that specific groups retain a privileged place in the government at all costs. There is a ratio pre-determining which groups are to be included in state institutions. Such corporatism can be achieved through a system which deliberately obliges voters to vote only within their own segment for their own ethnic parties, and where seats are reserved to ethnic parties in advance of elections. In Cyprus (1960–1968), for instance, citizens had to opt to be either Greek Cypriot or Turkish Cypriot when they voted. Cross-community political parties hosting candidates from numerous ethnic groups were proscribed from standing for election (Horowitz 2008). As such, individuals became mere agglomerates of stagnant communal ethnic identities. Such corporate or pre-determined prescriptions to power sharing are illiberal or even primordialist in its narrowest sense: it essentializes ethnicity and reifies group identity to properties immune from social relations thereby disavowing any potential for change or the amelioration of zero-sum conflict. Corporatism really does approximate to maintaining groups as 'clearly delineated and identifiable entities that coexist, whilst maintaining firm boundaries, as would pieces of a mosaic' (Benhabib 2002: 8). Such corporatism can store up future conflict since the permanently excluded are aggrieved and the potential for demographic shifts are unaccounted for (McCulloch 2009: 44). Power sharing agreements often reflect existing ethnic power relations and demographics at the time of signing. When these relations inevitably alter, corporate power sharing forms are too inflexible to withstand change. The power sharing system introduced in Lebanon in 1945, for example, gradually collapsed as it did not accommodate an increase in the Muslim population, thus leading to Muslim grievances and eventual civil war (Jarstad 2008: 120–121).

There is no corporate underpinning to power sharing in Northern Ireland. Voters in Northern Ireland can select any candidates they deem fit from a common roll and they can express first or lower-order voting preferences outside their ethnic blocs; there are no seats or political positions reserved for specific ethno-national groups; executive places are distributed among parties based on their performances in free and democratic elections (McGarry and O'Leary 2006). Groups are self-determined rather than pre-determined. In practical terms, this means that ethno-national blocs could disappear if voters decided to put their support behind parties who advanced non-ethnic issues which cross-cut cleavages. Groups are not rendered as 'fixed and unchanging entities in the moral universe'; a liberal consociation allows scope for the fact that 'groups are constantly forming and dissolving in response to political and institutional circumstances' (Kukathas 1995: 232). Having said this, it could be argued that some institutions of the Agreement sail close to the rocks of corporatism. The system of group designation and mutual group veto can be interpreted 'as a proxy for corporate guarantees' (McCulloch 2009: 221). This particular problem would easily be solved if the designation system was abandoned in favour of a simple weighted majority of 65 per cent of all MLAs irrespective of group identity (see also Wilford and Wilson 2006: 39). It is doubtful, though, whether this change would effect any substantial change to the balance of parties in the Assembly.

Hindering a politics of economic redistribution

Another critique of consociationalism is that it stymies the formation of class based politics in favour of ethnic resource competition.

Consociationalism is further seen as weakening the welfare state by eroding the sense of pan-ethnic solidarity needed to sustain society-wide economic redistribution. A key argument articulated by socialists is that the Agreement 'validates political parties based on communal identity and stiffens the sense of separateness' (McCann 2009b), thereby keeping the workers disunited on ethnic lines. In response to socioeconomic division, critics of the consociational Agreement call for a politics which will 'make the class we belong to more important than the community we come from' (Socialist Environmental Alliance 2005). Shirlow and Murtagh (2006) also argue that the Agreement has witnessed a 'stale and repetitive pattern of ethnically-divided competition over resources'. In Northern Ireland, fierce communal debates have arisen over distributive issues, like where hospitals and leisure centres should be sited (Horowitz 2008: 1221). Since the Agreement is accused of being unable to tackle the problems of endemic segregation across the region, a situation has emerged whereby public services are duplicated for nationalist and unionist areas. The 'cost of division', it is claimed, is £1.5 billion per annum (Deloitte and Touche 2007). The Alliance Party, a self-described non-sectarian party, has contested elections in Northern Ireland with the slogan 'Sharing Works; Segregation Costs'. Similarly, in some Bosnian cities, like Mostar, the municipal authorities are overburdened by a system supporting separate hospitals, postal services, fire stations and educational systems (McMahon and Western 2009). Such service duplication/multiplication can overtax a weak revenue base meaning that the government may have to enforce cutbacks on vital public services (Rothchild and Roeder 2005b: 39). In sum, recent research points to a grim conclusion for divided societies: cultural heterogeneity costs and such societies are associated with poor public services and low economic growth (Laitin 2007: 108).

A crucial problem with systems of governance which include a strong emphasis on group-differentiated rights is that it could compromise the effectiveness of the welfare state and the distribution of public goods. This concept of the welfare state requires us to make sacrifices 'for anonymous others ... whose ethnic descent ... differs from our own' (Kymlicka 2001: 225). The argument is that 'people are willing to make sacrifices for kin and for co-religionists, but are only willing to accept wider obligations under certain conditions' (Kymlicka 2001: 25). There must be, consequently, 'some sense of common identity and common membership uniting donor and recipient, such that sacrifices being made for anonymous others are still, in some sense, sacrifices for "one of us"' (Kymlicka 2001: 25). The easy way to create solidarity, it is argued by some liberals (Barry 2001), is by manufacturing a shared national or class based identity.

Proponents of consociationalism, on the other hand, counter socialist claims that 'transcendent class-consciousness can be easily or successfully promoted as an alternative to nationalist mobilization' (McGarry and O'Leary 1995: 364). In fact, a cursory review of the history of divided societies amply demonstrates how class alliances have 'been rendered hopeless by national, ethnic, religious, and communal divisions' (O'Leary 2005: 10). Intriguingly, O'Leary argues that if consociational arrangements had been tried in some countries, 'trust might have developed that would have fostered wider working-class or popular unity – for example, behind the welfare state or other forms of distributive politics' (2005: 10). It is left somewhat unclear by O'Leary, though, how consociationalism may be made to rhyme with class unity and welfarist policies. Nevertheless, the issue remains: it is unfair to state that consociationalism prohibits class based politics or pan-society economic redistribution; the major problem is the endemic persistence of ethno-nationalism as the major driver of identification. In divided societies, class tends to reinforce ethnic cleavages rather than providing a means for their amelioration.

Moreover, while division is costly, the price of engineering national homogeneity is even more expensive. Such uniformity is often wrought through the construction of strong assimilative policies designed to neutralize the differences of minority groups, which in turn can lead to heightened grievances and a violent backlash. Research also shows that divided societies tied together with consociational institutions outperform majoritarian democracies which exclude minorities from power, in terms of macroeconomic and welfare policies (Lijphart 1999). A more realistic proposition, then, might be to design institutions which encourage cross-cleavage cooperation to help distribute public services for the good of all society. Some recent research in the divided society of Uganda demonstrate that provided the opportunity to make anonymous donations of cash to randomly selected partners, individuals were just as generous to out-group members as they were to their co-ethnics (see Habyarimana et al. 2008). Yet when the pairs could see who their partners were, subjects discriminated strongly in favour of their co-ethnics. The research concluded that in-group peer-pressure rather than hostility towards the out-group determined levels of generosity. This may suggest that the forms of reciprocation required for distributive policies can be sustained in divided societies when institutions encourage cooperation while downplaying the deleterious consequences of in-group norms.

Providing weak and undemocratic government

The fifth critique concerns consociationalism engendering weak, divided and undemocratic governance. As Dryzek and Dunleavy (2009: 192) dryly note: consociationalism's 'democratic qualities can be questioned'. Taylor (2008: 185) goes further: 'there are processes integral to consociational politics that are inimical to liberal democracy'.

Broadly speaking, the structural underpinnings of consociationalism mean that the mandatory 'grand coalition' style of government consists of an élite cartel, guaranteeing representation from the various segments, which lacks strong opposition and accountability, a *sine qua non* of a democratic legislature. Although the point of a grand coalition is to transform 'opponents into partners', it is accused of lacking any discernible 'shared strategic vision' and instead resembling more a 'holding company' (Wilford and Wilson 2006: 27). According to one commentator (BBC 2009a), power sharing in Northern Ireland 'has brought a lack of decision making ... with no agreed underpinning ideology and decisions made on a lowest common denominator basis or by ministerial bargaining'. Due to the 'grand coalition' government triggered by consociationalism, only 8 of the 108 MLAs who sit in the Northern Ireland Assembly belong to parties outside of the Executive government, meaning that an effective system of opposition is distinctly absent.

The d'Hondt algorithm,[12] for selecting executive ministers to form a mandatory coalition, is accused of granting ministers with cabinet portfolios the power to operate *de facto* 'party fiefdoms' (Tonge 2009: 52). Power is shared out rather than shared between ethno-national blocs; there is no real 'joined-up government' to ensure any cohesive policy across government departments. Ministers can take autonomous decisions 'without sufficient cross-reference to the views of the other parties, something critical for an effective system of sharing than the carving up of power' (Farry 2009: 169). For one Northern Irish politician, the mandatory coalition represents a 'perversion of the basic tenets of democracy so monstrous that no self-respecting democrat should lie down under it' (Allister 2009).

The system of mutual vetoes, furthermore, is seen as inexorably leading to ethnic deadlock and brinksmanship. In Northern Ireland, stalemate has occurred over major issues like education, policing and justice, The Irish Language Act and the regeneration of a prison that once held paramilitary prisoners. In the worst scenario, veto logjam creates not only policy inertia but also precipitates violence. The frequent use of vetoes by the Turkish minority on Cyprus led the Greek majority to end power sharing resulting in civil strife and eventually a Turkish invasion and partition (Horowitz 2008 1221). Moreover, if we consider conflict to be the lifeblood of representative democracy, with its potential to generate progressive social transformation, consociational structures strive to tilt the balance too far towards deadlock thus rendering obsolete vigorous political competition and democratic renewal.

There is thus a nagging accusation that consociationalism provides a fractured form of democracy shorn of any real accountability. The inability of the Executive government in Northern Ireland to often act in a collective fashion replete with common political goals means that it is seen as a practically neutered type of legislature. Power has become increasingly centred in the axis of the two leading parties – the DUP and Sinn Féin – a coalition viewed as lacking accountability. Yet the inability of these two parties – representing the 'extremes' of nationalism and unionism – to compromise and work together on many issues has led to their partnership being called a 'dysfunctional office in a dysfunctional Executive' (see BBC 2009b). The example of the Bosnian Federation provides a salutary lesson in the negative impact of an illiberal consociationalism on democracy. Since every public office is allotted according to an ethnic quota, a spoils system has created extensive patronage networks, corruption, and inefficiency. With 160 government ministers and an engorged public sector which eats up nearly half of the country's GDP, corruption and inefficiency is rife (McMahon and Western 2009).

Critics of consociationalism's putative deleterious impact on democracy call for distinct changes to power sharing institutions. They request that 'government should be formed by [inter party] agreement, rather than by an automatic formula, to send out a clear sign of collectivity and commitment to the public good' (Wilson 2009b: 233). Instead of a government composed of a mandatory coalition, critics demand a voluntary coalition of moderates, who would be encouraged to engage in the politics of cross-cleavage compromise and conciliation as is the 'norm of coalition politics in societies generally' (Wilford and Wilson 2006: 29).[13]

Although many proponents of consociationalism recognize that 'consociationalism is difficult to love largely because it is not anyone's first choice' (Mitchell and Evans 2009: 146), they also depict a stark choice 'between consociational democracy and no worthwhile democracy at all' (Lijphart 1985: 13). Although they admit that 'consociational politics is…without "shared vision"' (O'Leary 2006: xxii), consociationalism is promoted as the only show in town. While the d'Hondt system of selecting ministers may not produce a joined-up government with a shared strategic vision for the common good, it is nevertheless a fair and inclusive system which encompasses moderates and hardliners alike (McGarry and O'Leary 2009). The task performed by consociationalism is not to exclude hardliners, as this would probably result in instability, but to accommodate them on the basis that they will moderate their actions as government partners.

Advocates also admit that while consociationalism places a premium on partnership, rather than on a system of parliamentary opposition, there is nothing to stop political parties from resigning from the government and acting as the official opposition (McGarry and O'Leary 2009). Although stalemates and unaccountability appear prevalent in consociational arrangements, this is common to all forms of democratic coalition government (Jarstad 2008: 129). Even when it comes to the competition for power, consociationalism measures highly in regards to the right to run for office, free and fair elections, and the responsiveness of institutions to votes (Andeweg 2000). Moreover, if we define democracy in terms of a system to engender broad representation of all segments of society, especially minorities, 'there is nothing in consociationalism that true democrats have to be ashamed of' (Lijphart 1985: 109). In many consociational societies, strong inclusivity is measured in terms of women's representation, criminal justice, political equality and voter turnout (Andeweg 2000: 531). As such, consociationalism improves upon majoritarian type democracies in which the competition for power provides a system of winners and losers with minority parties excluded from government. Although such a system may work where there are shifting parliamentary majorities and voters transfer between cleavages, in divided societies people consistently vote along ethnic lines meaning that minority ethnic parties are *de facto* absent from government. Furthermore, while consociationalism is accused of contributing towards a democratic deficit in Northern Ireland, the system of Direct Rule, with powers centralized in Westminster and the region led by the Secretary of State for Northern Ireland – ostensibly a consular figure able to make autonomous political decisions – is a system with much less accountability and inclusivity than power sharing.

An inability to contribute to long-term peace-building

The final critique of consociationalism is directed at its perceived inability to contribute towards lasting conflict resolution and sustainable peace-building. According to Horowitz (2000a: 256), consociational practices 'are inept to mitigate conflict in severely divided societies'. With its emphasis on political élites, consociationalism is accused of not addressing the need for 'bottom up' transformation, including intergroup contact and reconciliation, and civil society based approaches to the eradication of sectarianism that permeates virtually all sectors of society (Taylor 2006). The Agreement, hence, places the emphasis on 'mechanisms, institutions and legislation rather than engaging with the belief systems that underpin the conflict' (Mac Ginty 2009: 700). Neither, it is said, does consociationalism offer a clear vision in which antagonistic ethno-national identities can be emancipated so that new shared encapsulations emerge. Although consociationalism may have contributed to the diminution of extreme violence in Northern Ireland, the Agreement creates a matrix for the 'conflict to be pursued ... if anything with more alacrity than before' (Wilford and Wilson 2006: 5–6).

In a broad sense, consociationalism is not designed to immediately end conflict; a more realistic expectation is that consociationalism could eventually provide an institutional model to accommodate the conflicting interests of different ethnic groups so that 'incentives for cooperation and the nonviolent pursuit of conflicts of interest through compromise outweigh any benefits that might be expected from violent confrontation' (Wolff 2006: 134–135). In pluri-national societies, the main source of conflict between ethno-national groups – the issue of sovereignty – is rarely ever settled. As a condition to signing peace agreements and entering power sharing, ethno-national groups typically demand their right to maintain or pursue a change to the constitutional status of the state in which they reside. Consociational agreements are often designed with the purpose of accommodating two or more competing and irreconcilable claims to legitimacy and self-determination.

Clearly, however, consociational arrangements cannot simultaneously deliver a united Ireland and the maintenance of Northern Ireland within the UK. The trick of consociationalism is that it positively encourages such a paradoxical situation by allowing the leaders of unionism and nationalism to claim that the process will either inevitably consolidate the union or promulgate a transition to a united Ireland. A common description of the Agreement is that it is an exercise in 'constructive ambiguity', in which 'key documents of the peace process ... could be interpreted in various ways to suit the receiving audience' (Dixon 2002: 736). In order for consociationalism to give the appearance that it can satisfy mutually exclusive aims, it must allow for a relatively high degree of interpretative openness as to what the core legislative elements represent. In other words, many principles which underpin consociationalism are often so vague that they can be interpreted by the respective ethno-national groups as highly complementary with their own long-standing political aims despite their incompatibility *vis-à-vis* the rival group. The fact that consociationalism affords an opportunity for the respective groups to articulate discrepant readings helps the groups keep on board their own constituency of supporters who may be worried that forms of power sharing actually signal a defeat. Constructive ambiguity is accused of warding off any chance of a shared vision of politics and identity by ensuring that uncompromising ethno-national aims are maintained to keep all sides on board. Constructive ambiguity plays into the hands of those ethno-national entrepreneurs who deploy a creeping barrage, an attempt to make steady advances by slowly weakening the opposition. Wilford and Wilson (2003: 7) argue that because the Agreement accommodates mutually exclusive self-determination claims, it does little to 'mitigate intercommunal conflict. It also does nothing to establish overarching allegiance to a shared polity'.

On one level it seems churlish to chide the premise of constructive ambiguity; it provides a discourse of pluralism which allows former combatants to enter into peace agreements and power sharing in the first place. It is an exercise in *realpolitik par excellence*. Some research has demonstrated that combatants are 38 per cent more likely to enter into an agreement if it guarantees them a place in a future power sharing government (Walter 2002: 80). On another level, it cannot defer forever irreconcilable aims concerning how the polity should be governed. Only one side can realistically achieve self-determination. In this way, Rothchild and Roeder (2005a) have identified what they believe is a systemic problem with consociationalism. That is, while there are short-term benefits to power sharing, insofar as it entices the respective parties to end violence and enter into government, in the longer run it threatens the consolidation of peace. According to the authors, the incentives provided by consociational power sharing empower ethnic élites encouraging them to press ever radical claims and brinksmanship. 'Power sharing', they note (2005a: 9), 'may get ethnic leaders to leave the battlefield, but then after a short lull transforms the bargaining room into a new battlefield'.

Another way in which consociationalism is critiqued for failing to mitigate conflict in divided societies is that it does not try to and emancipate actors from sectarian ethno-national identities by creating new shared ones. Indeed, as Tonge (2004: 57) notes, the Agreement 'did not offer a model of assimilation of the ethnic identities of the two communities in Northern Ireland ... co-identity rather than shared identity, was a recurring theme'. The logic of critics is that unless there is a concerted effort to transform the binary logic of antagonistic ethno-national identities in divided societies, conflict will continually recur.

Proponents counter that consociationalism, 'in seeking political stability amid deep division, facilitating the inclusion and participation of a broad spectrum of the polity remains an invaluable conflict-managing device' (McCulloch 2009: 16). Although proponents of consociationalism often admit that it is designed primarily to regulate and manage ethnic conflict and identities, they also wish to retain a progressive potential for the system to 'provide a hospitable environment for the erosion of difference' (Coakley 2009a: 145). For O'Leary (2005: 19), 'the dissolution of (undesirable) collective identities and antagonisms may be more likely to occur after a period of consociational governance'.

In proponents' thinking it is very hazy the process by which consociationalism can move from a basis of accommodating ethnicity to one of fostering 'conditions where ethnicity will no longer be a primary identifier' (Higson 2008: 11). Mostly, the logic of consociationalists seems to be that the building of trust at élite level would gradually descend to envelop contending communities. This would, Tonge (2009: 53) summarises, 'have a beneficial impact upon societal ethnic rigidities, allowing differences to be managed peacefully and contributing to their eventual erosion'. The mutual recognition of ethnic interests is supposed to foster trust and intercommunal cooperation within the grand coalition. As Jarstad (2008:123) sums up, 'consociationalism is expected to depoliticize ethnicity and allow development of a common national identity'. Consociationalists, however, appear to be working from the most optimistic assumption regarding its ameliorative potential; it is never clearly specified exactly how consociationalism will eventually lead to the construction of shared identities.

Despite a lack of conceptual clarity here, it is possible to argue that consociationalism provides a matrix in which conflict and ethnicity *can possibly* be transformed. Accepting the point that conflict largely occurs between groups when inequality exists, and when identities are misrecognized or suppressed, accommodating groups on the basis of equality affords an opportunity for the regeneration of binary antagonistic relations. By endowing group based identities a sense of security creates an environment, paradoxically, not in which they flourish or generate heightened salience but where they can be modernized, dissolved or even fused in new benign combinations. More to the point, while it is conjectural whether consociationalism will lead to the complete transformation of conflictual identities, as we shall now see, we are on safer ground to claim that rival theories of governance in deeply divided societies are even less likely to bring about the sustainable conflict transformation their advocates claim.

Alternatives to consociationalism

The bulk of the criticisms levied against consociationalism in both the pre- and post-Agreement periods have come from those advocating various forms of social transformation and 'centripetalism' (Reilly and Reynolds 1997) as alternatives. Although their prescriptions differ, transformationists and centripetalists both emphasize the importance of civil society in their arguments (see Wilford 1992, Wilson 2009b). Social transformationists take issue with the idea that regulation through consociationalism has the potential to eventually alter a conflict's integrity; rather, they believe that transformation must precede any settlement (Ruane and Todd 1996, Taylor 2001). Ruane and Todd (1996: 15) advocate a process of 'social emancipation', whereby the people of Northern Ireland come together to transform the social, economic and political structures that, taken together, create a structure that 'determines, distorts, and limits their potentialities'.

In a similar vein, Taylor (2009b: 327) takes consociationalists to task for 'eschew[ing] critical confrontation with the underlying social structures that generate injustice'. Contending that these unjust structures – which he labels 'systemic sectarianism' – rather than ethno-nationalism, are responsible for the conflict, Taylor believes far-reaching affirmative action and economic policies, along with integrated education and the promotion of deliberative democracy, could provide the raw material for Northern Ireland's social transformation (2009b: 327–28).

Another perspective is provided by centripetalists who are aiming for moderation by bolstering 'the centre of a deeply divided spectrum' (Sisk 1995: 19). For this, centripetalists advocate the adoption of electoral methods, such as the Alternative Vote (AV) (Horowitz 2001, Wilson and Wilford 2003, 2006). It is believed that AV's high quota (50 per cent + 1) will force parties to adopt more moderate positions in an effort to obtain votes from across the ethno-national divide. It is further argued that AV may also result in the establishment of pre-electoral coalitions of ethno-nationally disparate, but moderate parties (for example, the SDLP and Ulster Unionist Party (UUP)) (Horowitz, 2000b, 2001, Reilly 2001, Reilly and Reynolds 1997, Wilson and Wilford 2003, 2006). Unlike consociationalism, proponents of AV argue that it does not reward extremists; rather they believe that it lays the foundation for accommodative behaviour by moderate parties, and this moderation will in turn help to neutralize extremists in all blocs. Moreover, its adherents argue that, in contrast to STV method of proportional representation, AV enables party leaders to agree to and deliver deals as it provides fewer incentives for internal party fragmentation (Reilly 2001).

While ostensibly promising, the arguments of social transformationists and centripetalists encounter difficulties when presented with empirical evidence. Social emancipationists' structural emphases risk treating violence as if it is merely derivative, and this in turn both obscures other sources of violence and paramilitaries' culpability (M.L.R. Smith 1999: 91, 96). Also, as the preceding sections have shown, ethno-national identities in Northern Ireland are not merely the product of élite machinations; while this does not mean that these identities are 'primordial' in the sense that many constructivists understand the term (Taylor 1994), it does not mean that they are infinitely malleable either. Failure to acknowledge this makes it difficult to imagine how Ruane and Todd's ambitious emancipation plan would be implemented in practice, and these practical difficulties may account for their recently modified position which acknowledges the Agreement's progressive potential (Ruane and Todd 2003).

The failure to acknowledge the strength and depth of ethno-national identities in Northern Ireland also complicates social transformationists and centripetalists' reading of civil society. As Belloni (2008: 189–91) notes, while there is evidence that multiethnic civil society organizations can provide the bridging capital that can further advance peace and democratization in post-conflict societies, these organizations alone are not constitutive of civil society; rather they coexist with 'uncivil' organizations (for example, paramilitary groups), and legal organizations that reflect the important ethnic and/or national divisions within a society. Many organizations in Northern Ireland reflect this divide, and it has been argued that many peace and conflict resolution organizations have consciously failed to develop their analysis of the conflict lest they offend portions of their variegated membership, and that members of cross-community groups often seek recognition of their ethno-national identity. As single-identity civil society groups often typify conflict transitional societies, and as 'uncivil' groups thrive in environments where the state is weak, it is likely that the cross-community associational life which critics of consociationalism believe will transform Northern Ireland may require a bi-communal settlement in order to develop (Belloni 2008, O'Neill 2007: 414).

Centripetalists' arguments also face an array of problems. Perhaps the most damning indictment of the centripetalists' central prescription, AV, is that it is rarely adopted by those drafting settlements in divided societies. Moreover, the disparate outcomes engendered by its utilization in Fiji led Horowitz (2006) to clarify that AV *can,* but *does not necessarily,* promote moderation. AV's ability to facilitate moderation rests upon the assumption that candidates are rational actors, and in the case of Northern Ireland, rationality would not necessarily dictate reaching across the divide for votes. Rather, the necessity of staying in the count could render it expedient to appeal for second preference votes within candidates' own blocs (O'Leary 2001: 72).

The application of AV to Northern Ireland also raises other specific problems. The adoption of AV in Northern Ireland would reintroduce a form of majoritarianism into Northern Ireland, and it would lead to the under representation of minorities in some constituencies. This majoritarianism would also have a similarly pernicious effect upon the smaller so-called 'non-sectarian' parties in Northern Ireland.

Horowitz's assertion that AV does not automatically foster moderation underlines the importance of examining a region's socio-political context before recommending it as an electoral method. The importance of context can be seen in the work of Reilly (2004: 18) who cites Papua New Guinea as an example of AV's moderating potential but does not recommend its application in Fiji, the salient difference between the two cases being that while the former is characterized by numerous micro divisions, the latter, like Northern Ireland, is largely split into two competing blocs (Reilly 2004: 18). One could cite other examples which expose proponents' uncritical acceptance of AV's moderating propensities, but this tendency is perhaps best revealed by the failure of AV's advocates in Northern Ireland to engage in quantitative analyses or simulations of its likely effects. When simulations of AV have been performed, it has revealed that not only would the smaller so-called non-sectarian parties be annihilated, but also that it 'would have undermined the inclusive and equitable electoral formula required for full-fledged power sharing' (Coakley 2009b: 272). Electoral institutions, as Reilly notes (2004: 16), 'cannot invent moderation where none exists'.

Conclusion

Consociational power sharing appears to have become the prescribed or default mechanism for conflict regulation in deeply divided societies. Its capacity to include élites from all prominent segments of the polity in government is seen as highly conducive to democratic stability and peace in places which have hitherto been viewed as unreceptive to any form of lasting settlement. In embracing consociationalism since 1998, Northern Ireland has been framed by some as a power sharing success story (see McGarry and O'Leary 2006, 2009). At the same time, consociationalism, as we have seen, has come under sustained attack from its critics, who accuse it, *inter alia*, of institutionalizing and aggravating sectarian division as well as engendering a democratic deficit. In response, many of the critics decry the hypothesis that consociationalism represents the only form of democracy for divided societies; they call for alternative forms of power sharing which engineer a more integrative approach to the existence of social divisions. They call for modes of power sharing which give incentives for moderation and cooperation across ethnic cleavages, which they expect will expedite the creation of shared identities and a more stable form of democracy. The logic here is that since identity conflicts are viewed as the product of social learning they can be ameliorated through a different form of social learning. Critics thus accuse consociationalism of perpetuating identity conflicts rather than their transformation (Dryzek and Dunleavy 2009: 194).

In reviewing the debates for and against consociationalism in Northern Ireland, in particular, we have argued that despite some of its seeming blemishes regarding a clear vision as to how to move from forms of conflict regulation to conflict transformation, it remains a robust system. Its ability to generate substantial inclusivity and proportionality across the polity, as well as recognizing the importance of self-determination claims in pluri-national regions, provide institutional mechanisms for contending groups to channel issues in a nonviolent form. The fact that other approaches to power sharing appear less likely to bring about stability and conflict transformation in deeply divided societies means that consociational prescriptions, though imperfect, will in all likelihood remain the preferred option of conflict management in the foreseeable future. In the next chapter, we explore how these leading issues concerning intergroup cooperation and group-differentiated rights relate to the sharing of key civic spaces.

3
'Our City Also': Sharing Civic Space

Sunday 8 August 1993 was eagerly anticipated by many Irish national-ists in Belfast, for this was to be the day when the security forces would grant permission for the first ever nationalist parade to enter the city centre. On that afternoon, parades from thirteen Irish nationalist areas across Belfast converged on Belfast City Hall in the heart of the city centre to commemorate the 22nd anniversary of internment.[14] Labelled a 'Nationalist Rights Day' by the organizers, the march attracted up to 10,000 Irish nationalists. Many of the marchers brandished placards stating 'Our City Also', and they cheered and gave clenched-fist salutes as they turned into Wellington Place, the thoroughfare leading directly up to the City Hall. The crowd sang the civil rights anthem 'We Shall Overcome' and a huge Irish tricolour was draped over the front gates of the City Hall, on top of which a Union Jack flag fluttered. A small contingent of marchers broke away from the main body of the parade and climbed above shops facing the front of the City Hall where they unfurled a banner proclaiming 'Ireland unfree shall never be at peace'.

Some unionist politicians, looking on at the event with incandes-cent rage, spent subsequent days pointing at the preponderance of republican and IRA paramilitary paraphernalia on display at what one newspaper called a 'tribal ritual' (*Belfast Newsletter* 9 August 1993). Ian Paisley, a unionist politician, claimed the event was 'nothing less than a recruiting parade for the IRA' (*Belfast Newsletter* 9 August 1993). Another unionist politician called the marchers 'scum' and accused the security forces of 'having one law for republican parades and another for loy-alists' (*Belfast Newsletter* 10 August 1993), particularly as, they argued, loyalist symbolism was increasingly proscribed from the city centre. A few weeks later a pan-loyalist group called Ulster Community Action invoked a commemorative occasion of their own,[15] to reclaim the space around the City Hall and to make visible the perceived shifting balance of political power by protesting at 'continuing social deprivation' in loyalist areas of Belfast.

The security forces, which had given the republican parade permission to take place only hours before its scheduled starting time, led the main contingent of marchers with three Land Rovers. On the grounds of the City Hall a police cordon stood armed with riot gear; army helicopters hovered overhead and a police spotter plane circled before and after the demonstration. The security forces stated that they granted permission for the parade when it was made clear that no organization – religious or political – had filed for authorization for a rival demonstration at the same time, one of the reasons given in the past for banning nationalist marches in the city centre.

The joyous scenes evoked by Irish nationalists on the afternoon of 8 August stood in marked contrast to nearly all previous nationalist efforts aimed at entering the 'sacred space' of the city centre surrounding the City Hall. On previous occasions, Irish nationalist parades and demonstrations would head towards the city centre aware of the inevitable conclusion awaiting them. At the perimeter of the city centre, the marchers were stopped by the security forces, which had erected barricades to seal off the whole city centre. In 1973, for example, the socialist/republican organization People's Democracy demanded authorization from the security forces to march into the city centre. The Minister of State, in consultation with the security forces, prohibited the march from 'within a radius of half-a-mile from the City Hall, Belfast' (*Irish News* 10 February 1973). Refusing to adhere to the ban, People's Democracy confronted the security forces, who responded by firing plastic bullets into the crowd attacking the barricades. For nationalist organizations, their continued exclusion from the city centre was seen as the spatial confirmation of their unequal status in Northern Ireland. On this issue, a nationalist leader wrote in 1973: 'one thing goes on forever – the ban on … any anti-unionist organisation marching to the City Hall in Belfast' (*Irish News* 10 February 1973). Nationalists asked whether 'it will ever be possible for an anti-unionist organisation to hold a march or parade outside the Catholic ghettoes of our cities and towns?' (*Irish News* 1 January 1973).

After decades of failed attempts, the authorities granted permission for the nationalist convocation on 8 August 1993 to enter the city centre and congregate around the City Hall. Publicizing the parade a few days beforehand, a republican leader, Alex Maskey, stated that one of the main injustices experienced by nationalists in Belfast 'was not being allowed into our own city centre unhindered. We're now taking that step' (Boyle 1993: 1). For many Irish nationalists, their presence in the city centre signified the equal esteem of nationalist identity with unionism in a 'sacred space' of the region.

'You have the right to your city'

At the conclusion of the 'Nationalist Rights Day' in August 1993, Gerry Adams, the President of Sinn Féin, addressed the crowd outside the City Hall. Adams told the crowd, 'you have the right to *your* city, the right to *your* city hall' [emphasis author] (*Irish News* 9 August 1993). Although it is not clear if Adams was aware of the provenance of his words, they can be directly traced to the proclamation of Henri Lefebvre (1996), the French radical thinker, who made a call for the 'right to the city as a cry and demand'. For Lefebvre, the 'right to the city' entailed the right for citizens not only to inhabit urban space but also to participate in a city as an *oeuvre*, an ongoing work of creation, production and negotiation. The *oeuvre*, according to Lefebvre, represented the highest form of participatory urban democracy required to overcome social divisions – a work in which all citizens participate; a collective, not a singular project emerges, and new modes of living and inhabiting are invented. The 'right to the city', stated Lefebvre, was for all members, regardless of whether they were *citadines* or *citoyens*. While *citadines* encompassed those who possessed citizen rights and preferential treatment because of wealth and status, *citoyens*, alternatively, included those urban inhabitants who might be illegal migrants, the homeless or even minority national groups who were explicitly and tacitly excluded from definitions of citizenship.

Lefebvre's demand to the 'right to the city' – the *oeuvre* – was not explicitly directed at cities and societies violently divided by ethnonationalism. Lefebvre's major concern was with how the forces of capitalism increasingly made the contemporary city a site of consumption, a place dominated by exchange value over use value. As part of this, Lefebvre argued that cities increasingly possessed centres of power and peripheries of exclusion. This process of centres and *banlieues*, continued Lefebvre, was largely part of the progressive extension of capitalist and statist production of space to concentrate the decision making centre while creating dependent colonies on the margins. Lefebvre (1978: 5) wrote: 'around the centres there are nothing but subjugated, exploited and dependent spaces: new colonial space'. The centre, Lefebvre (1976: 86) noted, was a site of social centrality in which authority is inscribed: 'the consolidation needs centres; it needs to fix them, to monumentalize them (socially) and specialize them (mentally)'. Processes of centralization aspired to be totally under contemporary capitalism, and in so doing attempts to expel 'all peripheral elements with a violence that is inherent in space itself' (Lefebvre 1991: 332). Such a process of excluding 'dissident elements', according to Lefebvre, would be met with subversion from 'countervailing forces'.

The struggle for dissident forces, Lefebvre believed, was to create a renewed centrality of inclusion and encounter. The right to the city is thus 'not merely a right of access to what the property speculators and state planners define, but an active right to make the city different, to shape it more in accord with our heart's desire, and to re-make ourselves thereby in a different image' (Harvey 2003: 939). While, as Harvey (2003: 939) notes, 'the right to remake ourselves by creating a qualitatively different kind of urban sociality is one of the most precious of human rights', the simple question remains: whose rights and whose city? In a city like Belfast, this question is not, as Lefebvre would have mused, one that is primarily resolved through the confrontation between the forces of capitalism and the excluded working-classes; in the ethno-nationally divided city the issue concerns the right of all groups and individuals to access public spaces to express their cultural and political identities. While initiating and maintaining equal access to Belfast city centre for Irish nationalists and British unionists is an obviously important step, the wider debate concerns to what extent a truly 'shared space' is being constituted. Is it possible to create public spaces that do not merely confirm nor valorise ethno-national separateness and immutable differences between groups? Alternatively, can a shared space be created as a truly public sphere that engenders the meeting and encountering of different groups to place their identities under scrutiny and debate their social value for the purpose of conflict transformation? (see also Nagle 2009b, 2009c).

Sacred sites of centrality

Hetherington (1998) argues that every society, no matter how complex, has a centre of values enshrined in sacred spaces. These sites of 'social centrality' are places in which a dominant group's hegemonic power is inscribed; the point of such spaces is to naturalize the group's control over the political and cultural institutions of the state. There is, accordingly, often a strong aura of the sacred imbued in such sites, which can make them seem timeless, unchanging and even beyond scrutiny and contestation. They rouse the deepest well of emotions and attachments from many actors. In sacred centres, 'actions take on an enhanced significance, in the eyes of the participants and witnesses alike…participants' emotions are heightened, orators' tongues are loosened, and citizens dream impossible dreams' (Sewell 2001: 65). With a sacred centre, 'we belong to it, as much as it belongs to us' (Smith 1991: 23). Such 'sacred centers are not just reflections or traces of political power: they are often instruments and sources of political power' (Friedland and Hecht 1998: 147). More marginalized groups often find themselves excluded from accessing or using these sites; the boundaries of the space are fiercely patrolled through discourses of purity and danger and their high status in society is typically defined in opposition to marginal spaces, which are framed as polluted and transgressive. Sacred places, like cathedrals, parliaments, monuments, state buildings, archaeological sites and other such places come to represent forms of authority in a society.

Yet because these 'sites of social centrality' can legitimize political power for the dominant group, they are open to challenge from marginalized groups. 'Conflicts over the social order will ramify in its sacred center' (Friedland and Hecht 1998: 147). In turn, the dominant group will go to great lengths to protect the vulnerability of sacred sites, for an attack of the site is perceived as an attack on the group. During spectacular moments, sites of centrality are the focus for revolt and revolution. Think of Wenceslas Square in Prague in August 1968, Tiananmen Square in Beijing and the Berlin Wall in 1989, and the Twin Towers on 9/11. These have been sites of protest and violence directed at the (perceived) central values of a society.

In societies characterized by violent ethno-national conflict sites of social centrality are particularly important in symbolizing the power of the dominant group over the minority. The ritualistic marking out of these spaces, in particular, ignites a unified and singular sense of community. If the minority group is prohibited from gaining access to these sacred spaces this will fuel grievances and provide a territorial metaphor of their alienation from the state. These spaces thus provide a matrix for conflict between groups over their control.

The history of ethno-national conflict in recent years is littered with sites of social centrality acting as foci for violence. It is often noted, for instance, that the rise to power of Serbian leader Slobodan Milosevic was crucially engineered by a speech at the Serbian sacred centre of Kosovo Polje in 1989. Later on, during the conflict in Bosnia, the Croat destruction of the Stari Most Bridge in Mostar in 1993, though a strategic act, had a symbolic function insofar as it destroyed the link between the Christian west side of the city with the Muslim east. The attack on the bridge became framed as an assault on a 'symbol of solidarity and coexistence' and the 'death of Yugoslavism' as a model of shared identity (Bose 2007: 110). Similarly, the bombing of the revered Shiite Al-'Askariyya Shrine in Samarra, Iraq in 2006 was a 'cultural atrocity that attacked Shi'a primary group identity on a deep level, and was perfectly calculated to provoke an intense and violent backlash from the Shi'a population against Iraqi Sunnis' (Kilcullen 2009: 120). In Jerusalem, the old city's holy sites, as Ross (2007: 154) notes, are the 'ground zero of the Israeli-Palestinian conflict', as Jews and Muslims contest their ownership, thereby mirroring 'the emotionally intense differences about political existence found in the larger conflict of which Jerusalem is just one part'.

Due to the way these sites are contested by ethno-national groups, they are also crucial places in which a shared society can be symbolized and enacted. The need to create a shared space in sites of centrality may be important in the search for sustainable peace. In the rest of this chapter we explore what a 'shared space' may mean in the context of a 'divided society'. It is in particular public spaces that different and contending definitions of identity and citizenship in 'divided societies' are made visible and placed open to debate and even transformation. Public space, moreover, is where people from different groups may come together to interact and even build relationships.

To help us understand the relationship between space, identity and citizenship, we track historical and ongoing struggles for access to public space surrounding Belfast City Hall, the *de facto* economic and political centre of Belfast. Indeed, while this space was once practically the preserve of unionist civic occasions, with nationalist events excluded by the state authorities, since 1993 nationalists have proclaimed their 'right to the city' by utilizing the city centre space for cultural and political events. Rather than uncritically celebrating this potentially inclusive definition of public space as the working out of progressive 'right to the city' struggles – in which public space is opened for dissent and competing identities – we investigate this process in terms of ongoing anxieties about the management of ethno-national division in Belfast during the current period of conflict transition. That is, to what extent are policies which promote inclusive uses of public space in Belfast city centre contributing to the formation of equal horizontal relationships between groups, thus enabling peace-building efforts? Or, alternatively, are group-differentiated claims to public space by Irish nationalists and

British unionists representative of the logic of institutional sectarianism, a dangerous politics of recognition as groups are placed in mutually exclusive cultural communities? It is important, consequently, to proffer ideas about what a 'shared space' may resemble, whether there have been any shared spaces in the past, and which groups and agencies should play a positive role in creating it. The task of turning the city centre into a shared space, accordingly, is not just a matter of ensuring that respective ethno-national groups and their events are equally accommodated, though this is an important step; there are also salient questions regarding the content of these forms, what these events may mean to other groups, what happens if events clash, and whether there should be efforts to create shared spaces which accommodate nationalists and unionists, and other groups together.

Divided space

To help explore the role of public space in constituting a shared society and peace-building it is important first to consider the fundamental relationship between public space and conflict in Northern Ireland. Issues surrounding the social reproduction of public space in violently divided societies should not be minimized since space is the central matrix upon which ethno-national separation and conflict is constituted. It is notable that conflict between groups is not only generated by incompatible claims over the same national territory, but also through the content of space, how it is imbued with forms of meaning which can make certain social actions and outcomes more predictable. The theory here is that rather than segregated space being the manifestation of ethnic hostility, violence is inherently produced by segregated spaces. Sack (1986: 19), for example, has written of the politics of 'territoriality', which he defines as the attempt to 'control people, phenomena and relationships by delimiting and asserting control over a geographic area'. Territoriality is underpinned by the presentation of 'fear' by certain groups, who aim to create purified and homogeneous spaces which legitimize a series of discursive activities and social group practices (Shirlow 2003).

Peace walls: segregated living

Defining practically every scale of Northern Ireland are forms of social segregation and divisive exercises in the politics of territoriality. The most obvious example of divided space is the number of districts in Northern Ireland which are either overwhelmingly Protestant or

Catholic. Although Belfast, in particular, has been a segregated city since the nineteenth century, a lasting legacy of violence of the 'Troubles' from the late 1960s onwards was the proliferation of territorial boundaries with sizeable population movements leading to residential segregation in single religion enclaves. The 2001 census showed that 66 per cent of Belfast's population lived in areas which were more than 90 per cent Catholic or Protestant (Shirlow and Murtagh, 2006).[16] In the most intensely segregated parts of the city, such as north Belfast, research has shown that as many as 68 per cent of young people say that they 'have never had a meaningful conversation' with people belonging to another religion (BBC 2002).[17]

Nationalist and unionist districts are also increasingly divided by 'peace walls' and security interfaces. These interfaces act as border areas between working-class nationalist and unionist districts, typically delineated by physical boundaries, such as 30 feet high walls or gates (Shirlow and Murtagh 2006), waste ground, business parks or derelict housing.[18] Perhaps most depressingly, in 2006 the Northern Ireland Office (NIO) constructed a 25 foot high 'peace wall' in the grounds of an integrated primary school (a purposely non-denominational school for Catholics and Protestants) in north Belfast. There are other zero-sum classifications of public space in Northern Ireland. The sheer volume of ethno-national representations of space which festoon parts of Belfast, like murals and paramilitary flags, are sources of group affiliation and identity reaffirmation that try to prohibit the emergence of alternative encapsulations. Rather than declining in number during the peace process, these memoryscapes have proliferated with circa 120 permanent murals, plaques and memorials constituted in Belfast alone since 1998 (see Viggiani 2006). The deleterious influence of paramilitary representations in public space on shoring up paramilitary power has been noted by Goldstock (2004: 7):

> As long as groups have the de facto privilege to colour communal rights of way, paint or maintain aggressive or sectarian murals on walls, fly provocative flags over thoroughfares, [and] place symbols at the entrance to housing estates…legitimate governmental power will be seen as secondary.

For some commentators Northern Irish society should strive to provide a radical and pluralistic vision of public space by reframing the divided ethno-national city away from its everyday manifestation as a site of social segregation, as 'spaces of hate', in which groups 'assert control over geographic areas and support ideas of enclosed or sealed places' (Graham and Nash 2006: 258). Although, it is not in the remit of this book to suggest a solution to the long-standing problem of residential segregation in Northern Ireland, it is possible to critically engage with civic spaces. In this way, Amin and Thrift (2002) have some interesting suggestions regarding how to begin conceptualizing public space as possessing the potential to frame the content of social relations between groups. They ask us to look at the effects that are generated in encounters, in 'the prosaic moments and daily rhythms of social life that have a decisive impact on racial and ethnic practice' (Amin and Thrift 2002: 292). Here, the authors (2002: 292) demand that our analyses take into account 'the intensity of racial or ethnic coding of daily life'. What is seen and said in schools, neighbourhoods, streets, shopping centres, workplaces and public spaces, they argue, provide 'the prosaic negotiations that drive interethnic and intercultural relations in different directions'. To begin considering the role of public space in generating relations between groups we now provide a historical overview of public space in Belfast city centre as a 'civic sphere'.

'The sacred temple of unionism'

In the early nineteenth century Belfast was a small town but the exponential growth of the city's industrial sector – particularly in shipbuilding, engineering, linen and ropeworks – quickly brought in hundreds of thousands of workers, including a number of Catholics. While the Catholic population of Belfast in 1800 was just 3 per cent, by 1900 the figure went up to 34 per cent (McIntosh 2006: 10). Between 1871 and 1901 the population of Belfast doubled from 175,000 to 350,000 (McIntosh 2006: 31). The arrival of thousands of Catholic and Protestant migrant workers into the city within a short period ignited sectarian conflict resulting in patterns of residential segregation that persist even today.

To reflect the city's growing economic and political importance, unionist civic leaders instigated the construction of a grand City Hall. Opened in 1906, the City Hall, a huge early Edwardian edifice demarcated the political and civic heart of the city centre, positioned at the epicentre of the commercial, financial and political quarters of the city. The City Hall and the long streets in its immediate environs became 'the stage for the political and social dramas of Belfast' (McIntosh 2006: 4). Mostly, the City Hall and the city centre were the focus for civic unionism. These events included Orange Order parades, celebrations of dominant Protestant and British rule in Ireland. After the First World War, a War Cenotaph and a Garden of Remembrance were constructed in the City Hall grounds. Within the grounds of the City Hall were also located a number of statues and symbols to remind the city of its great unionist heroes and its industrial and economic destiny. For instance, a statue of Queen Victoria 'guards' the entrance to the City Hall and on the façade of the piedmont above the entrance is a 'classical' relief which celebrates the city's mercantilist heritage.

The City Hall and the city centre were thus immediately marked 'in a high-profile and partisan way as a symbol of unionist power and Protestant culture' (McIntosh 2006: 73). For Irish nationalists, the unionist delineation of the City Hall and the surrounding city centre signified nationalist exclusion from political and cultural power in the city. Despite the architect of the City Hall hoping that the City Hall would become 'a monument to the character of the people of Belfast' (McIntosh 2006), shortly after its official opening the 'edifice', for nationalists, was 'now definitely recognised as the sacred temple of…Orangeism' (*Irish News* 30 September 1912) – 'Orangesim' being a popular sobriquet for unionism.

Protesting and celebrating in Belfast city centre

For unionist civic leaders, the space of Belfast city centre was seen as indisputably their space for cultural and political events. The sheer volume and content of these events is impossible to convey here. Nevertheless, it is important to give some flavour of the range. Perhaps the most visibly unionist events in the city centre are Protestant Orange Order and Apprentice Boys parades. Within days of its opening in 1906, the Apprentice Boys held a rally outside the City Hall (McIntosh 2006: 4). Although 12 July, the centrepiece of the Protestant 'marching season', encompasses eighteen major locations, the Belfast County Parade which has Belfast city centre as its focal point is the biggest event of the day (Jarman 1997, Bryan 2000). Entering the city centre on the '12th' fulfils a number of functions for participating unionists. As Jarman (1997: 102) notes, the city centre provides a focus for the ritual reunification of the dispersed unionist communities of Belfast. These communities, which are ordinarily decentralized and spread out across the city, 'are mapped out as a single body' (Jarman 1997: 102) when they congregate in the city centre. Also, on this day, shops and businesses are closed as the unionist marchers 'claim authority over the streets of the city centre' (Jarman 1997: 102). The city centre is thus claimed by marchers 'as theirs and theirs alone' (Jarman 1997: 102).

There have been other high-profile unionist ceremonial and commemorative uses of the city centre. Practices of remembrance for Ulster's dead from two world wars are powerful rites which instruct the faithful to never forget the ultimate sacrifice of the 'province's' sons and daughters in service of the Empire and state. In the grounds of Belfast City Hall lies the Garden of Remembrance and the Cenotaph, which was opened on Armistice Day 1929. On two particular days of the year, the Garden of Remembrance and the Cenotaph are the focal point for commemorative rituals.[19] Although these are official state-sanctioned events, representatives for the Ulster Volunteer Force (UVF), a loyalist paramilitary organization, have surreptitiously participated in Remembrance Day ceremonies by laying a wreath at the foot of the Cenotaph an hour before the main 'official' ceremony. Such 'social amnesia' – the forgetting of Catholics who fought in the wars – has helped leave unchallenged a narrative in which the 'fallen' were Protestant unionists who died for King and Country.

There were also celebratory civic occasions in the city centre that had the pretence of fashioning a shared space for all citizens of Belfast irrespective of religious affiliation. Royal processions through the city centre to the City Hall were particularly fêted by the unionist 'fathers' of the city; yet royal visits to nationalist areas could ignite riotous reaction (Purdie 1990). In the post-war decades, there was also an attempt by the unionist state and its business partners to fashion an image of Northern Ireland as technologically sophisticated and at the very vanguard of modernity. Belfast city centre became the showcase for the performance of this image. Under the aegis of the Belfast Junior Chamber of Commerce, a Belfast Lord Mayor's Show was initiated. Organizers claimed the event would muster as many as 500,000 attendees in the city centre. The 'show' was a literal advertisement for Northern Irish business and a display of military might, embracing 'fly pasts' of Phantom jet planes and attack helicopters, marching military musical bands and processional floats representing British army regiments. Despite its seemingly benign appearance, another post-war city centre civic ritual was hardly any less of a unionist platform. The ceremonial turning on of the lights for the City Council's Christmas tree, which stood tall in front of the City Hall, provided an opportunity for the unionist Mayor to make a political speech.

Exploiting the cracks

It seems easy to conclude that the city centre has been a site of unchallenged unionist hegemony and nationalist exclusion. In essence, this is similar to how dominant groups seek to control space in ethnocratic societies. Yiftachel and Ghanem (2004: 649) define an ethnocracy 'as a regime facilitating the expansion, ethnicization and control of contested territory and state by a dominant ethnic nation'. An open ethnocracy is a type of regime which is neither completely democratic nor authoritarian. It fails on the count of authoritarianism because it possesses partial democratic features, most notably political competition, some free media and some civil rights. It fails to be wholly democratic because these features fail to be universal or comprehensive, especially in regard to the state's minority ethno-national groups who are subjected to some forms of discrimination.

The structure of an ethnocracy is designed to expedite ethnic stratification and discrimination, with ethnicity rather than citizenship featuring as the main basis for resource and power. Furthermore, the dominant ethno-national group 'appropriates the state apparatus and shapes the political system, public institutions, geography, economy and culture, so as to expand and deepen its control over state and territory' (Yiftachel and Ghanem 2004: 650). In terms of space and territory, ethnocracies seek to fuse national identity with the boundaries of the state. By making ethno-national identity indivisible with a specified territory, the ethnocracy strives to render abstract its political power, making it appear beyond challenge. The process of ethnicizing territory also includes the utilization of structural segregation to facilitate the expansion of the majority group and the construction of minorities as a 'threat' to the project of 'purifying' ethnic spaces (Yiftachel and Ghanem 2004).

This is not the whole picture, however. Rather than rendering unionist power abstract, immutable and beyond dispute, the city centre became the very scene in which hegemony was exposed and contested. Yiftachel and Ghanem (2004) argue that a crucial characteristic of ethnocracies concerns how 'groups attempt to exploit the "cracks" emanating from the state's self-representation as democratic'. A particular place to illuminate this form of conflict, in which marginalized minorities use partial openings to challenge the regime, is public space. Importantly, the spatial challenge to unionism derived from groups who embodied shared interests by drawing support across the ethno-national cleavage and also from nationalist groups.

Cross-community challenges

In 1907, just months after the opening of the City Hall, Belfast was the stage for working-class, cross-community solidarity as 250,000 unskilled nationalist and unionist workers in the city united over trade union rights in the dockers' and carters' strike. The strikers marched on the City Hall where a deputation of dockers entered the council chamber to participate in a political debate. From then on, the City Hall and the city centre were used for a range of political protests and claim-making activities against the government at national and local level, which could often contain a cross-community nationalist and unionist constituency.

The price of rents for public housing in the city produced a perennial source of conflict between residents and the local state. In the early 1960s nationalist and unionist representatives of the large council housing estates in the city created the Amalgamated Committee, Belfast Corporation Tenants Association in order to pursue their claims (*Irish News* 21 July 1961). Such protests in the city centre could be quite critical of the unionist government. A march to the City Hall to demonstrate against municipal housing rents rises in 1965 featured a banner which read: 'Higher Rents, Higher Bus Fares, Higher Food Prices – Why Not Just Change the Name Belfast to Belsen?' (Irish News 3 August 1965).

Less rooted in class and issues concerning social reproduction, during the early 1960s the city centre was the focus for ban-the-bomb protests, which encompassed nationalists and unionists, religious leaders, socialists and trade unionists. These protests could also take a critical stance against the unionist government. For instance, in 1960, after the unionist Prime Minister of Northern Ireland, Lord Brookeborough, called for Polaris submarines to be built in Belfast's shipyards 'if it meant more employment', the ban-the-bomb movement held a series of demonstrations in the city centre and outside the City Hall (Nagle 2008b).

Notably, some spaces inside or at the fringe of the city centre were particularly fecund for inspiring radical protests. In the nineteenth and early twentieth century, Custom House Square, a civic space at the edge of the city centre hosted a speakers' corner, a space in which dissenting politics could be articulated in a public forum. During the 1960s, a space fondly called 'Blitz Square', located at the margins of the city centre, was a wasteland wrought by the Luftwaffe during the Second World War. As it was used by trade unions for May Day gatherings, it also attained the sobriquet of 'Red Square'. From here, the city's socialists would congregate and begin their parades which would journey into the city centre. Another space, Cornmarket, located within the confines of the city centre, was a forum for radical forms of street theatre. For instance in 1981, the Northern Ireland branch of the Campaign for Nuclear Disarmament (CND) held a street-theatre show in which

US President Reagan confronted Soviet leader Brezhnev and housewives tried to prepare for a nuclear attack (Nagle 2008c).

Interestingly, the unionist government tolerated many of these protests. This relative indifference was contingent on the protest groups being either unconcerned or at worst ambivalent about the 'national question' – Northern Ireland's constitutional position in the UK union. The reform these groups sought in the public and institutional arena, including demands for changes in the production of social goods and services, were not viewed by the state authorities as articulating a threat to unionism. Despite this, the state could be wary of the trajectory of these groups, fearful that they might be co-opted by more 'malevolent' nationalist infiltrators seeking to chart an anti-state direction. Access to the space of the city centre was thus dependent on whether dissenting groups were seen to represent a threat to the security of the state. Nationalist groups and events, however, were seen by the state as a decidedly different kettle of fish.

Nationalist challenges

After the foundation of Northern Ireland in the early 1920s, the minority Irish nationalist population were 'securitized' (see Chapter 1), meaning that they were constructed as a security threat actively seeking to undermine the survival of the state. As part of the strategy to securitize nationalists, unionism sought to limit the capacity of nationalists to challenge the cultural and spatial hegemony of the state. Such 'cultural' exclusion was most apparent in the Flags and Emblem (Display) Act (NI) of 1954 which forbade the public display of so-called 'provocative emblems' in Northern Ireland. This Act had the *de facto* intention of proscribing the use of nationalist symbols in public space without needing to formally specify nationalist symbols (Purdie 1990: 30).

An interrelated arena that nationalist groups were proscribed from was key public spaces, such as Belfast city centre, which were largely preserved for unionist civic events. In this way, access to public space surrounding the City Hall for cultural and political displays symbolized citizenship. Although there wasn't any official legislation which purposely prohibited nationalist events from entering the city centre, nationalist events were effectively banned because they were timetabled to clash with 'traditional' unionist civic events, which took precedence, or if the security forces judged the events to be security threats. Unsurprisingly, prior to the late 1960s very rarely would a nationalist group make an application to the security forces for permission to hold an event in the city centre. One rare example of an attempt was in June

1963 when a nationalist organization, 'The Political Prisoners Release Committee', applied for permission to hold a demonstration in the city centre. The application was refused by the security forces who stated that it could lead to a breach of the peace because it would potentially clash with unionist parades scheduled to take place at the same time (*Belfast Telegraph* 25 June 1963).

The immediate post-Second World War international dispensation was not favourable for minority ethno-national groups to challenge their exclusion within the state. Even in the aftermath of the Second World War, in which the issue of protecting minorities from genocide had been for some the *raison d'être* for waging war, minority specific rights were largely discouraged. The formation of a post-war international order to manage conflict across the globe, especially the UN, prioritized universal human rights as opposed to group rights for minorities. Although the Universal Declaration of Human Rights in 1948 was undoubtedly an accomplishment of immense moral vision designed to assail prejudice and Inequality, its corollary was also to disempower minorities from challenging state power both domestically and internationally (Kymlicka 2007: 29–30).

Despite endemic issues concerning post-war ethnic discrimination and inequality being dealt with through individual human rights, rather than the rights of special charter for minority groupings, struggles by minority groups for various forms of group recognition proliferated. Global struggles for decolonization and desegregation sought to contest the legacy of enduring racial and ethnic hierarchies. For some minorities historically subject to strategies of social discrimination, they demanded progressive integration into those social categories from which they had been excluded during the construction of the modern nation state (Melucci 1996). For other minorities subject to assimilatory policies, where they were stripped of their own language, culture and self-governing institutions, their struggle was the right to express their distinct identities (see Kymlicka 2007: 91).

Within this post-war milieu of minorities struggling for various forms of rights, Northern Ireland in the late 1960s witnessed the advent of a major civil rights movement. An ostensibly reformist social movement modelled on the African-American civil rights movement and the British Council for Social Liberties, the Northern Irish civil rights movement (CRM) campaigned for equal, singular and uniform rights under British law to be applied in Northern Ireland. Indeed, the formation of the Northern Irish CRM, rather than emphasizing differentiated group rights, defined its aims in terms of Universal Human Rights by demanding 'the basic rights of all citizens' and protecting 'the rights of the individual' (see Purdie 1990: 133).

Although these aims were largely targeted at addressing grievances regarding inequalities in the sphere of housing, employment and the electoral franchise, questions of public space were also prominent. The CRM underlined the importance of equal access to public space by calling for 'guarantees for speech, assembly and association' (Purdie 1990: 133). Certainly much of the CRM's activities were expressed through the occupation of public spaces with tactics gleaned from the international protest movements of the 1960s (marches, pickets, 'sit-downs', 'sit-ins'), and as such they sought a 'symbolic invasion of ancient territory' (Foster 1988: 588).

While prior to the CRM Belfast city centre was a space relatively uncontested by nationalist groups, from the late 1960s onwards it became a central crucible for testing claims to civil rights. On numerous occasions the CRM proclaimed their right to the city centre. Although many Northern Irish Protestants and even some liberal unionists were integral members of the CRM, the unionist leadership quickly viewed the movement as little more than a nationalist conspiracy aimed at overthrowing the state (see Purdie 1990). State-imposed restrictions on the CRM's ability to access public space was outlined in the Public Order Act (1951), which required parade organizers to provide forty-eight hours notice to the security forces of their intent to march. As a consequence, parades which could be viewed as threatening to public order could be peremptorily banned or rerouted.

The first attempt by the CRM to enter the city centre in October 1968 was banned by the authorities who claimed that it would cause violence as militant unionists threatened a counter-demonstration. A week later, two thousand civil rights marchers managed to bypass the restrictions by holding a sit-down protest outside the front of the City Hall (Purdie 1990: 205–07). This was to be their last success in gaining access to the city centre as the CRM marches were often halted by the security forces, which designated them 'illegal'. The restriction of access to the city centre to the CRM undoubtedly fuelled grievances that inequality remained endemic to the unionist state.

The CRM originally campaigned on the basis of undifferentiated, equal citizenship within the state. As noted before, this trajectory was ostensibly rooted in the post-war international dispensation of individual human rights. However, within the context of civil rights claim-making, Irish nationalists in Northern Ireland increasingly mobilized to demand recognition for group-differentiated minority civil rights.

Irish nationalists began to campaign, for instance, to have Irish culture better represented in the state media or for Irish cultural celebrations to be made into a national holiday. The issue of access to public space for Irish nationalist commemorative marches and political demonstrations became a *cause célèbre*. Unsurprisingly much of this focus was on Belfast city centre and from the late 1960s onwards nationalist cultural-political organizations increased claims to enter the city centre. In one example, on 3 June 1969 the 'James Connolly Commemoration Committee', a nationalist political organization, notified the city's Commissioners' Office of its intent to hold a commemorative parade in the city centre. The organizers also stated that the Irish tricolour flag, the flag of the Republic of Ireland, would be carried in the parade, a flag whose public display was *de facto* outlawed by the Flags and Emblems (Display) Act (NI) (1954). Although nationalist expectations were high that the march would take place, two days before it was scheduled the security forces rerouted the parade to a nationalist district after unionist gangs threatened to attack the parade. Subsequently, the unionist government could claim that it was not in principle adverse to nationalist gatherings in the city centre; however, for security reasons parades would be proscribed.

In order to further maintain control over the numerous challenges to public spaces in Northern Ireland, in 1969 the unionist government made crucial amendments to the Public Order Act, including banning many protest tactics used by the CRM, specifically making illegal 'counter demonstrations, the occupations of public buildings and sit-downs in the streets' (*Irish News* 13 March 1969). By criminalizing the CRM's core *modus operandi*, street politics, the demand for civil rights increasingly became focussed on the right to public space in Northern Ireland (Purdie 1990: 222–23). Although the unionist government originally considered applying a blanket ban to 'all processions and outdoor meetings,' crucially they decided to put a 'prohibition on all processions and outdoor meetings which include any street, road or highway and any place to which, for the first time being, the public have or have been permitted to have access' (*Belfast Newsletter* 26 September 1969). In other words, groups demanding the right of access to specific public spaces for the first time would be outlawed; on the other hand, events perceived to be traditionally related to specific places would not be affected. This effectively meant that unionist events which were traditionally routed through Belfast city centre would not be subject to the proscriptive Public Order Act. This can therefore be read to mean that group specific rights, those of unionists, were protected in law while those of nationalists were curtailed.

One of the major consequences of the onset of sectarian violence in the early 1970s was the collapse of the unionist controlled parliament as all political powers were transferred to the UK government at Westminster (Bew and Gillespie 1999: 50–51). The control of public space in Northern Ireland, invested in the Public Order Act, was placed under the jurisdiction of the Secretary of State for Northern Ireland, appointed by the incumbent Westminster government. Rather than lessening, disputes over access to public space in Belfast continued with violent intensity as nationalists continued to challenge their continuing exclusion from the city centre. Nationalist organizations habitually tried to force their way into the city centre for political demonstrations, and in response state security forces repulsed the marchers. In this milieu, violent clashes between nationalist marchers demanding access to the city centre and the security forces resisting them were a common occurrence.

At the same time as nationalist organizations were demanding the right to the city centre, militant republicans, like the IRA, were promoting a more destructive approach to it. Bolstered by the development of the car bomb, the IRA constantly targeted the city centre as it endeavoured to cripple the commercial, financial and symbolic centre of Belfast. On one infamous occasion in 1972, subsequently called 'Bloody Friday', the IRA detonated 26 bombs across the city, 11 in the city centre in the space of one hour, killing nine and injuring 130 people. In response to the bombing campaign, the security forces erected a 'ring of steel' around the city centre with armed checkpoints charged with stopping IRA car bombs. The advent of the security cordon placed around Belfast city centre made it difficult to enter without passing through armed security checkpoints. Shoppers underwent bag and body searches and the few vehicles allowed into the centre were subject to rigorous checks.

The security ring had another impact: it effectively guarded the city centre from proscribed demonstrations. Nationalist attempts to enter the city centre thus became largely aspirational. With little opportunity of the *de facto* ban on nationalist marches into the city centre being rescinded, nationalist groups adopted new tactics to make their presence known. In 1981, for instance, during the hunger strike protests for Irish republican prisoners, nationalist demonstrators sought to enter the sanctum of the city centre. One attempt in May 1981 involved hunger strike demonstrators joining the traditional trade union organized May Day parade. As the parade approached the City Hall, about fifty protestors broke away from the main march and unfurled placards and held a rally in support of the hunger strikers. A riot ensued when police moved in to arrest the protestors (*Belfast Telegraph* 2 May 1981).

During the late 1980s, a change occurred as Irish republicans and nationalists began to mobilize for increased inclusion within the local state (Bean 2008). Instead of viewing the City Hall purely in terms of an 'impenetrable bulwark of a "Protestant state for a Protestant people"' (Hayden 1999: vii-viii), nationalists, especially Sinn Féin, began advocating participatory input into formal politics at the citywide municipal level. Eschewing the rhetoric of exclusion, Sinn Féin increasingly articulated the politics of pluralism and diversity, speaking of 'a shared city of equals' and of seeking to physically reconstruct the city. From the 1980s onwards Sinn Féin began to increasingly frame issues regarding inequalities as necessitating an engagement with formal electoral politics. This process was augmented by the republican military campaign running out of steam and republicans looking to use politics to advance their objectives. The use of politics bore fruit as in the space of twelve years from 1985, Sinn Féin had almost doubled its number of electoral seats in the city council to transform itself from one of the smallest parties to the largest one in the city. In 2001 Belfast elected its first Sinn Féin mayor at the City Hall. Running parallel with this was an emerging Northern Irish peace process which sought to provide new democratic institutions and mechanisms to allow conflict to be expressed through nonviolent democratic means. As part of this process, it was hoped that in exchange for republicans abandoning violent means, they would be endowed with a place in power sharing in the region.

Shared space?

Since 1993, especially after the 'Nationalist Rights Day' described at the beginning of this chapter, Belfast city centre has become a space in which nationalists and unionists are made to feel that they have equal access for cultural and political performances. Belfast City Council, containing nationalist and unionist parties, and now responsible for the management of public space in the city centre, actively encourage the premise that public space is a palimpsest upon which any number of uses and identities can be constituted. The city council's policy on public space aims to 'encourage a tolerant and fair society, where people are respected and their differences are celebrated...it is very important that we remove any physical barriers, and break down social, political, cultural, religious and economic barriers' (Belfast City Council 2005: 18).

In recent years, Belfast City council has developed and funded a 'Celebrate Belfast' programme of selected, prestige events, many of which are performed in the city centre. These include a St Patrick's Day Parade and Concert, the Christmas Tree Lights Switch On, Halloween and The Lord Mayor's Carnival. The council thus views itself as in 'a key position to provide civic leadership,' including an 'integrated cultural strategy' to create a 'shared city'. In a display of optimism, the council has stated that these 'celebrations encouraged inclusive community involvement at all levels, creating a sense of ownership and pride in our great city' (Belfast City Council 2006).

While such sentiments are eminently worthy, a number of commentators (Graham and Nash 2006, Morrissey and Gaffikin 2006, Shirlow and Murtagh 2006) have asked whether state-funded projects are more often guided by the logic of 'benign apartheid', the confirmation of institutional sectarianism, which they see as resulting from the consociational structures discussed in Chapter 2. To be sure, much of this critique addresses what they see as the intensification of residential segregation during the post-conflict phase. Pertinently, however, key civic spaces, like Belfast city centre, are also subject to critical analyses. It is in both residential areas and civic public spaces, theorists note, that despite talk of diversity and integration by policy makers, the concept of 'identity remains vested in traditional principles of ethnonationalism that locate cultural belonging and citizenship in a "living space" defined by clearly demarcated boundaries and zero-sum models of space and place' (Graham and Nash 2006: 254).

In order to explore more closely the extent to which the public space of Belfast city centre can be seen as a successful form of sharing between nationalists, unionists and other groups, it is important to analyze some of the contemporary uses of the space. To begin with, it is possible to discern two parallel methods which underpin shared space in Belfast city centre. First, the notion of a 'shared space' has been evoked in public spectacles wherein the identities of the two groups are accommodated as much as possible on a basis of equality. The assumption here is that in many cases nationalists and unionists share a similar cultural repertoire and it thus follows that an important task of peace-building is to encourage the idea that the two groups have more binds of commonality than forms of difference. We call this strategy *common ground*. The second form of 'shared space' refers to the process in which nationalists and unionists should be endowed with separate but equal access to the city centre. The underlying assumption here is that nationalists and unionists maintain different cultural and political practices and it is therefore correct that they should be allowed equal recognition. We call this strategy *shared but different*.

Common ground

Of the two approaches, the *common ground* thesis appears particularly appealing because it seeks to foster cross-community dialogue and debate concerning issues of cultural similarity and common political needs. At its most attractive the approach offers a radical opportunity to forge alliances across the ethno-national cleavage and to deconstruct the very basis of separateness which can constitute ethno-national division. This perspective could fruitfully link with theorist Nancy Fraser's distinction between 'affirmative' and 'transformative' politics. Nancy Fraser (2000) argues that struggles undertaken to gain 'affirmation' for cultural difference in the multicultural paradigm serve not to 'promote respectful interaction within increasingly multicultural contexts, but to drastically simplify and reify group identities. They tend, rather, to encourage separatism, intolerance and chauvinism, patriarchalism and authoritarianism'. A 'transformative' politics, alternatively, is one which engenders 'dedifferentiation' by attempting to abolish 'economic arrangements that underpin group specificity' (Fraser 2000).

An example of a cross-cleavage social movement in Belfast which purposely seeks to use the space of Belfast city centre in order to try and deconstruct the ethno-national cleavage is the annual trade union May Day Parade. The May Day parade actively promotes diversity by embracing as wide a constituency as possible. By promoting cosmopolitanism embedded in the idea of the International Workers' Movement, organizers hope to challenge the competitive and divisive nationalisms which contribute to the sedimentation of violence and segregation in the city. We'll return to the May Day parade in Chapter 4.

Another strand to the *common ground* strategy is more problematic. This does not involve an attempt to deconstruct nationalist and unionist identities, but instead strives to accommodate them equally in a shared ritual. Belfast City Council has announced its intention to promote events which provide 'opportunity for input from both the major communities...within the city' (Belfast City Council 2005). Underlying this premise is that despite their political differences, out of encounters each community would discover that they possessed a shared civic identity that transcends the ethno-national binary. Belfast city centre has been identified as a key 'shared space' upon which the *common ground* can be forged. The problematic aspect of this approach to the *common ground* can be seen in the St Patrick's Day parade, which will be considered in

Chapter 5. In situations where ethno-national groups share identification with a cultural form, this is not guaranteed to engender a shared sense of identity. Indeed, these cultural forms are as likely to be the source of enduring ethnic conflict regarding which group should gain control and 'proprietary rights' (Harrison 2002) over the meaning of the event.

Another problem with the *common ground* is that it is often the case that the respective groups have very different ideas about what is shared between them. There is often a tendency within groups to believe that their own cultural and political identities are universal and therefore should be shared by all while the identities of rivals are particular and exclusive. For instance, many unionists claim that the wearing of the poppy to commemorate the fallen British soldiers in the world wars is universal because both Catholics and Protestants served in the army. The poppy symbol is thus presented by unionists as an 'inclusive symbol' and Remembrance Day commemorations should be shared by all (*Belfast Telegraph* 12 November 2009). Alternatively, for 'nationalists and republicans [the Poppy is] antagonistic and a sign of British oppression here in Ireland' (*Andersonstown News* 16 November 2009). Unionists' attempt to demand that nationalists share the same symbol and commemoration is viewed as coercive by many nationalists while nationalists' refusal to adorn the poppy is read by unionists as a sectarian gesture. Sharing, in this synopsis, becomes not so much about finding new ways of expressing connections between the groups, but of making one tradition universal and hegemonic. The goal of conflict regulation, as we will explore further in Chapter 5, is not always to create sharing, but to find ways in which symbols are not seen by members of groups as signs of antagonism and where difference can be respected.

The *common ground* approach is problematical because it is at this juncture where competing group-differentiated cultural demands most visibly clash and lead to conflict. Critics have argued that 'in Northern Ireland, the attempt to deal with sub-state patterns of ethno-sectarian antagonism though principles of parity of cultural respect and esteem has inadvertently created a legitimating vocabulary of "culture" and "cultural rights" for antagonistic expressions of separatist difference' (Graham and Nash 2006). In other words, group rights encourage conflict by allowing incompatible claims to clash in the public arena. To avoid conflict, critics of group rights argue that the alternative task is to ensure that the authorities remain neutral when considering competing cultural claims. As a corollary to this perspective, it is argued that politics should be driven by a process of rational deliberation, in which all relevant arguments are debated in the public arena before binding decisions are made for the common good of society. For this process to work, it is important that citizens debate issues as rational actors rather than in terms of their group based identities.

The search for the *common ground* in public events in Belfast city centre should not necessarily be viewed as incompatible with forms of 'deliberative democracy': how 'democratic Institutions are legitimate insofar as they embrace dialogue between relevant actors on a wide range of issues and that those discussions have a direct bearing on decisions made and the policies which emanate from them' (Little 2004: 89). In terms of conflict management in Northern Ireland, the task here is for interested groups to recognize not only that conflict occurs regarding the parity of nationalist and unionist identities in public spaces, but to commit themselves to debate and dialogue on the substantive issues to make sure that event is as fully representative of all groups in the city. An important initial step is taken towards conflict mitigation by eliciting a debate on how ethno-national identities should be represented in public space.

Even if forms of deliberative democracy are successful insofar as they lead to respective ethno-national groups debating and finding compromise on substantive issues in the public sphere, it is a decidedly different matter ascertaining whether the content of these deliberations have any lasting effect. This is particularly the case with how civic space is used and shared. In particular, 'staged spaces', such as festivals and carnivals, which are designed to build positive relationships and bridges between different social, economic and ethno-national groups, rarely act as 'levers that will magically spark interaction between groups' (Lownsbrough and Beunderman 2007: 28). They do not create the sort of lasting behavioural shift which is generally needed to make a qualitative difference to separate communities. At best, staged spaces can be viewed as 'a point of entry for making crucial first connections' between groups (Lownsbrough and Beunderman 2007: 28). What seems more realistic in the short term is to create spaces which create systematic discursive encounters between groups. Such encounters, at best, can help with the attempt to 'replace the *antagonistic* politics of sectarian enmity and grievance with a new *agonistic* politics', which 'seeks to optimize the solidarities and compromises of civic association, while avoiding the contrived conviviality of a dishonest harmony' [emphasis original] (Morrissey and Gaffikin 2006: 886).

Shared but different

The second strategy for Belfast city centre is *shared but different*, which is based on the premise that nationalist and unionist groups should show respect for diversity by tacitly accepting the right of each other to use public space, even if only sequentially. This largely refers to nationalist and unionist political and cultural events which are exclusive to their own constituency. Although this is ostensibly a fair arrangement, it is not without problems. Graham and Nash (2006), for instance, sum up anxieties by arguing that 'the post-conflict social geography of Northern Ireland is predominately conceived in terms, not of a radical departure from segregation but of ' "interconnected separation"; "benign apartheid"; "separate but equal"; containing conflict by working together to live apart; or even "malign apartheid" '.

A problem which critics have identified with the *shared but different* formulation is the extent to which it becomes the focus for zero-sum conflicts over space and identity, wherein the claim for space by one group is perceived as a loss by the other group. For some Irish nationalists, gaining access to the city centre has been a victory, an act of abandoning a past characterized by unionist hegemony. Returning momentarily to the 'Nationalist Rights Day' in August 1993 described at the beginning of the chapter, the entrance of nationalists into this hitherto proscribed sacred space ended a central grievance for the group. The *de facto* exclusion acted to perpetuate nationalist feelings of injustice. After one failed attempt to access the city centre in 1973, nationalists concluded that 'the city centre is banned to "Taigs" ' [nationalists] (*Irish News* 10 February 1973). The seemingly simple act of allowing nationalist groups into the city centre for political and cultural events engenders a sense of equality which can help ameliorate a fundamental generator of violent conflict: the exclusion, non-recognition and denial by one group of another group's identities. Significantly, the 'Nationalist Rights Day' in 1993 came at a crucial juncture in the unfolding peace process. At that point Irish republicans were engaged in secret dialogue with the British government and less than a year later the IRA declared a ceasefire in expectation of multi-party peace talks. The decision of the British state to grant permission to the 'Nationalist Rights Day' could be viewed as an important confidence-building gesture which pointed to the guarantee of nationalist rights in any new political dispensation.

Yet while it could be argued that the 'Nationalist Rights Day' played some part in securing the IRA ceasefire the following year, it also perpetuated uncertainty and conflict. For unionists and loyalists, the triumphal entrance of nationalist groups, especially republicans, augured their own loss of control of a sacred space, thus symbolizing a wider scenario in which unionists were losing political command of the state itself. Unionist political parties – excluded from the secret talks between

Sinn Féin and the Irish and British governments – expressed fear that the security 'go-ahead' for the parade had been made under pressure from the two governments (Sullivan 1993: 6).[20] This augmented broader unionist concerns that the two governments (British and Irish) were willing to grant nationalists any number of concessions at unionists' expense in exchange for a cessation of violence. For many unionists there was also outrage that the entrance of nationalist events in the city centre was also accompanied by a concomitant lack of respect for unionist symbols. Some nationalists had, for instance, adorned Irish tricolours on the gates of the city hall and in the 'hands' of the statue of Queen Victoria, who stood guard near the entrance to the city hall. If nationalists have welcomed their 'right to the city' as indicative of 'a city of equals', some unionists have viewed it as not only an example of loss of power but also representative of the new political dispensation which now acts to discriminate against them.

In a clear sense, the differing perspectives delineated by unionists and nationalists on sharing Belfast city centre is indicative of a wider picture in which power sharing is viewed by the two groups. The concept of 'shared space' for some unionist groups has therefore been reframed to outline the process as one of loss. The sharing of public space continues to be portrayed in terms of 'winning' or 'losing'. The use of the city centre by one group can be seen by the other as an example of the other being favoured thus contradicting the ideal that the 'state should be neutral between competing cultural claims' (OFMDFM 2005). An example of this was when a republican march for victims of the Troubles in August 2007 was granted permission to take place in the city centre. Unionist politicians accused the parade of containing 'depictions of I.R.A. terrorists and participants carrying guns', and was in contravention of the notion of 'shared space' (McCausland 2007). Moreover, unionist politicians argued that the presence of a threatening nationalist parade in the city centre was an example of unfair treatment, since official procedures make sure that any unionist parade, such as Orange Order parades, 'that enters any shared space in Belfast…is marked "contentious"' (McCausland 2007).

Despite the *shared but different* strategy to Belfast city centre causing some zero-sum conflict, could the strategy be conducive to conflict management? The idea of equal group rights to public space, however, is countered by Sennett (2005: 2), who argues that what is constituted by differential group rights is in fact 'civility based on indifference…fragmentation as a form of freedom. A social compromise which works against shared citizenship'. In response, there has been a call for the need in divided societies to foster a sense of common belonging that is not based on ethnic or cultural roots, but rather on a shared commitment to the political community. This emphasis can be seen, for example, in a report by the Commission for Racial Equality (Lownsbrough and Beunderman 2007), commissioned to provide strategies to deal with 'ethnic' division in Britain. The authors of the report state that a 'vision of living together, by forging 'common belonging to a citizenship that can embrace diversity but still engender solidarity is crucial to twenty-first century Britain'. The aim is to thus foster 'civic engagement and a richer notion of what it means to be a British citizen' (Johnson 2007: 3–4). This perspective bears some similarity to what McGhee (2005: 163) has called a 'differentiated universalism', which depends on ethnic 'boundaries remaining present, but requires that they must be flexible, and, importantly, open to change'.

The applicability of 'differentiated universalism' for 'divided societies' noted for contests over national sovereignty is limited. In Northern Ireland, in which the 'state is itself the subject of apparently irreconcilable political differences' (Graham and Nash 2006, 25), attempting to forge a common political and civic British (or Irish) community seems implausible. The aim of 'encouraging flexible or complex meta-loyalties above and beyond competing micro-loyalties' (McGhee 2008: 84) in ethno-nationally divided societies must, consequently, involve an alternative to the glue of national identity. The *shared but different* strategy offers the opportunity for diverse identities to be granted equal recognition and as a corollary it further helps build social stability and reduce ethno-national conflict. It is important, however, that this occurs in a transparent milieu and that the respective groups can engage in dialogue about how space can be used.

Addressing whether group-differentiated uses of public space can help with conflict mitigation, it is notable that conflict over the control of city centre has lessened in recent years. This has been assisted by how the city centre has lost some of its salience for nationalists, simply because it's no longer a site of exclusion and nationalist convocations in the city centre have waned. At first, after the *de facto* prohibition of nationalists was lifted there was a tendency for nationalist groups to enter the city centre at every opportunity, thus eliciting a counter demand by unionist groups. There was also an accompanying tendency to mark the city centre as nationalist, which included 'maladapting' unionist symbols, such as on a number of occasions draping the Irish tricolour over the statue of Queen Victoria that stands at the entrance of the City Hall. In more recent years, nationalist groupings gaining access to the city centre have realized that if they are to rightly demand recognition for their cultural identities then they are required to show equal respect for the precepts of diversity. The leaders of ethno-national minorities may appeal to the values of groups rights to challenge their historic exclusion, but 'those very ideals also impose the duty on them to be just, tolerant, and inclusive' (Kymlicka 2007: 93). This precept applies for all groups using public space and is elaborated in legislation which calls for groups to 'behave with due regard for the rights, traditions and feelings of others in the vicinity; refrain from using words or behaviour which could reasonably be perceived as being intentionally sectarian, provocative, threatening, abusive, insulting or lewd' (Parades Commission 2005: 8).

Conclusion: the *oeuvre*?

In this chapter we have explored the vexed schemes to promote 'a shared space' in Belfast city centre and to augment peace-building efforts in a 'divided city'. After decades in which nationalist events were prohibited from accessing the city centre, the chapter has noted two heuristic categories which have been tried in recent years to engender a shared space: *common ground* and *equal recognition*. While the chaper has noted that neither of the approaches has terminally ended conflict, crucially they do provide an opportunity for respective groups to participate in peaceful dialogue regarding the meaning and validity of their cultural and political identities as well as space to transform identities, if so desired. This is assisted by mutually agreed legislation and monitoring structures which provide a basis for the usage of public space to be informed by the values of liberal multiculturalism: individual human rights, tolerance for the claims of others and democratic responsibility. The construction of shared space – a truly public realm – involves not only the constitution of a more cosmopolitan politics in which 'pluralities, hybridities and multiple identities of a complex diverse world offer an alternative to the fundamentalisms of fixed identity' (Gaffikin et al 2008). A shared space is also one wherein the particularistic politics of 'recognition' can be negotiated peaceably.

Returning to Lefebvre, his conception of the city as an *oeuvre* was a site of renewed centrality, a place of encounter, an assemblage of difference which permits the full usage of moments and places. Yet in violently divided societies the space of encounter can be one of conflict as much of amicable sharing and engagement, especially when the space of meeting holds such symbolic value for the respective parties. The *oeuvre*, if it is to be re-imagined for divided societies, requires strategic thinking to allow groups to perform their specific identities without being experienced as intimidating or a loss to other groups. Specific preconditions, wrought through engagement between sections of society, should be encouraged concerning how space is to be used by groups. Although this will not necessarily end conflict, it at least will provide room for groups to discuss their meaning of how their identities are expressed in public space.

4
Unity through Diversity: A Shared Civil Society

'Globalise resistance'

At midday Tuesday 1 May 2001– May Day – up to one hundred anti-global capitalism protestors stormed Gap, the US based clothes retailer, which had opened a branch on Royal Avenue, the commercial thoroughfare of Belfast city centre. Calling themselves Globalise Resistance, located within the Global Justice Movement, the group has sought to create a broad based mobilization to 'oppose the neo-liberal policies of the G8, IMF, World Bank and WTO'. A decentralized yet globally linked movement, they 'seek to increase the involvement of Trade Unions and to increase collaboration between different strands of the movement, including environmentalist, NGOs, progressive faith groups and other campaigning organisations' (Globalise Resistance 2007).

On Tuesday 1 May 2001, the Belfast branch of Globalise Resistance initiated a sit-down occupation of Gap for a few minutes, where they blew whistles and chanted. After being forced out by the security, the protestors ran across to the opposite side of Royal Avenue to McDonald's, the fast-food chain. As in Gap, the protestors sat on the floor and waited until security arrived to push them out onto the street. The police had arrived by now. Once on the street, the protestors were quickly on the move. This time they headed up Royal Avenue in the direction of the City Hall until they arrived at the Disney Store; however, the security had been alerted and they managed to shut the doors of the store before the protestors arrived. Standing outside the Disney Store, Globalise Resistance proceeded to hold an impromptu 'rave' until the police managed to peacefully disperse them.

The Globalise Resistance protest in Belfast on May Day 2001 was part of a number of similar demonstrations in numerous other locations across the globe that day. May Day had been carefully chosen as the time to initiate the protest because it is the traditional day that socialists, anarchists and trade unionists celebrate the International Workers Movement. Although the Globalise Resistance demonstrations in Belfast were ostensibly against certain global franchises for their alleged exploitative use of Third World labour, the protests performed another crucial function. The attempt to challenge the logic of global capitalism in Belfast city centre was not just an outgrowth of an insular nationalism, but also a cosmopolitan act to 'jump scales' from the local to the global. In this way the Globalise Resistance' protestors were seeking to show that local/national issues regarding the constitutional position of Northern Ireland were superfluous to the larger and more pressing issues of 'planetary interdependence' (Melucci 1996). As one protestor wrote:

> May Day's protest was very significant in Belfast, not only as part of the global protests, but also because it gives lie to the notion that all politics here are either orange or green [unionist or nationalist]. The people on the streets on May Day were both Catholic and Protestant but their priority was not justice for one cause or one community, instead it was about justice for the whole of humankind. (Globalise Resistance 2002)

Social movements and peace

It has been noted in Chapter 2 that a host of theorists have argued that the consociational politics of the Good Friday Agreement have encouraged the dominance of 'identity politics', which give succour to inter and intracommunal conflict by institutionalizing difference at the political level, stifling diversity in the name of communal identity and for failing to recognize cross-cutting identities. In this apparently divisive milieu the task, according to some commentators, is to encourage 'those movements that crosscut social divisions, and challenge and erode the clash of ethno-nationalisms and create new relationships of mutuality through networking and debate' (Taylor 2006: 47). Some civil society groups and social movements seek to provide an alternative to ethno-national division by promoting a politics of solidarity, a shared identity capable of mobilizing across the cleavage and policies of economic redistribution for all groups. In the case of the Globalise Resistance demonstration described at the beginning of this chapter, they seek to go beyond ethno-national politics by making us see the wider, 'joined-up' global picture: how the neoliberal political economy connects us at the scale of the high street to the sweat shops of the Third World. Alongside 'Globalise Resistance', there is a long history tradition of social movements in Northern Ireland which have managed to secure cross-cleavage support, such as trade union mobilizations and public housing tenants associations. There are other social movements, which are not primarily rooted in the politics of class and economic redistribution; they hope to pluralize society with expressive forms of understanding and diverse communities which critique the perceived limitations of competitive and divisive nationalisms. These movements, located at the scale of civil society rather than institutional party politics, include Lesbian Gay Bisexual Transgendered (LGBT) groups, ban-the-bomb associations, green environmentalists and street carnival practitioners.

In this chapter we assess what impact, if any, some of these social movements can contribute to the project of a shared society and peacebuilding in Northern Ireland. To aid this, we look at social movements in Northern Ireland which, in different ways, seek to either end ethno-national conflict, to pluralize society and make it more tolerant of difference, or force it to come together face-to-face with the reality of broader global issues which confront humanity. Notably, these groups do not confine their struggle to institutional party politics; the groups in this chapter endeavour to bring about change through altering the traditional values and identities of social actors in a divided society.

At the most utopic these movements are identity involving and transforming; they manipulate symbolic spatial arrangements and challenge entrenched sectarian values. Such social movements have been called 'prophets' (Melucci 1996: 1) because they are key agents for recognizing and even bringing about change within societies. In the face of social change, they may more likely appear to be 'proverbial canaries in the mine, except they sing out rather than quietly expire' (Jasper 1997: 13). 'Movements…call for changes in our habits of thought, action and interpretation' (Crossley 2002: 9). Lefebvre's (1991: 54) argument that 'a social transformation…must manifest a creative capacity in its effects on daily life, on language and on space' links satisfactorily with many contemporary social movement projects.

Yet while social movements located at the sub-institutional level are important generators of alternative politics and new inclusive identities in divided societies, they can also be key protagonists in igniting ethnic conflict and for providing meddlesome attempts to stymie peacebuilding efforts. These movements, although they may reject violent methods, advance zero-sum ethno-national politics and reject attempts to bring about compromise and cooperation between groups (Belloni 2008). To adequately address both the progressive and reactionary character of social movements, it is necessary to understand how the framework of 'civil society' contributes to the production of non-state actors in divided societies.

Civil society

Although there is no consensus underwriting the concept of civil society, a standard definition refers to 'all associations and networks between the family and the state, except firms' (Edwards 2004: vi). This inclusive remit includes, *inter alia*, cultural and faith organizations, protest movements, trade unions and voluntary groups. In recent years there has been an interest in the role that civil society can contribute to the social well-being in two distinct ways: the *associational* and the construction of a *public sphere* of political deliberation.

In an era in which traditional social institutions (like the welfare state, labour unions and nuclear families) have been progressively dismantled, leaving individuals disconnected from society, civil society is identified as rectifying the imbalance. Voluntary associations can provide a reassuring oasis of solidarity and mutual support among like-minded people. The *associational* aspect of civil society thus refers to how members of society can come together in groups and breed the important civic values of trust, reciprocity, sharing, tolerance and nonviolence. Civil society groups are further empowered when they are linked together in ways that promote collective goals and mutual accountability.

Civil society can further provide a *public sphere* of deliberation, rational dialogue and the exercise of collective citizenship in pursuit of the common interest. The realm of civil society, here, allows citizens to debate the nature of the 'good life': through the institutions and practices of politics, governance and everyday life, civil society can provide the raw material required for individuals to live peacefully by reconciling individual autonomy with collective aspirations, by 'marrying pluralism with conformity so that complex societies can function with both efficiency and justice' (Edwards 2004: 6).

Conflict and peace

There is much above that is apposite to the process of peace-building and creating a shared identity in divided societies. The associational aspect is particularly salient because in divided societies ethno-national identities provide 'criteria for the organization of social relations at all levels, including community and family linkages' (Della Porta and Diani 2006: 96). This means that opportunities to bridge 'sectarian barriers are infrequent and people involved [in cross-community movements] are regularly met with ostracism from their own community' (Della Porta and Diani 2006: 96). Ethno-national cleavages are, hence, fundamentally rooted not only in voting patterns but also in a combination of group traits and associational relationships linking members of a collectivity to each other (Diani 2000: 391). These associational relationships are expressed in 'concentric' circles: group relationships are concentrated within 'specific circles consisting of overlapping primary and secondary groups, associational and private, often family ties' (Diani 2000: 396). Importantly, Diani (2000) notes, 'concentric relationships' shape people's identities and social representations and thus 'support cleavages to the extent that they reinforce actors' world views and identities while reducing the possibility of their accessing other social milieus with conflicting views' (2000: 396).

If cleavages are characterized by relationships which are 'concentric circles', then new forms of relationships which cross-cut cleavages and engender new types of solidarities are the product of 'intersecting circles'. For Diani, social movements can be shaped by 'intersecting circles': relationships are voluntary, multiple and overlapping, thus contributing to the creation of new models of communitarian and organizational action. Such 'intersecting circles' can contain relationships which cut across established social and political polarization. These movements are able to 'draw upon, or generate, new solidarities and group memberships which cut across the boundaries of any specific traditional political cleavage, and thus undermine current forms of encapsulation' (Diani 2000: 399). Diani thus points to the 'patterns of social relations they generate through the overlapping memberships and personal linkages of their activists, and through the alliances between the different groups which identify with a given cause' (2000: 387). In addition, while ethnic conflict is perpetuated by high levels of mutual uncertainty, vulnerability and distrust between groups, the formation of new associational relationships across the cleavage can help generate the emergence of trust and the binds of reciprocity.

The capacity of social movements to construct alternative public spheres is also important. While consociational power sharing can create a government with power concentrated amongst political élites (see Chapter 2), civil society can play a crucial counterweight by promoting transparency, accountability and other aspects of good governance.

Civil society, furthermore, can sustain a public sphere hospitable to democratic civic life – curbing the power of centralizing institutions, fostering trust, tolerance and dialogue, advancing plural interests across cleavages, and providing many public services which are beyond the capacity of a weakened state. In the public sphere, pluralism is also advanced and protected in the face of ethno-national homogeneity and centralizing institutions. The public sphere further allows for conflicting ethnic and cultural claims to be deliberated by respective groups to facilitate the peaceful resolution of differences.

The contributions of civil society to mitigating conflict is seen in Varshney's (2002) comparative research on Muslim/Hindu civil society linkages in a number of Indian cities, which demonstrates that ethnic violence is less likely to occur when strong civil society ties bind the two groups. According to Varshney (2002: 9), 'a vigorous associational life acts as a serious constraint on the polarizing strategies of political elites'. When such networks of engagement were missing, 'communal identities led to endemic and ghastly violence'. Social movements have even been identified as bringing down violent ethno-national regimes. An example of this was the group 'Otpor!', the Serbian word for resistance. In the wake of Serbia's attack on Kosovo and NATO's bombings of Belgrade in response, Optor!, a radical student movement took the opportunity to channel war weariness and disillusionment among Belgrade's Serbs during 2000 into open, radical sedition. Inspired by a mixture of Serbian anti-Nazi guerrillas during the Second World War and the nonviolent direct action student movements that paralysed many parts of the globe during 1968, Optor! was instrumental in leading the successful campaign to remove Slobodan Milosevic from power (Collin 2007).

Despite the potential importance of social movements in peacebuilding, an overview of civil society in divided societies provides a more ambivalent picture of its input. While it can nourish movements important for sustaining peace, equally civil society groups can foment discord and violence (Belloni 2008). For instance, during the 1980s in Croatia and Serbia, an emerging civil society bred single-identity groups tied to their respective nationalisms, which were instrumental in bringing ethno-national entrepreneurs into power on the basis of nationalist politics. The so-called anti-bureaucratic revolution of 1988 and 1989 witnessed hundreds of thousands of Serbs rallying across various parts of Yugoslavia with the intention of securing Serbian political control of strategic provinces and republics. The movement helped reawaken Serbian nationalism and paved the path for Milosevic's inexorable rise to power (Sell 2002). A multitude of voluntary associations in Lebanon and Rwanda (prior to the genocide in 1994) also fuelled intergroup violence. The vast majority of associations in Lebanon during the 1970s and 1980s were 'exclusionary', divisive and constantly at war with each other (Belloni 2008, Edwards 2004). Rwanda had the highest density of civil society associations in sub-Saharan Africa; yet from such associations emerged the *interahamwe*, originally a soccer fan club which evolved into a Hutu militia responsible for the deaths of hundreds of thousands of Tutsis during 1994 (Gourevitch 1998: 93).

Even when the conflict has ended, the role of civil society in ensuring that peace prospers is unclear. While some peace agreements have actively encouraged the consultation of civil society, many more have been élite driven thus excluding civil society for fear of overburdening the process. Some agreements have provisions for civil society to help provide services for post-war reconstruction and to help embed peace. In Rwanda the *gagaca*, an adapted citizen tribunal system at the community level, has contributed to post-genocide reconciliation by relieving the local justice system of trying tens of thousands of perpetrators (Belloni 2008: 191).

Northern Ireland civil society

What has been the role of civil society in Northern Ireland regarding conflict and conflict management during and after the Troubles? The outbreak of civil violence in the 1960s led to the problem being defined by the British state as a problem of poor community relations between Catholics and Protestants. In response, an attempt was made to build up a community development sector to encourage harmonious relations between the groups. The logic here was that community development work would encourage each group to gain self-confidence as a precondition to the 'coming-together of community groups across the sectarian divide to agitate on issues of common interest and concern' (O'Dowd et al. 1980: 154). In essence, the paradigm of 'good community relations', a batch of anti-racist initiatives designed to foster contact and appreciation of the cultures of minority ethnic groups in Britain, was transported over to Northern Ireland (Hayes 1972, Mitchell 2009). The underlying rationale of the good relations industry was that conflict arises from individuals lacking information about the other group and from lack of opportunities. A 'contact hypothesis' was developed which formulated that conflict resolution could be achieved by encouraging and promoting contact between ethnic groups, resulting in more tolerant and positive attitudes, a position endorsed by the UK government and many academics (see Hayes et al. 2007: 461).

Another strand to community relations work developed in the aftermath of the arrival of Direct Rule government in Northern Ireland in 1972 (Cochrane 2006, Adshead and Tonge 2009). At that time Northern Ireland was governed by the UK Secretary of State, which many critics called a form of 'consular government'. In an attempt to counter this democratic deficit, a state sponsored voluntary sector was set up to offer on the ground expertise as well as providing some public services. A nexus between the military and the 'community' was also formed through civilian-military committees, which were supposed to facilitate communication between the local population and the security forces (O'Dowd et al. 1980: 156).

During the 1980s and 1990s, civil society organizations mushroomed under state patronage. While there were 800 voluntary organizations in Northern Ireland in 1975 (O'Dowd et al. 1980: 160), by 2000 the number had risen to over 5000 (Adshead and Tonge 2009), and employing over 30,000 people with an annual turnover of £657 million (Cochrane 2006: 257). Civil society, consequently, became a crucial space for conflict transformation attempts in two distinct ways. First, the British state, as part of counter-insurgency initiatives, tried to marginalize Irish republicans within their own 'communities' as community development policies were designed to build up the 'moderate' sphere of civil society, providing a 'more effective channelling of expressions and grievances' than intercommunal violence (Community Development Review Group 1991: 2, Mitchell 2009, Bean 2008: 27). Second, sections of civil society began to take a more proactive approach to the emerging peace process. For instance, in the aftermath of 25 killings in a short period of time in October 1993, trade unions and other civil society groups held massive peace rallies across Northern Ireland. Although civil society was not set a place at the negotiating table for the 1998 Agreement, it was charged with ensuring that the Northern Irish public supported it in the referendum by campaigning for a 'Yes' vote.

Despite the growth of civil society during the Troubles and the peace process, some commentators fear that the consociational politics of the Northern Ireland Agreement has been élite driven at the expense of civil society (Taylor 2006). Yet while some commentators lament the lack of civil society's critical input into Northern Irish politics – as it is hope that it could deliver an alternative public sphere of reconciliation – the capacity of the sector to deliver such goals is distinctly dubious. Civil society, broadly speaking in Northern Ireland, can be both progressive and reactionary. For instance, although a large body of groups mobilized to campaign for the 'Yes' vote for the 1998 Agreement from the public, many Protestant unionist groups, however, coalesced as a 'victims' movement to act as 'spoilers' opposed to the Agreement (Nagle 2009d). Neither is it clear that that the political preferences of Northern Ireland's 'civil society', that is, its large numbers of civic associations, differ from those of its political parties. The most popular civil society organizations in Northern Ireland, the Orange Order and the Gaelic Athletic Association (GAA), are bastions of unionism and nationalism, respectively (McGarry and O'Leary 2004). Aughey (2005: 76) has also argued that the idea that community associations held society together during the Troubles is a 'benign myth'.

What this all illuminates is that it is difficult to make a definitive verdict on the impact of civil society on peace-building. Even adherents of peace and reconciliation groups admit their contribution is difficult to quantify (Schubotz and Robinson 2006). Nevertheless, it can be said that civil society positively augments peace-building efforts when *associational* aspects are aimed at engendering cross-cleavage relations to transform ethno-national relations from 'communities of strangers' to 'communities of neighbours', as well as constituting a critical *public sphere* which allow for various interests to be debated in the light of the common good. These associational ties, however, have to be deeply and profoundly embedded to adequately work (Varshney 2002).

For the rest of this chapter, we assess social movements in Northern Ireland that have purposely sought to challenge and undermine ethno-national division by creating new associational networks which transcend 'binary identities'. These movements have also often encouraged the formation of a critical public sphere designed to encourage pluralism and the reconciliation of antagonistic ethnic interests by forging a shared identity. One particular way in which we explore how these movements strive to create associational networks and a public sphere is their use of space. In particular, we examine the way in which these social movements mobilize to challenge the seeming naturalness in how segregated space is reproduced in Belfast. Lefebvre's (1996: 159) assertion that the most important thing is to multiply the readings of the city, that the city contains plentiful detritus to construct different stories which provide an antidote to normative discourses which underpin ethnic division and inequality is a good way to think of this project.

May Day

One of the most persistent attempts to forge a non-sectarian shared identity in Northern Ireland and Belfast has come from socialist and workers' movements. In a city increasingly ruptured by sectarian violence,

1892 witnessed a solidarity march of trade unionists, encompassing Catholics and Protestants, in support of linen workers who wished to join a trade union (Cradden 1994: 69). As mentioned in Chapter 3, a formative moment for the movement occurred in 1907 when Catholic and Protestant workers mobilized together during the dockers and carters strike which brought Belfast to a standstill.

After the formation of Northern Ireland in the early 1920s, the workers' movement found a focus for solidarity in an annual May Day 'demonstration', a parade of trade unionists and socialists which marched in tight, almost military formation, into Belfast city centre and back to its starting point for a political rally. Organized by the Northern Ireland Committee for the Irish Congress of Trade Unions (NICITU), the parade in the 1960s and 1970s was an attempt by the city's socialists to provide a model of working-class unity. This logic of unity was in contrast to the acrimony promulgated by the competing narratives of ethno-nationalism. Belfast's May Day parade was indicative of the prevailing socialist interpretation of the conflict as fundamentally driven by a class dynamic. For Belfast's socialists, capitalists were blamed for hindering the alliance of working-class nationalists and unionists by creating a form of false-consciousness, that of ethno-nationalism. In this analysis, the capitalist class was able to benefit from a fractured working-class by keeping wages deflated and the two ethno-national groups separated in the workplace.

The May Day 'demonstration' was thus a focus for dissenting politics which could be highly critical of the unionist government. In one keynote speech at a May Day rally in 1963, a speaker demanded that a socialist government be installed in Northern Ireland and that 'a state of war exists between the Northern Ireland Tories and the working class movement' (*Irish News* 6 May 1963).[21] May Day speakers also urged for class unity to transcend the ethno-national divide and the march was seen as providing an opportunity to 'bury the shibboleths' (*Belfast Newsletter* 9 May 1960) of sectarian division. The march thus gave expression 'for united action by all trade union members in support of our common objectives' (*Belfast Newsletter* 7 May 1962).

Unity through exclusion

Perhaps paradoxically, the most palpable way in which May Day in the 1960s articulated unity was through processes of exclusion and hierarchy. This trope could be seen in the range of groups allowed to participate in the parade. Only trade unions formally affiliated to the NICITU were allowed to march. Members of a diverse array of groups operating in Belfast at the time (such as CND, Anarchists and the Women's Communist League) were only allowed to march as part of their trade unions and not as individual units. Exclusivity performed another powerful function: it tried to prohibit 'single-identity' nationalist or unionist groups from participating in the parade thus potentially rendering May Day as a focus for sectarian interests and division. In 1965, for instance, the NICITU barred the Republican Party, a socialist Irish nationalist grouping, from participating as a single unit.

Ultimately this exclusionary practice caused conflict. Groups who viewed themselves not only as socialists but also as belonging to an ethno-national identity were excluded from the May Day parade by the NICITU. In the mid- and late 1970s, as the conflict in Northern Ireland intensified, these proscribed groups organized their own alternative May Day parade and up to three separate parades occurred on the same day. One of the contending 'rebel' parades was organized by the Irish republican socialist group, People's Democracy. One march, in 1971, featured 300 people. A car preceded the marchers, who carried placards calling for 'Workers of the World to Unite'. The apparent fracturing of the May Day parade revealed the lack of cohesion in the working-class movement in the face of an eruption of violent ethno-national conflict. The salience of the unified model of class collectivity to provide an alternative to sectarianism foundered as polarization sharpened.

Unity through diversity

The development of the Northern Irish peace process in the 1990s provided impetus for the NICITU to reimagine itself in terms of diversity and peace-building. Rather than a day of class homogeneity, there is a stress on diversity to embrace a wide possible constituency. By promoting cosmopolitanism enshrined in the idea of the International Workers' Movement, trade unionists hope to challenge the competitive and divisive nationalisms which contribute to the sedimentation of violence and segregation in Northern Ireland. One of the May Day organizers summed up their conception of the parade:

> I would see it as challenging the two community idea. What we have strived to do is to create a safe space for people of all religions and none to come together to mark their relationship as working people rather than as Catholics, as Protestants, as atheists, whatever…We have said 'it's a non-sectarian, non-denominational march'. The

biggest May Day parade in the British Isles is in Belfast. That tells you something. It also tells you this: the May Day parade continued through the entire period of the Troubles in various formats, there were splits, there were difficulties, there were rows, but the point is it continued, I think, because there are enough people here who are determined to show their faces and say: 'I'm not going to be shoehorned into one sectarian corner the way the Good Friday Agreement, for example, thinks we ought to be'. (Interview, 2007)

The diversity of May Day is expressed in terms of the issues it represents. An organizer defined them as: 'economic justice and workplace justice. Increasingly as we move into a global market, globalized society, issues of global solidarity and justice and racism are important as well as issues of Third World debt, issues relating to child poverty, HIV AIDS' (Interview, 2007). Its diversity is further expressed through the range of groups who participate: not only trade unions but also anti-war groups, nationalist and unionist groupings (such as Sinn Féin and the Progressive Unionist Party (PUP)), the Anti-Racist Network, the Campaign Against Water Privitisation, the Anarchist Black Cross, Environmentalists, the Anti-War Coalition, The Northern Irish Gay Rights Association (NIGRA), the Cuba Support Group Ireland, amongst many others. One of the most successful mobilizations in recent years was in 2005 when 6000 people marched to protest against rising levels of racism and to proclaim solidarity with the city's ethnic minority groupings. May Day is now a carnival type event; it elaborates the forms of cross-cutting, intersecting circles of relationships noted by Diani (2000) in network movements which transcend cleavages and offers a shared identity. For the 2003 May Day celebration, the organizers described its remit thus:

This year's theme [is] based on rejecting sectarianism and celebrating diversity in Northern Ireland. Today's parade is seen as one of the few marches in Northern Ireland which has been designed to embrace participation from people of different backgrounds. (*Belfast Telegraph* 5 May 2003)

This process of networking is also representative of nascent trends within the global trade union movement to forge links with other civil society groupings. Termed 'Global Social Movement Unionism' (Lier and Stokke 2006), this strategy of constructing alliances outside the traditional remit of trade unionism is responsive to contemporary processes of 'state deregulation, informalisation and flexibilsation, all in the context of neoliberal globalization' (Lier and Stokke 2006: 802). The attempt to internationalize May Day in Northern Ireland in terms of trade union struggles against the neoliberal world economy also provides a focus to transcend the particularism of the local ethno-national cleavage.

LGBT: unity through diversity

The next movement concerns the Lesbian, Gay, Bisexual and Transgender (LGBT) mobilization. They have mobilized on their basis of their unequal citizenship status in Northern Ireland; subjected to intolerance and state regulation because of their sexual identities, the movement has campaigned with a range of groups to make the celebration of diversity and difference an activating feature of a potential post-sectarian society in Northern Ireland.

It is often argued that Northern Ireland is historically a homophobic society (Kitchin 2002, Kitchin and Lysaght, 2004, Conrad 2006). This homophobia is seen as stemming from how ethno-national encapsulations can be entwined with religious identities. The holy alliance between religion and politics has meant that there has been a strong current of homophobia in Northern Ireland. Expert exponents of this are the DUP, currently Northern Ireland's largest party. Regressive views continue to permeate the DUP's *weltanschauung*. In 2005, Maurice Mills, an elected DUP politician, branded gays as 'abominable and filthy' and to blame for AIDS in Africa and Hurricane Katrina (Chrisafis 2005). Then in 2008, Iris Robinson, then an MP in the Westminster Parliament, was asked in a radio interview to comment on a homophobic attack that had recently occurred in Northern Ireland. Robinson answered that homosexuality was 'disgusting, loathsome, nauseating, shamefully wicked' and 'an abomination' (see *Mail on Sunday* 8 June 2008).

Although there are no Irish nationalist parties which are inextricably linked to the Catholic Church, the two are most clearly connected in so far as the vast majority of Irish nationalists are Catholic. Catholicism has historically taken a strong reactionary line against homosexuality. As Kitchin and Lysaght (2004: 87) note: 'homosexuality was deemed to be a crime against nature, an "objective disorder"; a bodily expression of sin and evil that had to be disciplined'. This view of homosexuality shows little sign of abating. In late 2008, Pope Benedict XVI suggested in a speech that homosexuality is as much of a threat to the survival of the humanity as climate change.

In this milieu an important LGBT movement has mobilized in Northern Ireland. If ethno-nationalism is defined through homogeneity and exclusivity, and homophobia is but one manifestation of such division, then the LGBT movement has sought to create a broad based inclusive movement which challenges not only their omission from the public sphere, but also to contest the nature of the dominant two-community model.

Mobilizing for equality

While homosexuality had been decriminalized in England and Wales in 1967, it remained criminalized in Northern Ireland. In this situation, mobilizing for equality was an inherently difficult practice for Northern Ireland's gay men. Paradoxically, however, the intensification of civil violence during the early 1970s presented an opportunity for a nascent movement to organize, especially in Belfast. Although prior to the Troubles, Belfast city centre was a hub for social activities, with its numerous bars, clubs, theatres and restaurants, the chronic violence which befell the city ensured that many people only felt safe within their own districts and few felt confident to travel into the city centre to socialize. While Belfast had hitherto never possessed a definable LGBT 'space', the emptying of the city centre due to violence provided an opportunity for LGBT activists. In particular, the bars which remained open in the city centre became places that LGBT members could use. An LGBT activist recounted the city centre was an LGBT space during the 1970s:

> Gays were one of the few groups who used the city centre and we had more courage than other groups. So quite often the only people on the move on a Saturday night in Belfast city centre would have been us going to the Chariot Rooms or the Europa [bars]. There was a cordon around the city centre which meant that anybody going into the city centre would have been searched, which gave us a certain sense of security. (Interview 2008)[22]

Importantly, the city centre space gave an opportunity for the construction of new networks and the basis of political action. In the 1970s the first LGBT political lobbying groups formed. Of these, the Northern Ireland Gay Rights Association (NIGRA), the Campaign for Homosexual Law Reform (CHLR) and CARA-Friend provided complementary services. CARA-Friend, formed in 1974, was initiated to provide a voluntary and confidential counselling service, befriending and a social space for LGBTs. A key organizer during the 1970s explained that although CARA-Friend was not an explicitly political organization, by facilitating the opportunity for LGBTs to come together for the first time, this allowed LGBTs to articulate their sense of grievance with having to suppress their sexual orientation:

> Over 30 years ago, there was total invisibility for gays in Northern Ireland. If they knew they were gay they didn't know how to meet other people or what to do about it. We were the first generation to come out to ourselves. That part was relatively easy but coming out to other people was impossible unless you had the wherewithal. I think a lot of us had a great anger about early years being misspent, no purpose and being denied a love life or sex life even from until the movement began in 1975. So when CARA started, the gay befriending group, they only started with putting ads in the papers and posters on walls. And we received a torrent of letters from people who had been waiting 20 to 30 years for that moment when they could find out how to connect with other gay people. It was heartbreaking and it accentuated our anger. (Interview 2008)

It was at this point when a more politically focussed movement began to emerge. In particular, the CHLR was formed in Northern Ireland in January 1974 with the intent of pressurizing the British government to decriminalize homosexuality by extending the *Sexual Offences Act 1967* to Northern Ireland. The CHLR was then reorganized in 1975 as the NIGRA, which concentrated on lobbying for a national gay rights bill.

The British state's justification for maintaining the law which criminalized homosexuality in Northern Ireland was that there was an high degree of resistance in the region to any change of law. In 1978 the British Government published a proposal for a draft Homosexual Offences (Northern Ireland) Order 1978, which, if passed, would bring Northern Ireland law on the matter broadly into line with England and Wales. The proposal was put out to public consultation where there was a substantial degree of resistance. Public opposition to the reforms was articulated by a number of senior judges and district councils. The leader of the DUP, Rev. Ian Paisley, then an MP, collected nearly 70,000 signatures as he led a petition to 'Save Ulster from Sodomy'.[23]

Due to the continued criminalization of homosexuality in Northern Ireland during the 1970s, gay men continued to be harassed by the police and the crown prosecution services. The most conspicuous bout of police harassment occurred in 1976 when the police's drug squad raided the homes of up to thirty leading gay activists across Northern Ireland. As part of this they searched the home of Jeff Dudgeon, where they found personal correspondence and diaries in which he described homosexual acts detailing other gay men. After being questioned by the police regarding his homosexual activities, the police passed the investigation file to the Director of Prosecutions with the intent of charging Dudgeon with the offence of 'gross indecency between males'.

In the end, the Director of Prosecutions came to a decision that prosecutions of the arrested gay men would not be in the public interest. However, subject to criminalization, police harassment and potential public prosecutions, NIGRA stepped up their campaign by utilizing multiple access points to advance their claims. In an attempt to escalate the campaign, NIGRA began to challenge the criminalization of homosexual men in Northern Ireland in the European Court of Human Rights. Acting on behalf of NIGRA, Jeff Dudgeon submitted a complaint against the United Kingdom of Great Britain with the European Commission of Human Rights (ECHR) on 22 May 1976 under Article 25 of the Convention for the Protection of Human Rights and Fundamental Freedoms.[24] NIGRA finally claimed success when, on 22 October 1981, the European Court of Human Rights declared that the criminalization of homosexual acts between consenting adults in Northern Ireland was a violation of Article 8 of the European Convention on Human Rights (ECHR).

Belfast pride

From the 1990s onwards the LGBT mobilization focussed on a number of interrelated issues: achieving equality in all spheres of social life, increased visibility in the public sphere and promoting diversity to foster mutual tolerance between all groups in society. If Northern Ireland's narrative has told of discrete, homogeneous and autonomous cultures, characterized by sectarian violence and exclusion, then the organizers of the LGBT mobilization believe that they are contributing to the notion that cultural interchange and pluralism provides new models of interaction. Such movements have come to represent a myriad of shifting, interwoven alliances seeking to pluralize existing society. A particular focus for this politics of pluralism is Belfast 'Pride', a weeklong celebration encompassing numerous events.

Although there are a number of distinct LGBT groups operating in Northern Ireland, these groups come together each year to either organize or participate in Pride.[25] Since its formation in June 1991 the first six days of Pride are concerned with indoor events. Since the late 1990s, however, the focus of the indoor events has been on 'increased access to information, rights and resources' (Queerspace 2007). This emphasis on information resembles Melucci's (1996) analysis of contemporary social movements as concentrating on information in two senses. On the one hand, the social movement tries to gain information on 'things', such as trying to gather data on the number of homophobic attacks in Northern Ireland; on the other, the social movement challenges incorrect information, such as disputing negative representations of LGBTs. The acquisition and disputation of 'information' is facilitated through contact and networking between LGBTs and groups outside the LGBT 'community'. These networks are forged through a highly diverse array of events, which cover, for instance, arts events; workshops on safe sex; tackling homophobic violence; addressing spirituality; lesbian and gay parenting; drug awareness; 'meet the police' talks to discuss policing; gay swimming groups; fashion shows; photographic exhibitions organized in conjunction with Amnesty International. To assist with relationships between nationalists and unionists, Belfast Pride has held events in nationalist and unionist arts and community centres, hoping that members of these two ethno-national groups will be encouraged to visit and explore a 'space' that is perceived to be hostile because it belongs to the other community. The organizers of Pride have stated that such events are 'a celebration of the rich diversity within all communities' (*Irish News* 16 June 1997).

Beat carnival

The final social movement we assess is that of 'Beat Initiative', a group of carnival practitioners. Formed in 1993, 'Beat Initiative' is a compilation of street artists. When asked about the organization's formation, David Boyd, 'Beat's' director, said:

It was to create a means for people to get together on the streets in a different form of expression, and particularly to have that gathering of people led by artists rather than led by politicians ... Whenever we have parades or gatherings, whether it is riots or protests, it is usually something political, so that's where the street leadership has been seen ... I believe there are other forms of leadership that are important that you get on the street, including from artists ... While that holds true anywhere it was particularly important in a place like Belfast which is very much divided by conflict and confrontation. (Interview 2007)

Like May Day and the LGBT movement, 'Beat Initiative' purposely strives to facilitate networks which transcend the ethno-national cleavage. A fundamental way in which 'Beat' creates these networks is by bringing together nationalist and unionist groups from interface areas to work together to prepare and perform street carnivals. As David Boyd explains:

> We don't just want to be seen as dressing up for just a bit of craic [fun]. There are the stories behind it about groups, say from east Belfast and north Belfast, who would never have met before…but…it is significant there are…people from north Belfast travelling over here to be part of the event in east Belfast for the first time, or *vice versa.* (Interview 2007)

Analogous to May Day and Belfast Pride, the temporary occupation of public space engendered by their carnivals provides a concrete alternative to single-identity uses of space or top-down attempts to manage intercommunal conflict. Boyd elaborates:

> social work…can get bogged down in just trying to manage difficult situations, keeping a lid on things…Arts work is more about looking at doing something and transforming situations. So for me that was the carnival activity was about in terms of the street. It was about transforming what happens on the street, giving people a reason to get together. Certainly when it started, it was really an alternative to what was happening where everything was so polarized before in terms of creativity, in terms of communal activity. (Interview 2007)

The interface margins

In this chapter we have so far considered a number of social movements in Northern Ireland, paying particular attention to the ways in which they have struggled to create mobilizations which cross-cut the ethno-national cleavage. Turning now to the potentially radical possibilities imagined by Lefebvre (1991), especially his conception of 'reappropriated space' to critique dominant uses of space, the chapter considers whether these groups can contribute towards peace-building by challenging different spatial formations that underpin segregation. In the context of Belfast, we note how social movements reappropriate marginal interface spaces as well as the social centrality of the city centre.

The concept of 'reappropriation' was vital to Lefebvre's radical thinking to reimagine the fracturing of the city into discrete, alienated parts. Reappropriation referred to how spaces could be occupied or reused by groups which challenged representations of space which were programmed to allow only specific functions to be performed at the expense of others. In analysing reappropriation, Lefebvre concentrated on marginal sites and sites of social centrality.

The notion of marginal spaces being reappropriated for radical politics is often concerned with sites at the edge of society. Lefebvre wrote of a quest for a 'counter-space'. According to Lefebvre, when a community organized to 'demand amenities or empty spaces for play and encounter', the 'counter-space can insert itself into spatial reality' and fight against 'specialized space and a narrow localization of function' (1991: 382–83). Marginal space thus refers to spaces identified by 'marginal out-groups' for investing values embedded in lifestyles which express their alternatives to existing society. This utopic conception of the margins views it as a 'space of freedom, resistance, alternative moral order and authenticity' (Hetherington 1998: 129). However, as Hetherington points out, 'marginal space' should not be viewed as a simple binary just between the margins/mainstream; margins can also be 'in-between spaces, spaces of traffic' (1998:107). Marginal space can host exchange and flux, in which fixity is challenged as identities are subject to new forms of symbolic ordering. For this reason Hetherington is interested in the ritualistic process of liminality, the middle, margins stage of the *rites de passage*. The margins can therefore be hybrid spaces which contain an unstable identity position existing between two states before a new form of encapsulation emerges. In the context of Belfast, marginal spaces are contested buffer zones, fiercely patrolled boundaries which are marked by fixity rather than the site of mixing. These marginal spaces are called 'interface areas', which we discussed in Chapter 3. Rather than spaces which facilitate radical alternatives to segregation, interfaces are the everyday manifestation of sectarianism and separation.

A challenging spatial politics would have to transgress the margins of interface space. One group which purposely seeks to do this is 'Beat Initiative', the carnival practitioners. Notably, the premises of 'Beat' are located on an interface in east Belfast, an area which has hosted extensive bouts of violence, even in recent years. One project instigated by 'Beat' is their Lantern Parade, which has been performed annually from 2003 in east Belfast. The Lantern Parade involves nationalist and unionist groups working towards and performing a street carnival.

Under the aegis of 'Beat', groups design and create their own costumes and music which is performed in the carnival. According to David Boyd from 'Beat':

> The Lantern Parade was introduced as a way of changing what happens on the streets here and putting different images on the streets, because so much of the images going out from here were still confrontation between the different communities across the interface…and still there were shootings going on…The lantern parade was very much about communities coming out and doing something different, doing it together. (Interview 2007)

The fact that the Lantern Parade takes place on the interface is highly important. A 2005 write-up of the Lantern Parade stated:

> Mention a parade, drums and fireworks on an interface and most people would…prepare for the battle ahead…the Lantern Parade was to prove not only a perfect model of how interface communities can work together, a wonderful fun-filled and colourful event in an area that could be described as contested space…this event became a test of how relationships which had been fostered behind the scenes had created real change. (Beat Initiative 2005:np)

David Boyd from 'Beat' has further elaborated how the Lantern Parade can sustain long-term changes:

> Interface relationships [between nationalists and unionists] had broken down, even the telephone network which is specifically there to keep things in control had broken down and the only thing that was keeping cross-interface relationships going was the Lantern Parade, which I think is very significant. It was actually an arts project that was enabling people to talk to each other and keeping work going, keeping people working together towards the same goal, which was to have the Lantern Parade. (Interview 2007)

Coming out

This section examines how social movements try to reappropriate another form of contested space: Belfast city centre. As we highlighted in Chapter 3, for over a century the city centre has been a sacred space, a site which defines citizenship and political power. For this reason, it has been a profoundly contested space, as groups have sought to challenge their status and/or exclusion from society. The social movements we have described so far in the chapter also identify the city centre as a site of social centrality. They have hosted protests or festivals in the city centre to express alternative forms of identity from ethno-national exclusivity. For the May Day organizers, specifically, their very presence in the city centre is therefore a literal demonstration of the visibility of socialists in public life, and their willingness to challenge the dominance of sectarianism:

The May Day march is a way of reclaiming the streets, ending violence and that. In a way, one of the reasons I love marching in the parade is that you hold up traffic and say: 'actually, this is our town and our streets for this day'. (Interview, 2007)

Another organizer of the May Day parade compared the march to a 'coming out' event similar to LGBT 'Pride':

May Day is a once a year thing where people who are walking the street and are proud to be associated with each other. It's a very good thing coming out and saying: 'my identity does not necessarily come from the religion I was born into or my perceived political baggage, or my past, or my age, or my race, or my gender, or for that matter my sexuality'. What you do when you take part in that May Day parade is that you are expressing notions of your identity; the people you feel solidarity with are based upon our class and also our common humanity. I think that is quite important that it happens every year, especially in Belfast...In Northern Ireland it takes a hell of a conscious choice to go out and say, 'right, this is the one day every year I'm going out and I'm going to walk through the middle of the town' and I'm going to say, 'I ain't like the rest of you'. The role of May Day, then, is a public outing; it's a once a year public outing. We are a community of interest in that we are there to reflect the interests of all working people. We do not see that as being open to crude divisiveness, such as sectarianism...a lot of people who are active in the trade union movement are alternative role models that are not always properly appreciated. There are many people involved in the trade union over the years who live in areas that are strongly attached to one identity or the other dominant identity. At the same time a lot of these people have taken risks because of their commitment to two basic socialist values, such as equality and solidarity. (Interview 2007)

The act of 'coming out' in the city centre is also of vital importance to the LGBT movement. As part of its agenda the LGBT Pride parade seeks to pluralize public space. Belfast Pride has developed from just over 50 participants singing 'gay rights anthems' in 1991 to over 6500 participants and 12 carnival floats in 2006. The conditions for mobilization in 1991 compared to those in 2006 have substantially changed. The first small parades were indicative of a slowly forming 'gay' scene in Belfast which followed the decriminalization of homosexuality in Northern Ireland. One of the organizers of the first parade in 1991, which was the first ever public demonstration of LGBTs in the city, stated at the time: 'it has taken us eight years since the law was changed in Northern Ireland to reach the stage where we can organize a march at all' (*Sunday Life* 13 June 1991). The focus of Pride during the early years was explicitly political. Rather than concentrating on establishing networks and relationships across the ethno-national cleavage, Pride was directed towards making LGBTs visible in public space and for initiating claims for funding from statutory bodies. As such, decriminalization was not seen as a mandate for equality, but as a mere act of toleration. Whereas equality represents approval and acceptance, tolerance is a tacit form of disapproval and tolerance has limits, which once reached, 'the tolerator has the power to criminalize and punish the tolerated' (Wilson 1993: 174–75).

The growth of Belfast Pride, however, has been aided by its ability to create networks and alliances with a myriad of non-LGBT groups and by expanding the remit of Pride away from a specific mobilization of LGBT 'issues'. Pride has thus developed as a celebration of all forms of diversity to challenge ethno-national polarization. This focus on networks and relationships across the cleavage is given emphasis through the theme given each year to Belfast Pride, like: 'Unity through Diversity' (1998); 'One Community, Many Faces' (2001); 'Let's Respect Diversity' (2003). A Pride organizer, Andi Clarke, explained that rather than this sentiment being limited to promoting sexual diversity, 'an event like this is particularly relevant in a city like Belfast. This parade transcends all barriers, we have all religious persuasions coming together to celebrate the community' (Bourke 2005).

The scope of groups who participate in the Pride Parade reflects the call for diversity. Apart from nationalist and unionist LGBT participants, a range of groups participate in the parade, including the Belfast

Humanist group marching behind the Rainbow River, a 50-foot flag signifying diversity. Amnesty International has participated to draw attention to human rights abuses of gay people around the world who face torture and imprisonment for their sexuality. Trade unionists and socialists, like the Socialist Environmental Alliance, participate to show solidarity with LGBTs. Such has been the growing success of Belfast Pride that the Northern Irish Tourist Board advertises the parade as 'family friendly' and several airlines promote it as a reason to visit Belfast.

Commemorative space

Apart from merely becoming visible in a constricted space, these groups make use of tactics, salient memories rooted in specific locations and alternative identities embedded in ritualistic performances. The performance of parading and carnival forms by non-sectarian social movements is a particularly potent way of demarcating public space because unionist and nationalist commemorative parading traditions often attain a sectarian, territorial function, representing symbolic invasions of ancient terrain.[26] These single-identity nationalist or unionist parades are viewed by David Boyd of 'Beat' as 'images of contrived confrontation, perpetual division and frozen tradition' (Interview 2007).

In order to challenge segregated space, the May Day organizers have used commemorative practices that emphasize memories to stimulate cross-community solidarity. The 2007 May Day parade, for instance, was a commemoration to mark the 100th anniversary of Belfast's 1907 Dockers and Carters' strike, which mobilized nationalists and unionists. The route of the 2007 May Day parade which journeyed through the city centre also skirted outlying working-class districts, purposely reproducing the massed marches of 1907. When the 2007 march passed the bottom of the Shankill Road (a working-class unionist district) and the Falls Road (a working-class nationalist district), which are separated by a 'peace wall', the organizers left a wreath to commemorate all workers killed in sectarian conflict since 1907. Such use of commemorative practice inscribed through the performance of street performance can provide alternative visions of history for present exigencies. A May Day organizer explained to us:

One of the lessons of 1907 that were looking at now: Catholics and Protestants of the workplace are better off when they are not divided; that the boss class will always try and divide us along sectarian lines as they tried to do so in 1907; as an organization we can have a commitment to do anything we want. (Interview, 2007)

Carnivalesque space

Belfast Pride has engendered the performance and constitution of new, inclusive and cosmopolitan forms of cross-communal networks and relationships. The space of the city centre is transformed by the Pride Parade into what Rose (1993) would call a 'paradoxical space'. Paradoxical space refers to the process by which groups seek to transform sites that are of centrality to the mainstream into places which marginalized and even transgressive identities and relationships can be composed. These spaces become 'elective centres', subjected to new and alternate symbolic forms of ordering. Paradoxical space further facilitates carnivalesque forms of social drama, especially those based on the possibility of momentary social transformation.

Importantly, the carnivalesque, with its emphasis on what Bakhtin (1998) called *'monde á l'envers'* (the reverse side of the world), is a site of disorder and transgression against the conventions of hierarchy, the performance of monstrous and grotesque identities. Humour – especially mocking authority – challenges the conventions of social order and spatial relations. Because of its inclusive structure, the carnivalesque can assist in the formation of networks and relations across traditional cleavages. As Hetherington (1998: 103) argues, the carnivalesque allows actors to engage in status reversals, of constituting and understanding the position of the 'other'. The Belfast Pride parade utilizes the carnivalesque to engender status reversals and symbolic forms of transgression which are given further emphasis by being performed in the city centre. The mocking of hierarchy and convention can be seen each year in Pride. Led each year by the newly crowned by the 'gay queen' and 'lesbian king', the parade has become synonymous with displays of humour enacted in alternative identities.

Despite the success of 'Belfast Pride' in engendering new cross-cleavage alliances and the pluralization of the public sphere, in response a reactionary section of civil society has mobilized. In 2004, a number of different far-right and Christian groups decided to picket 'Pride'. One organization, calling itself the Christian Coalition Against Perverted Pride Marchers picketed the 2004 'Pride' by shouting at the marchers through microphones. The British National Party (BNP), a far-right political organization, also turned up to threateningly photograph marchers. Shortly after, a number of fundamentalist Christian organizations coalesced into the Stop the Parade Coalition (STP). According to the STP in 2005, 'the nature of the [Pride] parade and the filthy behaviour and lewdness of its participants would not be tolerated in any other circumstances' (*Irish News* 19 July 2005). LGBT participants responded to the protestors with placards that stated 'Religious Fundamentalism Kills', 'Doing Our Bit to Piss-off the Religious Right' and sporting t-shirts showing Iranian men killed for their sexuality.

Notably, the example of STP illuminates that although 'Pride' can enable new types of cross-cutting alliances between different groups, it can also stimulate new alliances in response. Under the umbrella of the STP, Protestants and Catholics have joined to take a 'hard-line' Christian stance against 'homosexuality'. This alliance cuts across the cleavage of religious polarization in a city where there has been a famously strong anti-ecumenical movement designed with the purpose of stopping dialogue of common religious issues between Catholics and Protestants.

Conclusion

In this chapter, we have assessed what role a number of disparate social movements in Northern Ireland may contribute to the project of peacebuilding. Movements can organize across and even disrupt dominant cleavages with mobilizations which reflect typical contemporary social movement concerns, like quality of life and post-material social issues. In fact, by focussing on issues not confined to the question of Northern Ireland's constitutional status, groups can purposely transcend and undermine ethno-national cleavages by providing 'real' alternatives to counteract cultural and political homogeneity.

This point also links to a core concern of social movement theorists: that of structure-agency dualism (Melucci, 1996). Why are only certain members of a social group mobilized even though the group as a whole may experience the same structural conditions? Ethno-national groups, in contrary to claims of homogeneity, are themselves riven with internal cleavages, like class and gender. Could, then, the social movements this chapter has examined be fundamentally middle-class in constituency, a class that theorists have typically viewed as dominant in social movements? This appears particularly applicable for examining social movements in Belfast because the conflict mainly impacted upon working-class areas with the middle-class often immune from the ravages of violence. This left the middle-class seemingly more disposed to engage in so-called cross-community work. While class factors may play some part in determining the membership of social movements in Belfast, as Shirlow's (2003) analysis of working-class districts in Belfast highlights, many working-class informants articulated a keen desire, whether it was for religious or for class, gender and radical ideological reasons, to forge intercommunal identities.

Movements, like the recent 'Pride' mobilization are thus purposely pluralistic and heterogeneous, struggling to blend together multiple orientations. This emphasis on creating networks across the ethno-national cleavage has typically meant that many similarly minded groups based on cross-community action can be viewed as part of a broad family of movements in the city which are characterized by a high degree of membership overlap. For example, the Environmental Socialist Alliance regularly takes part in Belfast Gay Pride to show solidarity with LGBTs. This constant process of networking has more recently helped to form new protest movements which feed into contemporary global mobilizations, like the Anti-Iraq War Coalition or anti-capitalist movements, as well as for local issues, such as anti-racist formations. Another group, the Global Action Movement, has helped to form other campaigns, like the Dump the Debt campaign against Third World debt and the Justice Not Terror campaign, which was instigated to protest against US/British intervention in Afghanistan and Iraq.

The salient question, though, is to what extent do these activities really constitute a radical politics of social transformation? There is certainly a danger in overemphasizing their transgressive potential. The occupation of public space by alternative identities might only have a temporary impact. A participant in the 2007 May Day parade articulated this perspective. While he stated that 'it's great to see so many from different sections of the community coming together and stay together for this day', he also argued that 'unfortunately when they go home, as I say, they forget about it, you know'. In other words, the display of solidarity across the cleavage is for the period of the parade and a return to sectarian mindsets follows its completion. Moreover, and this is an important point, although many of these movements may be able to embrace actors from both nationalism and unionism, this does not mean these people wish to abrogate their national identities. Far from it, as O'Neill (2001: 225–26) has commented in regards to the women's and LGBT movements: 'even politically active feminists in Northern Ireland seek to be recognized as one of the national communities by women from the other traditions…most feminists freely acknowledge the political primacy of the national struggle…The same point may be made about activists in the gay and lesbian communities'. The May Day and Pride movements, as we have seen, furthermore, have developed not by trying to eradicate differences between groups, but by ensuring that they are equally accommodated, and it is from this point where dialogue can be constituted regarding cooperation on issues.

David Boyd from 'Beat', alternatively, argues a different trajectory of long-term change, noting that the Lantern Parade is:

> a year long and ongoing developmental process of building up skills within the communities that we're working in and then getting them out on the streets as a visible demonstration of creativity. We suffered greatly from a lack of creativity here. So much of what has happened on the streets and in social life and political life is based on the past all the time... Part of creativity I think is about developing new ideas and making new connections of people and new connections with other communities. (Interview 2007)

What this suggests is that the capacity of civil society to contribute towards the mitigation of chronic ethno-national conflict works best when the associational ties amongst groups not only cross cleavages, but also are fashioned in such a way to ensure that engagement between groups is constant, formal, mutually reciprocal and deeply embedded rather than transient and fleeting. This perspective underscores Varshney's (2002) research on civil society networks between Hindus and Muslims in India. Varshney makes a distinction between civil society networks based on everyday and associational relations in urban India. In the former, events like public festivals and public meeting places may expedite chance, quotidian encounters between groups, but they do not have the capacity to make a difference when the exogenous shock of ethnic riots occur. In the latter, associational ties, if profoundly rooted in societal relationships, do have the ability to act as a bulwark against the spread of ethnic antagonism by allowing sustained relations and trust to build. While civil society may not be a place where a shared identity can be generated, it does at least provide a fora in which animus can be defused, relationships can be constructed and common interests fought for.

5
Shared Rituals and Symbols

New Jerusalem or new *Ustaše*?

On Palm Sunday 1990, Franjo Tuđman, the newly elected nationalist leader of Croatia addressed a crowd of thousands of supporters in the French Republic Square in Zagreb. Tuđman spoke: 'On this day, Christ triumphant came to Jerusalem. He was greeted as a Messiah. Today our capital is the New Jerusalem. Franjo Tuđman has come to his people'. With this, Tuđman released a flock of doves and the *šahovnica*, Croatia's red-and-white checkerboard national emblem, was unveiled to the singing of the Croat national anthem, 'Lijepa naša domovino' ('Our Beautiful Homeland') (Glenny 1992: 89, BBC 1995, Kaufman 2001: 183). For Croats, the pageant represented the rebirth of Croatian nationalism after years of proscription. Under the control of the former leader, Josip Broz Tito, Croatia, like the other Yugoslavian federations, was forced to mute its ethno-national identity in favour of the unifying socialist chorus of 'brotherhood and unity'. Even the singing of Croat nationalist songs was enough to have an individual imprisoned and Croat cultural institutes were severely curtailed (Silber and Little 1995: 82). On Palm Sunday 1990, Tuđman, who had once himself been gaoled for Croat nationalist sentiments contrary to the spirit of 'Brotherhood and Unity', augured the resurrection of a proud independent Croatia, replete with the symbols of Croat nationalism.

For many Serbs resident in Croatia – known as the Krajina Serbs – Tuđman's spectacle generated altogether different emotions. The sight of a rejuvenated Croat nationalism, especially the unveiling of the *šahovnica*, evoked the memory of the feared *Ustaše*, the Nazi backed Croatian nationalist movement which massacred hundreds of thousands of Serbs during the Second World War while brandishing the *šahovnica* (Glenny 1992: 92). Serbian ethno-national entrepreneurs were quick to remind the Krajina Serbs that Tuđman's nationalism was in fact the renaissance of the *Ustaše* led genocidal state which would once again butcher Serbs in their thousands. Within months Serbs could point to how their grim forecast was being fulfilled as Serbs were dispelled from the judiciary, government and the police and replaced by Croats as part of nationalizing policies (Ignatieff 1993: 27). In mainly Serb populated areas, like the Knin, Serbian nationalists responded with their own symbolic answer to Croat nationalism: they bordered off their territory with trees – disparagingly labelled the 'log revolution' by Croats – and replaced street signs with ones in Cyrillic, the alphabet used by Serbs (BBC 1995). Tuđman's nationalist government responded in turn by attempting to strip the Krajina Serbs of their cultural distinctiveness, a ploy once used in the eighteenth century by Maria Therese and Joseph II which had ended in armed Serb rebellion. While the Croat national-ists had originally hoped to keep Serbian areas of Croatia within the new nation by offering them some federal powers (Kaufman 2001: 186), the ritualized display of Croat nationalist symbols and the proscrip-tion of Serbian symbols had provided Serbian nationalist leaders the opportunity to quickly mobilize and 'demobilize'[27] the Krajina Serbs to demand that they remain in a Serbian dominated Yugoslavia (Wolff 2006: 78); within a year war had broken out between Serbian and Croat forces.

The Croat nationalist spectacle on Palm Sunday 1990, and the reac-tion of the Krajina Serbs, is testimony to the correlative power of ritual and symbols in ethno-national conflict. Although ethno-national con-flict is by no means over ritual and symbols, the ritualized evocation of symbols can provide a dramatic enactment of the core issues of the major antagonists, their innumerable aspirations and fears which gov-ern political and military action (Ross 2007: 3). Moreover, ritual and symbols can provide a matrix on upon which the rival groups come to misunderstand and distrust the other's intentions (Kaufman 2001). While for Croats the Palm Sunday spectacle represented their legitimate claim to an ancient nationhood – 'a new Jerusalem' – after decades of totalitarian repression, for the Krajina Serbs the same event signalled the resurrection of the dreaded *Ustaše* and thus a mortal threat to be repelled by all means necessary.

Ritual and symbols are therefore not just 'surface phenomena' (Ross 2007: 3); because of the fundamental emotions they evoke of group identity – people will die for a flag – they are a significant medium in which ethno-national conflict is manifested and expressed (Kaufman

2001). They can 'offer a window through which we can better understand the multiple layers and issues in long-standing intractable ethnic conflicts in which these disputes are embedded' (Ross 2007: 16). Ethno-national identities, and the boundaries between groups, are articulated through symbols and ritual; the correct manipulation of ritual and symbols can assist the prospective ethno-national entrepreneur build and consolidate power; ethno-national violence can be expressed in ritualistic and symbolic forms. As Kertzer (1989: 129) notes, 'human ritual is employed to exhort people to war and violence in situations where they would otherwise have no reason to harm others'. At the same time, ritual and symbols are equally adept for peace-building. This can be witnessed in the ritualistic drama of peace talks, who sits where and the location venue; the symbolic handshake between the once 'warring' leaders; and the formation of new symbols and rituals which foster reconciliation and a shared society.

In this chapter, we assess the capacity of ritual and symbols to perpetuate ethno-national conflict and its vital role in conflict transformation and peace-building. In terms of conflict transformation we assess what fruitful possibilities are engendered by constituting shared rituals and symbols in divided societies. While it is often argued that the idea of the respective ethno-national groups existing in hermetically sealed and mutually exclusive cultures is something of a misnomer, and that there is a lot more sharing of symbols and rituals between groups (Nic Craith 2002), and what is shared can be a focus for rivalry and contestation over which group has 'proprietary rights' (Harrison 2002) concerning their ownership. To illuminate this dilemma, we draw upon extensive research on some initiatives that have been imagined, and contested, to create shared civic rituals and symbols in Northern Ireland, especially regarding St Patrick's Day. It is worthwhile providing a brief definition and overview of ritual first and then its relationship to both conflict and the management of conflict.

Ritual, symbols and conflict

Ritual is often defined in terms of a formal action expressed in structured, repetitive acts (Kertzer 1989: 9). This definition, however, covers an almost inexhaustible assortment of human action. Yet ritual can include modes of recurring and quotidian activities as well as special, exciting and sensual occasions which mark out the extraordinary from the mundane. Different forms of ritual involve various cognitive faculties. Some rituals provoke boredom and are quickly forgotten; some rituals captivate the imagination, evoke strong emotions and live long in the memory. Importantly, because ritual is never purely an instrumental performance – the prescribed actions of the ritual cannot be regarded as exclusively technical procedures – it invites exegesis: multiple and often irreconcilable interpretations (Whitehouse 2004: 4). This means that ritual can be a form of action, in which the regulation of bodily performance is the most important feature, or as a type of symbolic form of meaning making, a construction of a narrative in which 'beliefs about the universe come to be acquired, reinforced, and eventually changed' (Kertzer 1989: 9). While theorists occasionally tend to concentrate on ritual as either a mode of action and form (Connerton 1989), or as a type of symbolic meaning and content (Kertzer 1989), it is best to think of ritual as often incorporating both elements (Jarman 1997: 18).

Due to the fact that ritual embodies symbolic meaning, it is a crucial *modus operandi* for delineating social and political goals, in short for moulding people's understanding of the political universe (Bryan 2000: 19). Despite the prevalent belief that formal politics involves instrumental and rational choices and the logical outcome of various interest groups competing for material interests, ritual and symbolism provide a key mechanism in which politics is played out and communicated in highly emotional forms (Kertzer 1989: 174). As Kaufman argues (2001: 28, emphasis original), people often make political decisions '*by responding to the most emotionally potent symbol evoked*'. Nowhere is this better illuminated than in ethno-national politics. The importance of ritual in ethno-national conflict can be seen in a number of interrelated spheres: how it imagines group identity in opposition to rival groups; its use of memory; how it seems to disengage individuals from their sense of agency to allow them to carry out activities which are ordinarily proscribed; its capacity to make symbols speak for wider political concerns; and its inherently contestable meaning.

Group identity

In Chapter 1 we explained that ethno-national conflict is not a mere epiphenomenon of ethnic and cultural differences between groups; practically all societies contain various ethnic and cultural groups, and such a state of affairs is not in itself cause for violence. When there exists between these groups disjunctures regarding ownership of material goods, irreconcilable claims over territory and other structural inequalities, then in many cases ethnic and cultural differences are stressed to justify immutable distinctions between the groups. This is especially relevant in areas riven by ethno-national conflict and yet the ostensible physiological and cultural differences between the groups appear minute, especially for undiscerning outsiders. In this situation, the particular ethno-national groups are required to dramatize what it means to belong to the collectivity as well as their core objectives in opposition to their antagonists. Ritual and symbolism, in short, are a perfect means for expressing group identity and boundaries. Ritual helps 'identify the enemy, recounting their moral inferiority, while glorifying the celebrants own group' (Kertzer 1989: 130, see also Ross 2007: 21).

Ritual is a means of linking the individual to the wider ethno-national group, ensuring that the 'individual's subjective experience interacts with and is moulded by social forces' (Kertzer 1989: 10). Ritual binds the participants together and reminds them of their moral commitments, stirs up primary emotions, and reinforces a sense of solidarity with the group, a 'we-ness' (Jasper 1997: 184). Ritual can represent the move to universality and ever greater unity, an identification among members which is so absolute as to be tantamount to the stripping away of all the social impedimenta that would otherwise divide and distinguish them (Cohen 1985: 55). As such, groups need to socialize their members to the values and expectations that make up its culture and ritualized activity, such as initiation ceremonies. The sense of collectivity imagined through ritual elaborates the numeric strength of the group and its capacity to mobilize. These are what Tilly (2004) calls 'WUNC' displays: participants' concerted public representations of worthiness, unity, numbers and commitment (WUNC) on the part of themselves and their constituencies.

It would be mistaken, however, to think that displays of solidarity represent consensus within the ethno-national group as to what the ritual means. As we have seen, ethno-national groups are internally diverse and mask a range of different cleavages, especially class, faith and gender (Kertzer 1989, Jarman 1997, Bryan 2000, Ross 2007). The power of ritual is that it can serve political and ethno-national groups by 'producing bonds of solidarity without requiring uniformity of belief' (Kertzer 1989: 67, see also Nagle 2005a, Ross 2007: 19).

The iterative nature of many ritual performances is also salient in generating ethno-national division. The almost obsessive habit of ethno-national groups to ritualistically mark out territory, commemorate and use their bodies and symbols in highly regulated ways are almost like forms of obsessive-compulsive-disorder (Whitehouse 2004: 32), which act as protective forces against contaminants, like the despised, rival ethno-national group. As such, compulsive ritual activity helps the ethno-national group demarcate the boundary between purity and danger, pollution and cleanliness and defines the terms of 'us' and 'them', 'hero' and 'friend' (Kertzer 1989: 92).

Memory

The second important facet of ritual in ethno-national conflict is its ability to conjure up the memory of the past. The group, as Jarman (1997: 6) notes, 'must have a memory of itself that recounts a sense of origin and distinctiveness'. Ethno-national groups are thus 'communities of memory'. The performance of memory and continuity with a past, propelled primarily through ritualistic acts of commemoration, provides the group a sense of timelessness, naturalness and unchanging primordial belonging. Ritual can achieve these aims in a number of ways.

The repetitive character of many ritual forms can mean that memory and identity become inscribed into the body (Connerton 1989). When ritual is strictly prescribed and regimented, leaving no scope for improvisation in bodily action, it becomes part of 'social habit memory' (Connerton 1989). Memory and identity are thus incorporated into the performer helping to link the individual to the wider collectivity. This helps to endow the group with a feeling of security; by linking the past to the present and the present to the future – the group appears the same as it was a hundred years ago as it will be in a hundred years time thus giving them confidence that the world in which they live today is the same world they lived in before and the same world they will have to cope with in the future (Kertzer 1989: 9). Paradoxically, however, although the form and content of the ritual may appear to be unchanging over time, its meaning can undergo subtle transformation in service of present political projects (Jarman 1997: 11).

Another essential way in which the past is utilized by groups is through the performance of social memory: how the idea of past is actively and selectively used, abused, reworked, transmitted and received in the context of specific groups. Groups remember and shape the past in specific ways to justify contemporary political exigencies: 'by placing the present in the context of the past and of the community, the myth of descent interprets present social changes and collective endeavours in a manner that satisfy the drive for meaning' (A.D. Smith 1999: 62). As Cimet (2002: 146) notes, memory is identified as key to institutionalizing acrimony by ensuring that the original, seemingly primordial clash of groups is re-enacted constantly as the old conflict of opposing ethnic groups. As such, 'the characters that confront each other must be polarized in a representation that imagines the past, even when these are renewed actors at each point in time'. This view of history helps locate the activated memory of a group in an ongoing structure of difference. This discriminating use of the past is as much about forgetting or – disremembering as it is about remembering. Groups purposely perform 'social amnesia' – they elide details and histories which do not fit into their neat, linear narratives. They may, for instance, ignore a past in which peaceful social interaction with their present opposition was routine.

Symbols

The ritualized performance of symbols is another essential feature of ethno-national identity and conflict. The saliency of symbols is that they allow groups to give meaning to the world around them (Kertzer 1989: 4). The power of symbols, hence, is not that they carry meaning inherently; it derives from giving us 'the capacity to make meaning' (Cohen 1985: 16). For ethno-national leaders the act of identifying themselves with a national symbol, or even creating a new one, 'can be a potent means of gaining and keeping power, for the hallmark of power is the construction of reality' (Kertzer 1989: 5).

Symbols are also vital for how they personify political power and ethno-national groups. Because state power is essentially abstract and invisible, 'it must be personified before it can be seen, symbolized before it can be loved, imagined before it can be conceived' (Walzer 1967: 194). Flags, monuments, landscapes, national stereotypes all come to symbolize the *sui generis* nature of the ethno-national group. Symbols are also the means through which groups dehumanize despised rival ethno-national collectivities to ensure that their extermination is little more than an act of cleansing the moral community from unwanted vermin (Blok 2000: 29). Nazi propaganda compared Jews with rats and Hutu Power labelled Tutsis as an 'inyenzi' (cockroach) before going out to butcher hundreds of thousands of them (Gourevitch 1998). In many divided societies, like Northern Ireland, 'the exchange of violence is the principle economy of symbolic exchange' between groups (Feldman 1991: 191). A great deal of ethno-national hostility also comes in the form of devaluing, desecrating and destroying the other group's core symbols – what has been termed 'ethnocide' (Ross 2007: 37–38).

Displaced agency

On many occasions ritual appears to displace agency; that is, participating individuals often seem to be carrying out a traditional rite which has been performed unchangingly in *aeternum*. Such rituals, as Connerton (1989: 102) argues, 'contain a measure of insurance against the process of cumulative questioning entailed in all discursive practices'. Moreover, because ritual can relate to supernatural entities, individuals can seem to be governed by external bodies or even possessed by otherworldly spirits. We have to be careful here. Although on the surface ritual seems to divest individuals of their agency, 'in ritual one both is, and is not, the author of one's acts' (Humphrey and Laidlaw 1994: 99). Extreme ethno-national violence is often recorded as being performed in ritualistic acts in which the participants appear to be invoked by forces they claim to no longer control. As Blok (2000: 29) notes, 'one can detect in the ritualization of violence attempts to avoid moral responsibility for killing "fellow" human beings'. The most extreme example of this is perhaps the carnivalesque aspect of violence. The carnivalesque typically allows actors a temporary license and release from ordinary constraints and rules in which extremes of behaviour are common. Sporting toxic coloured clown wigs and flamboyantly coloured pajama suits, the *interhamwe*, the Hutu militia in Rwanda responsible for murdering hundreds of thousands Tutsis and moderate Hutus, 'promoted genocide as a carnival romp' (Gourevitch 1998: 93). The carnivalesque aspect of the genocidal spree could allow individuals to practically dissociate themselves from any personal responsibility of the violence they conducted. One Hutu killer claimed: 'We were taken over by Satan. When Satan is using you, you lose your mind. We were not ourselves… You wouldn't be normal if you start butchering people for no reason. We had been attacked by the devil' (cited in Wolff 2006: 21). This is not to say that ritualized violence lacks an instrumental objective. For instance, in the Bosnian war during the 1990s, status degradation rituals were conducted by Serb militias to make Bosniaks appear non-human as part of ethnic cleansing strategies to ensure that healthy relations between groups could never be restored (Gagnon 2004).

Contestation

Finally, ritual and symbols are central to ethno-national conflict because they are intrinsically open to contestation from vying groups regarding what they mean or who should rightfully own them (Harrison 2002). Although, as we have seen, ritual can bring a group together and bind them despite obvious internal cleavages, it can also cause serious and irrevocable fracture. A fundamental reason for this is because of the polysemic nature of ritual and symbolism: it simply means different things to different groups because of their varied political and historical experiences. As demonstrated at the beginning of the chapter, while for Croats the Palm Sunday pageant augured a 'new Jerusalem', for the Krajina Serbs it ushered in a new holocaust. Similarly, when in 1999 a group of Protestant unionists embarked on a protest march for their 'group rights' across Northern Ireland calling it a 'march of pride', Irish nationalist groups lined the streets with banners proclaiming it a 'march of shame' (2009a). Ritual is thus a natural home for 'framing contests' as contending groups attempt to 'rebut, undermine, or neutralize a person's or group's myths, versions of reality, or interpretative framework' (Benford 1987: 75). When there is a gross disjuncture regarding the esteem to which a ritual is evaluated, this leads to intergroup misunderstanding, suspicion and no small dose of hostility (Ross 2007). This narrows the range of permissible actions allowed by groups and the ground required for reconciliation. In divided societies it is also often the case that the respective groups share a repertoire of symbols and rituals. This situation, though, does not mean that the groups can achieve cultural compatibility or have commensurate values regarding what the ritual and symbols mean. In fact, the 'sharing' of symbols and rituals between ethno-national groups can provide a focus for acrimonious competition to 'trademark' and gain exclusive ownership over (Harrison 2002). In this scenario, groups fashion historical narratives which clash and are incompatible (Ross 2007).

Ritual and peace

A shared culture and ritual does not automatically generate reconciliation between protagonists in divided societies. Yet it is often suggested that shared cultural forms are important in helping to bring about a shared identity and even eventual peace. Hammell, for instance, reflecting on the conflict in the Balkans during the 1990s argued that the diffusion of 'cultural and symbolic systems across social groups' can help soften the hard edges of ethnic boundaries, thereby reducing social divisions:

> Especially under the homogenizing influence of the much maligned mass media, ethnic groups in many countries share large parts of major symbolic systems. The sports and entertainment industries are cases in point. Football and baseball in the U.S., soccer in other countries, basketball in many, the cinema, and musical forms such as jazz and rock are great unifiers and diminishers of cultural distance. (Hammel 1997: 7–8)

Indeed, sporting rituals can provide a symbolic depiction of national reconciliation after decades of disunity and intergroup violence. The sight of Nelson Mandela adorning the Springbok jersey of the South African rugby team in 1995, a team hitherto seen as the embodiment of a racist Afrikaaner identity, is often evoked as the foundation of the 'Rainbow nation' and a unified post-apartheid South African identity (Ross 2007: 45–46). Of course, such shared cultural and ritualistic forms can provide a matrix for ethno-national conflict. In Northern Ireland, sectarian rivalries are mediated through the support of soccer teams. Similarly, in Yugoslavia Croat/Serb allegiances were antagonistically expressed through their respective support for the soccer teams Dinamo Zagreb and Red Star Belgrade.

Are we then to abandon any hope that ritualistic forms can play a positive role in contributing to a shared identity and peace-building? Addressing this precise question, Ross (2007) has formulated some interesting ideas. Ross believes that if we are to create an holistic approach to peace-building we have to take seriously the function of culture – like ritual – in exacerbating and mitigating ethnic conflict. Ethnic conflict, he argues (Ross 2007: 21), involves 'both material interests and collective cultural identities and understanding a conflict's cultural frames is a central challenge to the analysis and constructive management of them'. Ross (2007: 21) is careful to stress that he rightfully rejects the simple hypothesis that 'conflicts are about cultural differences'; conflict involves 'tangible interests and power, constitutional arrangements and values' (2007: 21). Cultural expressions, like ritual, are important in conflict because they are crucial in framing interests and demands, heightening the salience of group differences, facilitating the mobilization of people to action and polarizing the parties. For Ross (2007: 21), ritual can be a 'psychocultural drama': practices which represent one group to its members become polarizing when their expression is felt as a threat by a second group, and/or when attempts to limit the practices are perceived as a threat by the group performing them. This exacerbates conflict as 'opponents frequently operate from such different frames that they misunderstand each other and fail to see how their own actions might be contributing to the escalatory spiral' (2007: 83).

At the same time, Ross argues that ritual is an essential part of conflict management. Ritual, he argues, can link interests between groups, or rituals which are threatening can be redefined to be less menacing or exclusive as part of a constructive management process. Ritual, however, does not act in a vacuum; it works best when it acts as an auxiliary to political movements on 'the ground'. In other words, the de-escalation of heightened emotional feelings surrounding 'cultural conflicts', such as the flying of flags and parades, can help to smooth the path for opponents to enter in peace talks or new institutional arrangements. For instance, in the context of Northern Ireland, when conflict is avoided during the summer over the Orange Order 'marching season', this is often seen by the media as auguring well for political dialogue between nationalists and unionists in which concessions can be made. The key here is not to force groups to abandon their cultural identities and ritualistic practices because they are wrong or provide erroneous accounts of history, for this would only exacerbate feelings of inequality and fear; group differences have to be honestly acknowledged and addressed. Because ritual and symbolism, within limits, can be made malleable for different readings, new narratives can be developed 'which do not directly challenge older ones, but which reframe them in more inclusive terms that deemphasize the emotional significance of differences between groups and identify shared goals and experiences', such as civic values or a past of coexistence (Ross 2007: 31). For Ross, it is important that the 'narratives' enshrined in ritual forms can be constructed so as to allow more nuanced views of the other side. Central to this dynamic, states Ross, is mutual acknowledgement of each other's perceptions and concerns; such acknowledgement is often implicit rather than explicit, and may not involve acceptance of the other's point of view. Such gestures, however, require at least a modicum of goodwill between the groups.

For the rest of this chapter, we examine an attempt to create a shared public ritual in Northern Ireland. In particular, we assess how rituals which have been subject to exclusion, conflict and contest can possibly be reframed to allow for nuanced views, inclusivity and a public sphere of debate and dialogue regarding the value of respective identities.

St Patrick: a contested symbol

We now turn to exploring the ritual surrounding St Patrick's Day celebrations in Northern Ireland. We look at this because St Patrick, as a symbol and a ritual, is shared by Catholics, nationalists, Protestants and unionists alike. However, such 'sharing' does not provide evidence of consensus; as we shall see, nationalists and unionists have proclaimed divergent and clashing narratives regarding the 'essential' meaning of St Patrick and the celebration, which has caused some conflict. Indeed, the celebration of St Patrick in Northern Ireland has rarely 'been an occasion in which all differences would be sunk in a single and spontaneous unity of spirit. Both sides [nationalists and unionists] claim St Patrick but in many ways he remains a divisive rather than a unifying grace' (*Belfast Newsletter* 17 March 1977). At the same time, there has been another narrative running parallel, with cross-community groups and ecumenical movements seeking to frame the significance of St Patrick's Day as one of peace and harmonious coexistence between all the peoples of Ireland. Illuminating these multiple narratives, we wonder if it is possible, and desirable, to reconcile them in a common ritual form, and if so, how might it contribute towards peace-building.

Who is St Patrick?

It is worth briefly describing who was St Patrick and some of his teachings in order to show how the 'symbol' and ritual can be the focus for ambiguity and multiple, even contradictory readings. Indeed, one of the strengths of St Patrick, regarding how the symbol can be fashioned for different political projects, is that there are few facts we know about the saint; most of what has been passed down from the past is shrouded in myth and allegory. This is the potency of the symbol: groups seek to link their history to its ancient character so that they claim historical descent; yet its mythological quality means it can be made a 'floating signifier' open for semiotic guerrilla warfare.

In tracing the origins of St Patrick the Apostle, Cronin and Adair (2002: xxvii) note how there has long 'been dispute about the life and lore of St Patrick', including debate about the basic aspects of his existence. There is uncertainty among some scholars as to whether the St Patrick legend has fused more than one person into a homogeneous narrative or whether there were as many as five Patricks or even none (Cronin and Adair 2002: xxviii). Taking the common understanding that there was one Patrick, this is still not altogether helpful since what we know about this character derives from two texts, his *Confessio*, a spiritual autobiography, and a 'letter to the soldiers of Coroticus', and even then the earliest surviving copies of these writings date from at least three hundred years after their original composition (Duffy 2000: 37). Patrick's writings further present problems for scholars, especially his *Confessio*, which utilized metaphors and symbols as he described his life in a series of key incidents which he viewed as a result of God's direct intervention in the form of dreams. Since Patrick provides no factual information, this leads to gaps, ambiguities and fecund opportunities for competing interpretations.

The common history of Patrick was that he was born in Roman Britain, probably Wales, circa 416AD. At the age of sixteen he was kidnapped and taken to pagan Ireland where he was enslaved. In Ireland he worked as a shepherd either on Mount Slemish in County Antrim, in the north of Ireland, or in Killala Bay, County Mayo in the south (Duffy 2000). While a shepherd, a visit by a heavenly messenger prompted Patrick to negotiate his captors into letting him free. He then absconded to France where he became a monk. Another visit by a celestial being impelled Patrick to return to Ireland, this time as a Christian missionary, though it is unclear whether he was a self-appointed bishop or sanctioned by Rome. Although there were other important Christian missionaries in Ireland at the same time, Patrick paved the way for the adoption of monasticism as the norm of church organisation in the century after his death. The final details concern his death – 17 March (St Patrick's Day) – and his burial place, identified as Downpatrick in contemporary Northern Ireland.

The 'cult' of St Patrick began in earnest 200 years after his death. Monks in Armagh in the north of Ireland wrote a hagiography of Patrick and in the process elevated him to the level of national apostle, and then later on he became the patron saint of Ireland. The debate concerning Patrick heated up in the seventeenth century when the Anglican Church of Ireland and the Roman Catholic Church sought to establish the nature of the true church in Ireland (McCormack 2000: 20). The two churches appropriated St Patrick as evidence of the early origins of their respective churches in Ireland. In the eighteenth century this contest took on a particular ethno-political character. For Protestants, Patrick was the founder of the Church of Ireland and also a representative of the Protestant political nation. For Catholics, he was the evangelist, a link to Rome and the embodiment of a distinct and separate Irish nation. The main reason for these conflicting narratives is due to a lack of clarity whether Patrick had been an emissary of the Pope or had been an independent missionary.

After devastating conflict in Ireland during the early nineteenth century, government authorities decided to promote St Patrick's Day as a national festival in recognition of its shared appeal across the religious cleavage (Walker 1996: 77–78, Jarman 1997: 35). Despite this, St Patrick continued to be adumbrated by sectarian interests as the symbolism became the focus of divergent readings. Patrick had taught the pagan Irish the concept of the Holy Trinity; later folklore stated that Patrick had done this by using the shamrock, a three-leaf clover, as a symbol of the Trinity. For Irish nationalists wearing the shamrock on St Patrick's Day was a visible symbol of the unity of Ireland and Irish national self-determination, and thus the public rejection, for one day at least, of British rule in Ireland

(Cronin and Adair 2002: 97). For unionists, alternatively, the shamrock was also a unionist symbol, and in the late 1890s Queen Victoria, in appreciation of the valour of Irish soldiers serving in the British army, initiated the tradition of members of the royal family presenting shamrocks to Irish regiments on St Patrick's Day (Walker 1996: 79).

After the partition of Ireland in the early 1920s, St Patrick's Day continued to be celebrated in both jurisdictions by nationalists and unionists alike. However, celebrations in the north and south of Ireland were gradually vested with more or less salience. While in the south the day was marked by the President attacking Northern Ireland or declaring Ireland's attachment to Rome, in the north the unionist leadership began to neglect the celebration (Walker 1996: 83) and the day became 'business as usual'. This trend in the north was generally indicative of the idea that St Patrick's Day was increasingly an Irish nationalist celebration. To understand how St Patrick's Day celebrations became a source of conflict between nationalists and unionists from the 1960s onwards, it is necessary to provide a context for how symbols and ritual were highly regulated in Northern Ireland.

As noted in Chapter 3, Irish nationalists in Northern Ireland were 'securitized' (see also Chapter 1): constructed as an existential threat to the very survival of Northern Ireland's position within the union. As part of the strategy to securitize nationalists, unionism sought to limit the capacity of nationalists to mobilize. Such 'cultural' exclusion was most apparent, as mentioned in Chapter 3, in the Flags and Emblem (Display) Act (NI), which forbade the public display of so-called provocative emblems in Northern Ireland. Unsurprisingly, prior to the Troubles, 'one of the principal causes of communal conflict was the provocative use of flags and emblems' (Purdie 1990: 28). On one infamous occasion in 1964 an Irish nationalist flag was placed in the window of an Irish republican office in a nationalist district of Belfast. The loyalist leader, Ian Paisley, threatened to lead a mob to remove the flag if the police did not intervene. In front of a large crowd of angry nationalists, the police removed the flag and as a result severe riots wracked parts of Belfast for days (Purdie 1990: 30–31). St Patrick's Day parades could also be subject to bans. Although St Patrick's Day symbolism was not banned by the unionist authorities, parades could be proscribed if they included nationalist symbols. For instance, in 1958 a unionist politician banned a St Patrick's Day parade in Derry city because he feared that nationalist emblems would be present.

The prohibition of Irish nationalist symbols in ritualized demonstrations thus became a central issue of nationalist grievances in Northern

Ireland. Alongside the civil rights movement's demand for equal treatment regarding the allocation of jobs, housing and voting rights, there was a dual demand for the cultural identities of nationalists to be given more official recognition (see Chapter 3). During the height of the civil rights campaign in 1969, Irish cultural nationalists began protests demanding that public broadcasters allocate a percentage of their airtime to Irish language programmes. There was also the demand that Irish cultural/political organizations be allowed to access important public spaces and display their proscribed symbols. As part of this, in 1969 a St Patrick's Day parade took place on the Falls Road, a nationalist district in west Belfast. After the outbreak of civil conflict a 'traditional' St Patrick's Day parade was instigated again on the Falls Road in 1977.

As we can see, although St Patrick, the symbol and the ritual, is historically shared by nationalists and unionists in Northern Ireland, it has also provided a matrix for contention and division. We turn now to examining three central narratives surrounding St Patrick's Day in Northern Ireland during the Troubles. We look at how some of these narratives have clashed and been the focus for ethno-national conflict, and then we explore the potential of the ritual to foster a 'shared identity' and to contribute towards peace-building.

Irish nationalists

The first narrative concerns Irish nationalists and St Patrick. In the mid-1970s three Irish nationalists in Belfast set up the St Patrick's Day Association, the mission of which was to organize an annual St Patrick's Day parade in nationalist west Belfast. The Association stated that 'the parade is open to any individual, group or association with an Irish identity' (*Irish News* 16 March 1981). The first parades encompassed the Irish nationalist 'community' without clarifying exactly what that might actually mean. Amongst those participating in the early parades were a motorcycle cavalcade, over twenty Irish traditional music bands and dancing groups, floats advertising local businesses, Walt Disney characters and figures from the Muppets, community associations highlighting local issues, and on one occasion the parade hosted a group of skinheads who had dyed their scalps green (*Irish News* 17 March 1984). St Patrick was typically portrayed in banners dressed as a Catholic Archbishop. Although the organizers claimed 'this is not a political parade' (*Irish News* 18 March 1983), the parades undoubtedly contained a platform for Irish republican political protests on the various issues of the day. As such, the parades would feature republican banners brandishing slogans criticising the British government and the security forces, a republican colour party, and republican sponsored floats urging people to vote for them. In the late 1970s and early 1980s parades were used by republicans to illuminate the status of political prisoners. In 1981, during the hunger strike campaign, marchers were wrapped in blankets and seated inside a wire cage. During the parade a group of two hundred protestors attempted to enter a police station, where they planted an Irish tricolour. The protestors dispersed when the security forces discharged a number of baton rounds.

Outside of Belfast, in a number of other Northern Irish towns, Irish nationalists organized St Patrick's Day parades. In Derry, Northern Ireland's second city, the parade was purely a political operation. Organized by the Irish Front, an Irish republican umbrella grouping, up to two thousand republican protestors would march on the issue of political prisoners and Irish unification. On many occasions the protestors would confront the security forces or loyalists in a riot. The 1978 parade concluded with British soldiers battle-charging protestors who tried to dismantle a security checkpoint. Violence also occurred in the town of Portadown during the 1985 parade when a nationalist accordion band was stopped from parading past a Protestant housing estate by the police force and a group of loyalists. For Irish nationalists the ban on the parade was indicative of the security forces supporting unionists rather than supporting the right of nationalists to march. Later that summer, in direct response to the ban, nationalists in Portadown protested against the Orange Order from marching down a Catholic street.[28]

Although there was no clear narrative concerning the meaning of the Irish nationalist St Patrick's Day parades, it provided a vehicle for Irish nationalist and republican grievances and protests, as well as a day of Irish pride and the image of a cohesive community. A distinctly different bundle of 'frames' were developed by unionists in response.

Unionists

The second narrative concerns unionists and St Patrick. During the 1980s unionists began to reassert their interest in St Patrick. A clear narrative was gradually woven by the interested parties, which mainly concentrated on challenging the idea that St Patrick's Day was axiomatically an Irish Catholic and nationalist ritual; unionists offered an alternative frame in which St Patrick was portrayed as a purely Protestant and even a British unionist figure. For one unionist newspaper, St Patrick was even 'the first British personality in history' (*Belfast Newsletter* 16 March 1982).

As mentioned earlier, Protestant identification with St Patrick began in the seventeenth century. The Protestant churches in Ireland claimed their roots back to St Patrick and then he was subsequently fashioned to symbolize Protestant and British control in Ireland: 'Patrick's teaching became a guarantor of stability and the bringer of a rational social principle. He epitomized the established church and state as rational and enlightened, and non-Roman' (McCormack 2000: 32). In a similar way, unionists from the 1980s onwards constructed a similar narrative. A particular exponent of this was the St Patrick's Day Heritage Association, an organization linked to the exclusively Protestant Orange Order, which seeks 'to educate the Brethren of our Institution and the general public in the truths and principles of the Reformed Religion, and our historical and cultural heritage' (McCausland 2006). In one of its publications, entitled *Patrick – Apostle of Ulster* (McCausland 2006), the 'Protestant view of Patrick' was articulated. This narrative sought to challenge the idea that Patrick was an exclusively Irish and Roman Catholic symbol: 'Patrick wasn't Irish. He wasn't sent to Ireland by the Pope. He didn't wear a bishop's mitre' (McCausland 2006). The alternative view, adumbrated by the St Patrick's Day Heritage Association, emphasized that Patrick was a figure whose missionary area was limited to Ulster and who interpreted the scriptures in a fashion analogous to Protestant evangelical preachers. Following on, one unionist politician, Ian Paisley junior, has stated: 'we should proudly proclaim St Patrick as ours [as a Protestant] and I think there is a willingness to not allow people to hijack him…Anyone who has factual knowledge of the history of St Patrick knows that he was a prototype Protestant' *(Belfast Newsletter* 13 March 2003).

The attempt by some unionist organizations to reappropriate St Patrick is seen in a range of initiatives. In 1985 the unionist Orange Order inaugurated St Patrick's Day parades in Antrim Town (Walker 1996: 85, Cronin and Adair 2002: 191) and in some unionist areas of Belfast. Discussing the parades, Thomas Passmore, an Orange Order leader, stated that 'Orangemen had been marching in honour of St Patrick for years long before republicans made anything of it…after all he was British, not Irish, and we regard ourselves as his successors' *(Irish News* 18 March 1985). By 2000, unionist identification with St Patrick was complete after a mural of St Patrick was unveiled in unionist east Belfast, proclaiming him to be a 'Proud Protestant and Ulsterman'.

Peace and reconciliation

The third main narrative surrounding St Patrick's Day in Northern Ireland involves the symbol being interpreted as a sign of peace, reconciliation and ecumenical relations between the national and religious groups in Ireland. During the 1970s, peace groups, such as the Peace People, embarked on a pilgrimage on St Patrick's Day to Mount Slemish in Northern Ireland, where St Patrick was reputed to have worked as a slave. On one occasion the Peace People spoke of how St Patrick's shamrock 'has a new meaning today. The three leaves stand for repentance, reconciliation and renewal'. Other groups repeated the same broad narrative, emphasizing the capacity of St Patrick's Day celebrations to help 'foster understanding and respect within the communities in Northern Ireland' and the 'hope that our national feast day in years to come will be celebrated in an atmosphere of peace, reconciliation, friendship and respect' (*Irish News* 17 March 1978). St Patrick as a unifying symbol of peace, 'acceptable beyond all others even in the tribalism of our time', became a recurrent theme (*Irish News* 16 March 1985).

Running alongside this was the positioning of St Patrick's Day as an event for good relations between religious groups in Northern Ireland. On St Patrick's Day, from the 1970s onwards, the leading representatives of the Church of Ireland, Catholic, Presbyterian and Methodist Churches held an ecumenical service in Down Cathedral, Downpatrick, the site where St Patrick is said to have been buried. The narrative of St Patrick's life as a Christian missionary bringing peace to Ireland became a common theme of the ecumenical movement. In 1986, the Archbishop of Armagh stated that 'St Patrick was an apostle of peace and reconciliation' (*Irish News* 15 March 1986). A similar message was expressed a year later: 'St Patrick loved Ireland and its people. That love…is his legacy to us and in that spirit, we must unite to reject the men of evil in our society whose little egotisms can only bring, as they have already brought in cruel abundance, the shame of division and death' (*Irish News* 18 March 1987). In 1988 the Church of Ireland Primate Archbishop Robin Eames argued that if St Patrick was alive today he would want reconciliation and a shared identity for his people:

> Reconciliation means we must recognise diversity and realise that we can exist together. The message is a simple one – that we have much in common. On St Patrick's Day we should emphasise the things that unite us rather than what divides us. (*Belfast Newsletter* 18 March 1988)

As part of the ecumenical spirit, a successful cross-community parade began to emerge in Downpatrick during the 1980s, which included both Catholic and Protestant groups.

In the sacred space

It is hardly surprising that groups in conflict will have competing claims of ownership over the same symbols and rituals. This struggle is especially acute when the contested symbol is mired in antiquity and relates to the historical origins of the disputed territory. By proclaiming an ancient affiliation with the symbol, the group seeks to legitimate its own claims to the territory as well as its historical destiny as the predominant ethno-national grouping. By linking itself to St Patrick, the group desires to gain what Smith (1991: 22–23) has called a 'descent myth', a narrative which inextricably connects the *ethnie* to a particular territory. Symbols rooted in ancient mythology contain, as Cohen (1985: 99) notes, a particular efficacy for stating political legitimacy which derives from its 'ahistorical character': 'myth is beyond time… it blocks off the past, making it impervious to rationalistic scrutiny'. Claiming Patrick, shrouded in myth, thus enables a group to confer 'rightness on a course of action by extending to it the sanctity which enshrouds tradition and lore' (1985: 99).

The issue which is particularly significant to conflict management and peace-building is what happens when the rival narratives demand equal or predominant recognition in the same public space. This dilemma clearly has a resonance with quandaries regarding shared spaces in 'divided societies' that we explored in Chapter 3. This issue, though, is more acute when it comes to rituals which are shared by different groups, though they have distinctly different and often seemingly incompatible views of what the ritual represents. Simply put, while spaces can be shared sequentially by different groups at different times, the same situation cannot always apply for commemorative rituals, like St Patrick's Day. Because St Patrick's Day always falls on the same day each year (March 17), celebrations to mark the saint are concurrent. When there is a situation where rival groups wish to celebrate the same symbol in the same space at the same moment the emphasis of conflict management undoubtedly needs to be placed on sharing and accommodation rather than on attempting separation. For this to happen, there needs to be willingness from the respective parties to mutually acknowledge and recognize each other, the legitimacy of their concerns and their rights to coexist peacefully with their distinct identities (Wolff 2006). While it is not advisable to demand that groups surrender their identities, it is possible that identities, expressed through symbolic acts, can be reframed in such a way that they encourage shared concerns and even superordinate goals among opposing groups (Ross 2007). The narratives which underpin identity performances need to be altered so as that they provide more nuanced representations of the other group which in turn enable new opportunities for linkages to occur between the groups (Benford and Snow 2000). The goal of peace-building, as Ross (2007: 47) argues, is not to develop consensus around a single narrative, but to explore what basis there is for shared concerns to emerge so that the respective groups can peacefully negotiate the different ways that they view the same ritualistic and symbolic forms. This means, Ross continues, that group based differences need to be acknowledged. To explore the issues that arise when groups who hold opposing ideological views of the same symbol demand recognition within the same ritual, we turn to the example of St Patrick's Day celebrations in Belfast city centre since the late 1990s.

As we noted in Chapter 3, a core Irish nationalist grievance was their historical exclusion from specific civic spaces, most especially Belfast city centre, a sacred space in which political and social power was vested. This *de facto* prohibition generated a number of protests. Some of these protests concerned the demand to have a nationalist St Patrick's Day parade in the city centre. In 1978, for example, the SDLP, a moderate Irish nationalist political party, called for St Patrick's Day to be made a public holiday in Northern Ireland. They complained: 'what celebrations [St Patrick's Day] do take place generally reflect the divisions within our communities and in the city of Belfast the freedom of the town centre, which is the focal point for such celebrations elsewhere in the world, is denied to those whose tradition, background and upbringing is Irish' (*Irish News* 17 March 1978). After the first Irish nationalist political rally in Belfast city centre in 1993 (see Chapter 3), Irish nationalists began to increasingly mobilize on the issue of a St Patrick's Day parade being held in the city centre. Notably, by the mid-1990s, the nationalist St Patrick's Day parade in west Belfast was slowly losing popularity. The organizers thus hoped that moving the event to the city centre would help breathe new life into the celebrations.

The first St Patrick's Day parade to take place in the city centre occurred in 1998. The parade, however, evinced distinctly discrepant readings from nationalists and unionists. For some Irish nationalists the 1998 event was portrayed as being almost akin to a civil rights parade, the moment when Irish cultural identities were endowed with equal recognition after years of second-class status in Northern Ireland. A republican newspaper stated:

The tens of thousands who turned Belfast city centre black with green on Tuesday were doing more than scribbling footnotes, more

> than even contributing whole chapters to our history. They were
> shedding the pages of past wrongs, binning the Belfast of…second-
> class citizenship. (Ó Muilleoir 1998)

Alternatively, for unionists the celebrations appeared little more than
a display of nationalist 'triumphalism' and were distinctly exclusivist.
DUP Councillor Nelson McCausland typified the unionist view by noting in a council meeting that the celebrations had not been inclusive
and expressed particular concern at the flying of certain flags and the
political element of some floats (Nagle 2006: 38). The organizing committee for the first parade was led by Catríona Ruane, a member of Sinn
Féin. Her leading role led unionists to accuse the parade of being little
more than an exclusively Irish nationalist event. Although the parade
organizers had banned the display of political symbols, speeches and
bands at the event, the unionist media noted the presence of Irish tricolours and a republican ex-prisoners' group. Even though the Irish tricolour was not used in an official form during celebrations, the sight of
many in the crowd, and some in the parade, its presence in the crowd
was evidence that the space and celebration was not neutral and inclusive. The fact that some nationalists decided to adorn unionist symbols,
such as a statue of Queen Victoria, with tricolours further underscored
the notion that nationalists displayed little respect for unionism.

As the event was publicly funded, a debate was generated concerning the city council's role in managing events in the city centre and
whether St Patrick's Day could be repositioned as a family and tourist
friendly event shared by all groups in the city. A few weeks after the
1998 celebration, a meeting of community groups at the city council
agreed that while it was counterproductive to ban national flags from
the event, there should be an effort to promote the flag of St Patrick
as the official flag of the event with a Belfast tourism logo superim-
posed on it.[29] It was further agreed that the event should be free from
political slogans or emblems (see Institute of Irish Studies 2006). To try
and encourage greater participation from all groups in the city, and
not just Irish nationalists, the council also set up a steering committee for the parade, which included representatives of groups from both
nationalist and unionist districts. The committee quickly ran into trouble when unionist representatives withdrew stating that none of the
suggestions by nationalist groups were sufficiently 'cross-community'.
In particular, they demanded that parade-goers should be banned from
flying national flags, especially the Irish tricolour, a motion rejected by
nationalists on the committee. The breakaway unionist representatives

formed their own independent committee – the St Patrick's Heritage Association – and demanded that they should be allocated public funds to organize the parade, claiming they could make the celebrations more inclusive and less dominated by nationalists. Due to the fact that public funding for the parade was contingent on the support of unionist and nationalist political parties in the council, the fracturing of the committee into contending nationalist and unionist blocs resulted in the council rejecting both nationalist and unionist claims for public funding (Institute of Irish Studies 2006).

Despite the exit of unionist representatives on the steering committee and a concomitant lack of public funds, nationalists continued to organize a parade for the city centre by campaigning for charity donations. Subsequent parades in the city centre, therefore, became largely nationalist dominated. While nationalist grievances remained fixed on what they perceived to be unionist ill-will, unionists widened their attack on all elements of the parade as nationalist triumphalism. If, during the celebrations, the hoisting of Irish tricolours was intolerable for unionists, the sight of thousands of youths sporting green Irish soccer jerseys was a grievous insult. Unionists were quick to identify these signifiers as clear evidence the event was undoubtedly nationalist in nature; 'it is difficult for unionists to feel included' (*Belfast Telegraph* 19 March 2003), one newspaper bluntly stated.

A survey (Nagle 2005b) found a degree of unionist dissatisfaction with the St Patrick's Day event in Belfast. One respondent summed up a typical unionist view of celebrations in Belfast:

> I went into Belfast city centre and I wish I had not. There were lots of drinking and drunk people…and lots of Irish flags being waved. I felt scared to look at anyone in the wrong way for fear of being attacked. I would like to see future events where unionists could be made feel welcome. As it stands at the minute, St Patrick's Day in Belfast is nothing more than a nationalist festival. (Nagle 2005b)

Another unionist respondent put the case in extreme terms: 'I feel like a Jew at a Nazi parade. I am excluded from Saint Patrick's Day as I am a Protestant. Parades are more republican than ever' (Nagle 2005b). In the media, on the other hand, Irish nationalists expressed frustration with unionist intransigence regarding the funding of the parade, going as far as to call their obduracy an act of 'blatant anti-Irish racism' and 'a step back to the dark days of unionist misrule and domination' (*An Phoblacht* 6 January 2000). For Gerry Adams, the President of Sinn Féin, the refusal of unionists to support funding of the parade was a denial of 'positive political positions on equality and recognition of nationalist rights' (*An Phoblacht* 6 January 2000).

The situation began to thaw in 2005. The nationalist organizing committee made attempts to create a more inclusive parade, including designing a multicoloured shamrock which was to become the official symbol of the parade. In recognition that the right steps were being taken to foster a cross-community celebration, Belfast City Council decided that it was then opportune to provide public funding for an 'inclusive' event for 2006. As part of the funding stipulation, the venue for the celebrations was changed as the concert moved from the front of the City Hall to nearby Custom House Square, where a purpose-built entertainment space, privately owned by the Laganside Corporation was designed to host outdoor events. At the same time a period of public consultation revealed that there was a preference for a St Patrick's Day 'carnival procession', which 'provides opportunity for the people of Belfast to participate, join together, and feel part of their city. Work together, walk together, celebrate together'. It was nevertheless noted that the 'Protestant community would not take part in a parade, at this stage, maybe next year' (see Institute of Irish Studies 2006: 26–27).

A few months prior to the 2006 event a *Sunday Times* (6 November 2005) article plunged the event into new acrimony by erroneously stating that there would be a ban on all putative divisive symbolism being displayed at the celebration, such as national flags, soccer shirts and people painting their faces 'green, white and orange, or in the colours of the Union Jack'. The newspaper article acted to obscure the council's message for inclusivity, which was based on the premise that different symbols (St Patrick's carnival shamrock t-shirts, Cross of St Patrick and multicoloured shamrock flags) could be included as an alternative to those which are perceived to designate national identity.

Just before the event began, though, Belfast City Council managed to reassert its message that the event should actively promote good relations and shared space, and that inclusivity could be achieved by careful management of symbols which could potentially be regarded as offensive or 'triumphalist'. Nationalists largely agreed and committed themselves to ensuring that their constituency should try to avoid as far as possible the display of nationalist symbols.

The carnival itself was relatively successful. Though the vast majority of the crowd who attended the parade and the concert were nationalists, it was stated by the independent evaluators that the event was not an intimidating environment for unionists. Certainly, however, there was little evidence of a substantial attendance from Protestants. Using an onsite survey as a rough indicator, only 31 of 257 (or 12 per cent) surveyed indicated that they were Protestant. Those attending the event, including those from the Protestant community, generally indicated that they viewed it positively (Institute of Irish Studies 2006: 5). However, the strategy of Belfast City Council to introduce alternative symbols in the form of St Patrick's carnival shamrock t-shirts, cross of St Patrick and multicoloured shamrock flags was only a partial success.

Conclusion

The ongoing issues surrounding St Patrick's Day celebrations generate a number of different approaches to conflict management and even transformation. One approach might be to advocate that the celebrations occur in a completely neutral public sphere. In this approach, national and partisan symbols are banned and the celebration is free from the dominance of particular group based identities. This approach is inherently fraught with problems. As we noted in Chapter 1, it is a quixotic task to try and create a 'neutral public sphere'; the public realm is always imbued with the signs of a particular ethnos. For instance, St Patrick's Day parades in Belfast have taken place in the shadow of Belfast City Hall, upon which a Union Jack has flown and unionist statues and symbols stand in the grounds of the Hall. The fact that some annual publicly funded events in Belfast take place accompanied with the strong presence of unionist paraphernalia has been noted by nationalists, who argue that this is an example of unionists getting preferential treatment.[30] Attempting to cleanse the public sphere of national symbols can alienate particular groups and strengthening the hands of ethno-national entrepreneurs who view identity as non-negotiable. Proscribing national flags and emblems is not a realistic option for conflict management and may even exacerbate tensions.

The second option would therefore take a more libertarian approach by actively welcoming the presence of all symbols and insignia regardless of what national groups and to whom they may belong. The task here is to encourage equal esteem and recognition for the various emblems. The problem here is that some groups, for one reason or another, may dominate a particular ritual and their symbols appear in the majority. Although members of the group may view the brandishing of these symbols as a legitimate expression of their national identity, for opposing groups they are seen as an attempt to make the ritual exclusive, unwelcoming and threatening. This makes it hard to achieve a representative festival which includes all groups with a measure of equality. The dominance of nationalists and nationalist symbols at the Belfast St Patrick's Day parade is seen by many unionists as an attempt to exclude them from the pageant.

What, then, are the possible solutions which may mitigate conflict and contribute towards peace-building? As we have noted, the shift from conflict management to conflict transformation requires groups to redefine their interests in such a way so that joint concerns can be articulated without groups feeling they have been defeated. By reframing the symbolic content of rituals, as well as paying attention to how symbols are used and in what context, provides potential for new linkages to be made between groups or, at least, for celebrations to occur without one group feeling marginalized or threatened. The goal of peace-building, as Ross (2007: 47) argues, 'is to find sufficient common ground and tolerance to allow the groups not to feel threatened by differences in how they see the world'. Differences remain; the key is not to make those differences the object of antagonism and conflict.

In practical terms this project could include a number of substantive initiatives. First, as we saw earlier, one of the three narratives we identified as being associated with St Patrick's Day since the 1970s has promoted the idea of the saint as a figure of peace, reconciliation and good relations between groups in Ireland. Where there is an already strong narrative of cross-community relations between groups, it should be promoted as far as possible. To enhance this, symbols can be designed to foster the idea of a shared celebration. For instance, the design of the multicoloured shamrock, although it was ridiculed by some sections of the media, marks a welcome attempt to introduce a new symbol that all sections of society could accept. The vitality of ritual and symbols is that, within reason, they can be redefined or left open to multiple interpretations. A shared ritual can be evoked without there being any consensus about what it means. The polysemic capacity of symbols, to encompass a range of not necessarily harmonious and congruous meanings, allows them to provide a cloak of solidarity under which a high degree of heterogeneity can flourish (Jenkins 2004: 116). What matters, notes Cohen (1985), is not that people see or understand things in the same way, or they see and understand things differently from other communities. The efficacy of ritual and symbolism is that people can participate within the same ritual and yet find quite different meanings for it. It is a delicate operation, however, to ensure such constructive ambiguity works: allowing different groups to jointly participate and the centre to hold without becoming subject to countervailing forces of fragmentation.

Second, it is nugatory and counterproductive to try and ban national symbols; however, it is possible to try and regulate them by making them less threatening. Consequently, national symbols should not be used in a provocative way. This is a difficult proposition because, as we know, for one person the waving of their national flag is a legitimate expression of a core identity while for another it is interpreted as a threatening political gesture. Context is everything. The attempt by members of one group trying to misuse the other group's symbols, or the usage of symbols accompanied by malevolent gestures and sentiments should be stymied. Where appropriate, group leaders should encourage group members to limit their usage of national symbols at ritual performances which include a number of groups. There should also be an attempt to foster an environment in which national symbols can be accommodated and tolerated without automatically being seen as a menace. To help this, in the spirit of parity of esteem, parade organizers could find a prominent place in the festival where the respective national symbols, as well as cross-community ones, are placed alongside each other. Henceforth there also needs to be a public sphere which encourages the various groups to enter into deliberation about the value of group based identities and how they are best expressed in public places. In short, for these initiatives to occur there has to be a degree of goodwill by the interested parties to reframe what is at stake in the conflict so that they do not become zero-sum contests in which there are only winners and losers. Only when these groups are satisfied that these cultural events can enable a scenario in which group identities are accommodated will conflict be successfully transformed.

6
Between Trauma and Melancholia: Shared Forms of Commemoration

The Janus-face of commemoration

Commemoration is Janus-faced. As much as commemorative practice often evokes an aura of timeless continuity with the past, commemoration can simultaneously serve as a rite to signify rupture from tradition. In the aftermath of the French and American revolutions, writes Gillis (1994: 8), 'the need to commemorate arose directly out of an ideologically driven desire to break with the past, to construct as great a distance as possible between the new age and the old'. In societies journeying through the liminal space of conflict transition the ruptured face of commemoration is often brought to the fore. This rupture is articulated as an exacting effort to abstain from ancient grievances by advocating healing and reparation, mechanisms to confront the wounds of the past and offering a new and shared future (Consultative Group on the Past 2009). The logic of dealing the past in many divided societies, as Hamber and Wilson (2002: 35) critique, is that it is supposed to 'facilitate a common and shared memory, and in so doing create a sense of unity and reconciliation'.

In classic *rites de passage* fashion, commemoration, in this sense, marks and then refashions the boundary from a previous generation which perpetuated acrimony and division with a new identity proclaiming reconciliation and a shared identity. In Northern Ireland the present task of commemoration and remembrance could be its possible role in ensuring that 'healing can take place for all people affected by the conflict in and about Northern Ireland' (Hamber 2001). By healing wounds opened by conflict, commemoration acts as a final break from, to paraphrase James Joyce, a 'nightmarish sense of history' which Northern Ireland currently is trying to awaken from.

This recurring nightmare has often been perpetuated through commemorative practice in Northern Ireland. Talismanic dates (McBride 2001), such as annual commemorations, are seen as ensuring that the Irish nationalist and British unionist protagonists are unable to escape from 'dancing to history's tune' (Bell 1993: 829), a choreography which creates an aura of timelessness surrounding conflict rendering it impervious to political solutions (McBride 2001). Social memory is thus identified as key to institutionalizing acrimony because it re-enacts and recreates the old conflict of opposing ethnic groups (Jarman 1997: 3–4, see Chapter 5). It is for this reason that Leersen (2001), following Freud, has identified the 'uncanny' aspect of Northern Irish commemorative practice. Commemoration in Northern Ireland has been in the form of 'nightmarish recurrences characterised by their combination of repetitive familiarity and their disconcerting repulsion' (Leersen 2001: 222). Vamik Volkan (1997), likewise, has written of a 'time collapse' in societies wrought by ethnic conflict, like the Balkans and the Middle East. In a 'time collapse' members of an ethnic group evoke past traumatic events for current political exigencies, because they are unable to deal with the consequences of what they have lost.

This chapter explores the role of commemoration in Northern Ireland as part of the peace process. The chapter asks whether commemoration, as a form of addressing Northern Ireland's relatively recent violent past, can, as Brandon Hamber (2006a: 562) asserts, 'bolster national attempts to "re-establish" society, and as such can have a healing and restorative dimension'. Or, alternatively, are the dominant themes of commemorative practice in Northern Ireland continuing to evoke a 'time collapse', thereby perpetuating damaging relations between groups? To address in greater detail these questions, the chapter assesses the commemorative practices of three groups: Irish nationalists, British unionists and civil society cross-community organisations. The role of the British state, as both an interested actor in the peace process and as a funder of groups involved in commemorative work is further illuminated.

For and against commemoration

This section provides an outline of the debate – for and against – commemoration as a key engine to generate a peaceful and a shared society. The idea that societies which have undergone sustained ethnic violence should undergo some form of healing process, typically by addressing its violent past, adds to the analysis of ethnic conflict as a type of extreme medical condition. According to David Lake (1995: 3): 'to use a pessimistic but apt metaphor, ethnic conflict may be less like a common cold and more like AIDS – difficult to catch, but devastating once infected'. In this analogy, ethnic conflict is a disease which requires some form of therapy and treatment. Due to this type of diagnosis, a body of theorists have concentrated on the need to heal both the affected society as a whole and those individuals most seriously impacted by the conflict.

For example, professional peace-builder, John Paul Lederach's (1997) analyses ethnic conflict as being rooted in psychosocial issues equally as much as it is about pervasive socioeconomic inequalities or national aspirations. For Lederach, the conflicting groups' animosity, perception of enmity, and deep-rooted fear and hatred of the other, cannot be dealt with without being germane to the protagonists' experiential and subjective realities which shape their existential perspectives and needs (Lederach 1997: 24). The immediacy of hatred and prejudice, of sectarianism and xenophobia, as primary factors and motivators of the conflict, means that its transformation must be rooted in social-psychological and spiritual dimensions which traditionally have been rendered irrelevant or outside the competency of international diplomacy.

Reconciliation, in this analysis, looks towards forging relationships by engaging the protagonists to view each other in terms of a common humanity, 'as humans in relationship' (Lederach 1997: 24). A central component of this project is concerned with methods which address the recent history for both groups 'without getting locked into a vicious cycle of mutual exclusiveness inherent in the past' (Lederach 1997: 26). This inclusivity is achieved through acknowledging the other's loss and the anger which accompanies the pain and the memory of injustices experienced. As Lederach (1997: 26) explains: 'acknowledgement through hearing one another's stories validates experiences and feelings and represents the first step toward restoration of the person and the relationship'. Simultaneously, such emphasis on the past as a means to fashion reconciliation works best when it provides a space for people to look forward and envision a shared future. Reconciliation, as Lederach explains, is thus a social space, an encounter in which narratives of the past and future can meet and become singular. Though Lederach recognizes that this simultaneous orientation of melding together the past and the future is paradoxical, this is to be carefully nourished. Instead of prioritizing either the past or the future, providing a space for examining the past permits a reorientation towards the future and, inversely, envisioning a common future creates a new lens for dealing with the past.

Another way that the healing dimension has been emphasized by some authors is through the use of commemorative practice, which is seen as helping the bereaved come to terms with their loss. Jay Winter (1995), in particular, elaborates how Great War memorials in Europe acted as a mediating and healing agent for the bereaved. Winter shows how individual and collective sorrows were alleviated through being symbolized in shared commemorative forms. Applying Freud's 1917 distinction between healthy 'mourning' and unhealthy 'melancholia', Winter asks if the bereaved reading the names of the fallen, and even touching those names, on war memorials 'were means of avoiding crushing melancholia, of passing through mourning, of separation from the dead and beginning to live again'? (1995: 115).

Healthy mourning for an individual experiencing grief is outlined as a teleological process. Though the individual 'goes through mourning', it is a fixed journey which reaches a definite conclusion. When completed, the individual can begin to move on. The mourning concludes when the libido has yielded its attachment to the lost object, leaving the individual free to form new attachments. 'Healthy mourning' is framed as a passage, although often difficult, from point A (attachment to the lost object) to point B (attachment to the new object).

The dire consequence of failing to remember and mourn healthily through commemorative practice has also been transposed onto whole societies. The danger of a society not commemorating, mourning and dealing in a satisfactory fashion with the horrors of the recent past were outlined by the Mitscherlichs (1975), two German psychoanalysts. Like Winter, they also applied Freud's distinction between 'mourning' and 'melancholia' to the collective inability of Germany to mourn through confronting the nation's recent Nazi past, thus contributing to the rejection of anything which entailed collective responsibility.

To assist healing at the individual and societal level a broad range of commemorative templates are identified by theorists to help with the shift from melancholia to mourning. More permanent commemorative practices, particularly statues and monuments, can be seen as assisting the mourning process by encapsulating and containing the sense of grief – relegating it to a certain location, for example. Greg Forter (2003: 139) argues that 'mourning helps us to relinquish *real* objects by building *psychic memorials* to them – the memorials we call "memories [emphasis original]"'. Physical memorials can help the mourner resign (decathect) the traces of the lost objects by rendering them memorable for the first time. In the context of conflict transition, memorials can provide what Hamber (2006a) calls 'symbolic reparations', of making amends and trying to redress in some way the wrongs meted out to individuals and groups. For the bereaved, symbolic reparations, like memorials, 'can help concretize a traumatic event, aid an individual to come to terms with it and help label responsibility' (Hamber 2006a: 566).

Many modern forms of commemoration seem to function best when they include a space in which individuals can make symbolic exchanges, votive deposits and gift-giving to and with the dead. Maya Lin's Vietnam Veterans Wall, for example, allows the individual to see and even touch the names of the dead as well as to leave secret messages. Other forms of votives can include 'flowers, flags, letters, poems, photographs, teddy bears, dog (identity) tags, wedding rings, high school yearbooks and other offerings' (Doss 2002: 66). Such symbolic exchange has almost become the defining feature of contemporary commemorative practices, many of which seem to spring up in spontaneous fashion overnight in what Jack Santino (2001: 1) has termed 'spontaneous shrines and the public memorialisation of death'. At the site of the demolished World Trade Centre in New York City, or at 'Memory Fence' (Doss 2002), as it was quickly called in the aftermath of the Oklahoma City bombing, people came to adorn sites with tributes as tokens of remembrance, while people who lost family and friends in incidents added personal belongings that they regularly attended to.

As Santino (2001: 81) notes, these spontaneous shrines mark the sites of untimely deaths. They function as a means of consecrating the death for the bereaved which maintain and attend the shrines by attempting to re-establish some kind of spiritual balance which was upset through sudden, violent or early death. While the spontaneous shrines mediate or appease the unquiet dead, they further help the living to reconcile the death. Similarly, Hass's (1998) survey of the inventory of items left at the Vietnam Wall shows that the process of leaving personal items helps mediate the dead and the living by creating an appropriate memory. Commemoration, thus, helps us make sense of a senseless war, and to make meaningful the ultimate sacrificed (Santino 2001: 81).

Against commemoration?

To state that commemoration can facilitate 'healing', without any recourse to critical enquiry, however, is to risk platitudes. Principally the issue for whom commemoration is supposed to dispense cathartic relief requires absolute clarification. Commonly, 'healing' refers to those directly affected by the conflict, whether the bereaved, people who have suffered injuries or been threatened with violence, or those who have been exposed to violence. Problematically, however, such lists run the risk of excluding others. Relatively recent, though highly contested, definitions of post-traumatic psychopathology have spread far beyond combat-related stress to include accounts or death of injury (in contrast to direct encounters), and this can be sufficient to constitute traumatic stressors (see Young 1995: 289).

If the relationship between commemoration and healing is complex and ambivalent, is it possible to argue against remembering and commemoration? Moreover, can we query whether healing ever really occurs? Indeed, as Winter and Sivan (1999: 32) note, '[m]ourning may never end, and when it seems to be completed, it may re-emerge'. Hamber (2006a: 567–68) also argues that the building of memorials to recognize and give a focus for victims to bereave, can be guilt-inducing for survivors, a 'disrespectful act that betrays the loss they have endured, or the memory of those killed'.

Presenting the case against commemoration and healing, Walter Benjamin, a social theorist, avowedly refused to mourn or hold any redemptive hope in commemoration. Considering the vast process of memorialization inaugurated in Europe after the Great War, Benjamin 'steadfastly defied all attempts to heal the wounds caused by the war' (Jay 1999: 225). Benjamin instead defended repetitive, never-worked-through remembrance. For Benjamin, the national memory sites constructed to commemorate the Great War – such as opaque and concealed forms like the Cenotaph, Pyramid and the Mound – appeared to justify the sacrifices made in its name. Simply put, never could the horror of the War be transformed into something elevating or ultimately progressive through commemorative practice. To parry shocks, through commemoration, 'purchases its fragile peace…at the cost of a deeper understanding of the sources of the shocks, which might ultimately lead to changing them' (Jay 1999: 226). It was not consolation, or a superficial anaesthesia induced 'closure', that Benjamin demanded, because this would cushion the trauma to the point where only forgetting would result.

Similarly, for Doss (2002: 60), the 'spontaneous and, often impermanent, and distinctly unofficial nature of many…grassroots memorials…seem less concerned with producing a critique of historical moments and tragic events than in catharsis and redemption'. Wholly fixating on the therapeutic, cathartic and redemptive aspects of commemoration can act to ignore and forget the messy and uncomfortable political causes and historical realities which created conflict. It is not enough, as Doss (2002: 69) argues, to assume 'that grieving, in and of itself, is a prescriptive political practice'. Assessing the memorials which sprung up in the aftermath of the Oklahoma City bombing and the Columbine High School killings, Doss notes that a 'superficial focus on psychic closure – on healing and closure – skirts the causal, historical dimensions of these visibly public deaths. It further fails to provide a shared set of rituals and commemorative forms that might allow citizens to consider critically how to change the conditions that contribute to the culture of violence in America' (2002: 71). Specifically looking at the memorial solutions offered to commemorate the Oklahoma bomb, Doss writes that the 'Symbolic Memorial' contains 'no references to why the bombing occurred and who was responsible, or to the nation's history of catastrophic violence' (2002: 74). Rather than 'opening a window' on traumatic events, thus expediting stages of mourning – from anger to closure, from mourning to acceptance – the memorials are 'anaesthetic because the historical and political context of why these deaths occurred has been effaced' (2002: 78).

Drawing a line under the past?

If it could be argued that commemorative practices offer little in the way of 'healing' in divided societies, is it possible to argue instead that collective processes of forgetting are of better use? In this scenario, it is good to draw a line under the past, let bygones be bygones and forgive and forget? Such social amnesia can be engendered by the state through mechanisms like blanket or selective amnesties for combatants as well as by demanding that the members of the vanquished group forget the grievances they have harboured.

An example of forced forgetting, or 'organized oblivion' of the memories of the defeated was in the aftermath of the Spanish Civil War. While the victorious nationalists initiated an extensive and intensive programme of monument-building, street-naming and commemorations, in honour of their own fallen – their soldiers and civilians killed – they also effaced any oppositional memory of what had been at stake in the war. As Ashplant et al. note (2000: 24), 'The nationalists treated half the nation virtually as a foreign conquest, drawing on the pre-existing discourse and iconography of the late medieval *reconquista* of Moorish Spain by the Catholic monarchs to help construct a memorial narrative of triumph'. For the vanquished republicans who remained in Spain, on the other hand, and their families, were not only subject to legal persecution but were denied the opportunity to express their grief in public; nor were they able to organize a collective memory.

Even after the death of Franco in 1975, and during the transition from dictatorship to democracy, Spain embarked upon the *pacto de olvido* [collective pact of forgetting]. The pact meant the past was to remain silent to supposedly ensure that outstanding resentments would not be reignited to enflame a new generation of conflict. The limits of disremembering terminally fractured in 2007 when the Spanish government introduced 'The Law of Historic Memory', which had the intention of addressing past wrongs.

The time collapse

One of the reasons why it appears impossible to forget the past in areas of ethnic conflict is due to the crucial role memory can contribute towards the genesis and sustenance of ethnic difference and conflict. Certainly, the conflict in Northern Ireland has often been framed as one in which memory – especially the capacity of the protagonists to conjure up historical grievances – has played a large part in its perpetuation and intensity. As we saw in Chapter 5, in Northern Ireland the performance of memory can be seen in the acute linkage between commemorative rituals, symbols and public space. These connections are moulded by nationalists and unionists to create a sense of origin and distinctiveness and thus political legitimacy. According to Jarman (1997: 6), commemorations and symbols are 'a central facet of the ideological armoury of the group, helping to legitimise and rationalise difference by rooting it in the far-distant past and thus placing weight on the primordial or essential nature of the antagonism or otherness'.

This process in which ethno-national groups use social memory for present political exigencies is not the preserve of Northern Ireland. Volkan (1997: 34–35) has written of how competing ethno-national groups – ranging from the Middle East, the Balkans and Rwanda – commit what he calls a 'time collapse' :

the interpretations, fantasies and feelings about a past shared trauma commingle with those pertaining to a current situation. Under the influence of a time collapse, people may intellectually separate the past from the present one, but emotionally the two events are merged.

In the time collapse, past 'traumatic events' are summoned up by protagonists, who make them sound:

as though they had occurred only the day before. The feelings about them were so fresh it was clear that genuine mourning for the losses associated with these events had not taken place. Furthermore, representatives of opposing groups acted as if they themselves had witnessed such events, even though some had taken place before they were born. (1997: 34–35)

Such time collapses, according to Volkan (1997: 35), are crucial in stimulating conflict because they represent the inability of the ethno-national group to accept, through processes of healthy mourning, the 'loss of people, land, prestige' and the 'feelings of fear, helplessness, and humiliation' which accrued from their loss. The perennial temptation to revisit past traumatic events provides a matrix upon which the group can blame their rivals for perpetuating ongoing injustices. Volkan notes how the time collapse becomes particularly relevant in situations, like peace talks, when the competing ethno-national groups confront and remind each other of historical grievances.

Importantly, however, it is possible to see how the time collapse purchases immense emotional and political power when it is dramatized and visualized through ritualistic, commemorative events. These events, as Ricoeur (1988: 187) argues, summon up what he calls the *tremendum horrendum* aspect of history. This speaks of the horrors of history, those events which because of their nature must never be forgotten. Horror attaches itself to these events. Horror constitutes the ultimate ethical motivation for the history of victims. These events are what Ricoeur has further termed as 'epoch-making'. These epoch-making events, often borne from violence:

> [d]raw their specific meaning from their capacity to find or reinforce the community's consciousness of its identity, its narrative identity, as well as the identity of its members. These events generate feelings of considerable ethical intensity, whether this be fervent commemoration or some manifestation of loathing. (1988: 187)

The performances of ritualized commemorative practices, which evoke the *tremendum horrendum* aspect of history, are numerous and potent forms in which ethno-national groups in situations of conflict express the irreconcilability of conflicting political identities. For instance, Slobodan Milosevic used the sixth-hundredth anniversary of the Battle of Kosovo – the Field of the Blackbirds – to address a crowd of over one million restive Serbian nationalists, many of whom were intoxicated with *šljivovica* (plum brandy). This battle and its location – Gazimestan near Kosovo Polje – have provided the central foundation myth and grand theme in which contemporary Serbs bolt on their own historical experience and destiny, comprising 'heroic struggle, often against hopeless odds, followed by betrayal and defeat, but also – eventually – rebirth and triumph' (Sell 2002: 70). At the commemoration of the Battle of Kosovo, where Serbs had been defeated by the invading Turks in 1389, Milosevic evoked these key narratives to demonstrate to the faithful that just as in the past Serbs were under mortal threat from rival ethnic groups, this time within Yugoslavia. Six centuries after the battle of Kosovo, Milosevic told the throngs: 'We are again engaged in battles and are facing battles; they are not armed battles but such things cannot be excluded' (Sell 2002: 70).

In Northern Ireland the performance of memory is often more perennial, continuous, even quotidian, enmeshed in the fabric of everyday life. Yet its omnipresence is no less potent for propagating fear, mutually exclusive notions of victimhood and ethnic animosity. The tradition of public parading, in particular, is one particular *modus operandi* in which claims to victimhood are articulated. This can be seen, for instance, in how the unionist traumatic experience is sometimes characterized by being constantly under siege, its survival relentlessly threatened. The unionist self-image, articulated through commemoration can be represented as 'an endless repetition of repelled assaults, without hope of absolve finally or of fundamental close' (MacDonagh 1983: 13–14).

This narrative is seen by some in the annual Apprentice Boys parade to commemorate the siege and relief of Derry during 1688 and 1689. The importance of this iconic date is due to the construction of a surrounding narrative wherein 'Protestant settlers' effort to survive and subdue the resistance of surrounding indigenous Catholics reached its zenith' (Cohen 2007: 956). On 18 December 1688 an attack against the Protestant city was initiated by forces loyal to the Catholic King James II, but thirteen young Protestant apprentices closed the city gates and managed to hold out until relief arrived with the forces of Protestant King William III on 12 August 1689. The annual commemoration of the siege and relief, when the Apprentice Boys ceremonially act out the closing of the gates of Derry, rearticulates with renewed vigour the unionist experience in Northern Ireland. As Jarman (1997: 76) notes, 'the story of the siege remains the powerful metaphor of Protestant sensibilities in Ireland'. While the narrative of the story has retained its basic structure, each generation finds meanings salient for contemporary political exigencies. Mostly its force derives from presenting a picture of eternal danger, of unionists forever being under siege from their Catholic enemies; the point reiterated is to never compromise and let the enemy have power, and that defensive action is legitimate to ensure the survival of the group (Jarman 1997, Cohen 2007).

Irish nationalist and republican commemorative parades, though markedly smaller in number than unionist parades,[31] are no less instrumental in how they inform contemporary ethno-political exigencies. This can most clearly be read in Easter Sunday commemorations, which remember the Easter Rebellion of 1916. On every Easter Sunday, the Irish republican faithful congregate at designated graveside plots across Ireland where paramilitary colour parties often precede the arrival of figures replete in military fatigues, berets and balaclavas. Here, one of them steps up to read an announcement on behalf of the leadership of the IRA where they remind listeners that an all-Ireland republic is an unfinished project requiring the legitimacy of 'physical force' for its completion. Nationalist commemorations, furthermore, which display their pantheon of dead wrought through blood sacrifices, are an expression of grieving and how ancient grievances sustain the recollection of conquest and persecution (McBride 2001).

Notably, in terms of Ricoeur's concept of the *tremendum horrendum* of history, unionist and nationalist commemorative rituals can conjure up frightening images, which stereotype as the other as the perpetuator of the most savage abuses against the group.

The past, especially evoked through the use of social memory, is thus a precious resource which contributes towards the instigation and maintenance of ethnic conflict. The question is whether shared ways of dealing with the past can also be used in Northern Ireland to fruitfully contribute towards conflict resolution and peace-building. In this regard it is important to note how this precise question has become central to the ongoing Northern Irish peace process. To start off, we assess the role of the British state in bringing questions of victims/survivors to the fore of current post-Agreement dispensation.

The British state

There has been a distinct policy change by the British state in terms of its obligations towards victims of the conflict and also concerning how the legacy of the conflict should be commemorated. Prior to the instigation of the Northern Irish peace process, there was a policy silence by the British State on victims. This inertia was confirmed by a government minister, Des Browne (2003: 6): 'in all that time [thirty years of conflict] there were no policies in relations to victims'.

The first policy shift came in 1997 – with the change from a Conservative government to a Labour one – when the then Northern Ireland Secretary of State requested that Sir Kenneth Bloomfield, a former public servant, 'examine the feasibility of providing greater recognition for those who have become victims in the last thirty years as a consequence of events in Northern Ireland' (Bloomfield 1998: 8). The report which emerged at the end of the consultation advocated 'memorial schemes in honour of those who have suffered and died, and projects for physical memorials of various kinds' (1998:8). Notably, however, the Bloomfield Report refused to argue for an 'inclusive' memorial form, one that would recognize all those who had died during the conflict. As such, the Bloomfield Report magnified the major fissure of the victims' field: there is a so-called hierarchy of victimhood in which some of the people who died can be endowed with the epithet of 'innocent victims', while others, especially paramilitaries, are excluded. This partisan approach to commemoration is generally reflective of survey evidence, which shows while there is strong public support for a memorial to victims of the Troubles, there is less support for an all-encompassing memorial which would include paramilitaries killed.

Since the release of the Bloomfield Report in 1998, there have been a number of important state initiatives for victims, including the establishment of a Victims' Unit to allocate funds to victims' groups; the formation of a Memorial Fund to pilot schemes for victims' groups; and the creation of regional Trauma Advisory Boards. Funding is another area through which the state has supported the formation of victims' groups. From April 1997 to March 2007, the British state has furnished, by its own calculations, £43,962,152 (see Nagle 2009d) on organizations they identify as providing support for victims. At present, it is estimated

Table 6.1 'Do you think that there should be a memorial to all victims?' (%)

	2000
Yes	64
No	26
Don't know	9
Other	1

Source: Northern Ireland Life and Times Survey 2000, Module: Political Attitudes, Variable: MEMVICT

that there are approximately sixty victims' groups in Northern Ireland (Nagle 2009d).

The British state has thus taken a proactive role in setting the victims' agenda. The reasons underlying this level of involvement are multi-faceted. On one level it stems from the perceived legal obligations of a responsible nation state. It is widely held internationally that protecting and upholding victims of injury is one of the state's primary duties, and if a government fails to attend to victims and their injuries it has defaulted (see Biggar 2003). Some analysis has shown that victims are less likely to suffer from illnesses, such as PTSD and depression, if their status is recognized and supported (see Hamber 2006a). On another level the state's contribution to the victim's sector relates to its desire to bolster sustainable peace-building. How societies deal with issues related to victims is seen as a barometer of its progress in trying to entrench peace (Hamber 2006a).

The specific context in which the British state has stimulated different initiatives and debates concerned with 'dealing with the past' stems from the Good Friday Agreement of 1998. While the Agreement emphasized group-differentiated rights as a means to ameliorate ethnic conflict, it lacked definite mechanisms for dealing with the past, especially in terms of examining human rights abuses or forms of 'truth-telling'. As such, the Northern Ireland peace process, enshrined by the Agreement of 1998, is something of an aberration from the general trend of other peace processes which included measures to engage with the legacy of conflict (Bell 2003). The conspicuous absence of specific statutory measures to deal with the past in the Agreement has meant what schemes it has offered are piecemeal. While some other conflict transitional societies – such as South Africa, Uganda, Argentina, Chile, Ghana, East Timor and Guatemala – have opted for Truth and Reconciliation Tribunals, there have been no similar state-led initiatives launched in Northern Ireland. Instead, the British state has initiated at the behest of some victims' groups a number of investigations and tribunals into its possible role in the deaths of a number of high-profile individuals.[32]

Despite its lack of a joined-up approach to the 'past', the British government has taken an increasingly involved role in the victims' sector. On 1 March 2005, the then Secretary of State, Paul Murphy, took the opportunity to announce – in line with one of the major recommendations of a consultation document – proposals to appoint a Commissioner for Victims and Survivors, as well as instigating a period of consultation on the detailed remit of the post, and on the wider future of services for victims and survivors of the Troubles. In order to appoint a permanent Victims' Commissioner, new legislation was required. On 14 November 2006, the Victims and Survivors (Northern Ireland) Order 2006 was given Royal Assent. The Order makes provision for the establishment of the post of Commissioner for Victims and Survivors for Northern Ireland, and sets out the Commissioner's role and remit. The Order has three sections containing 10 Articles altogether. Most notable among these Articles include the definition of a 'victim and survivor':

(a) someone who is or has been physically or psychologically injured as a result of or in consequence of a conflict-related incident;
(b) someone who provides a substantial amount of care on a regular basis for an individual mentioned in paragraph (a); or
(c) someone who has been bereaved as a result of or in consequence of a conflict-related incident.

The Consultative Group on the Past

One of the major consultative processes commenced by the British government regarding dealing with the past has been the so-called Eames–Bradley Consultative Group on the Past. On 22 June 2007, Peter Hain, the then Secretary of State for Northern Ireland, announced the formation of an independent Consultative Group.[33] Asked to describe their function at a press conference to launch the group, the group stated: 'This consultative group provides a platform for people to express their own views on how to address the violent legacy of the Troubles that impacted on so many across all sections of society' (BBC 2007).

In early September 2007, the Group announced a process of public engagement and consultation, inviting any individuals or groups to share their views on how Northern Ireland society could best approach the legacy of the past 40 years. The Group stressed that its role was to make recommendations about a process for dealing with the past and that the Group itself was not that process. Reviewing the lengthy consultation process at its conclusion, the group stated:

The past should be dealt with in a manner which enables society to become more defined by its desire for true and lasting reconciliation rather than by division and mistrust, seeking to promote a shared and reconciled future for all. (Consultative Group on the Past 2009: 23)

The report of the Consultative Group on the Past was released to invited victims' groups, politicians, police officers and the media in

Belfast on 28 January 2009. The start of the event was delayed by around 15 minutes as some bereaved relatives stood pointing fingers at one another and traded accusations over the deaths of their loved ones. The 190-page *Report of the Consultative Group on the Past* makes more than 30 recommendations. In its foreword, Eames and Bradley state:

> Northern Ireland has made tremendous progress out of the dark days of the violence towards peace and stable Government. But it became clear to us that finding a better way of dealing with the past would help cement that progress. To take now the final steps out of conflict will be difficult for many. However, the divisions that led to the conflict in the first place are all too present and only by honestly addressing the past can we truly deal with it and then leave it in the past. (Consultative Group on the Past 2009: 14)

Although the group's report made a number of proposals, one specific scheme became the focus for public debate and division. This was: 'The nearest relative of someone who died as a result of the conflict in and about Northern Ireland, from January 1966, should receive a one-off ex-gratia recognition payment of £12,000' (Consultative Group on the Past 2009: 6). Explaining the rationale behind the 'recognition payment of £12,000' at the launch of the report, Eames described it as a way of society saying to the families of those killed: 'We are sorry for your troubles…This is not compensation by another name. It is the acknowledgment of their loss and of their pain' (Moriarty 2009). Opinions on this particular recommendation widely differed. There was some support for the so-called 'recognition' payment. In one article, a nationalist writer argued 'The pain is equally shared between Nationalist families who had relatives die at the hands of Loyalist militants, or Unionist families who had members killed by the IRA' (N. O'Dowd 2009). There was also a high degree of opposition for the 'recognition payment', especially from unionist political parties and a number of victims' group. The main crux of opposition to the proposal was that the recognition payment would act to make a moral equivalence between those who had committed violence and those innocents who were the victims of such violence. An editorial in a pro-unionist newspaper stated that if we accepted the 'twisted logic' of the recognition payments, 'then the rule of law, which so many died to uphold, will have gone forever. Should the families of the bombers in London on July 7, or the terrorists who hijacked the planes in the United States on 9/11 be similarly "recognized?"' (*Belfast Newsletter* 2009).

Who are the victims?

The controversy which surrounded the 'Eames–Bradley Report', as well as many of the other British government led initiatives to 'deal with the past', has illuminated a major fault-line of the Northern Irish peace process: who are the victims? There has been, and continues to be so, a high level of contestation over which groups rightfully deserve the epithet 'victims'. Proclaiming victimhood on behalf of the group fulfils a number of related political and emotional functions. The innocent and blameless victim merits compassion, assistance and resources to help subdue their victimizer. Their inherent defencelessness means that any attack by the victim can be seen as legitimate self-defence. As such, groups who have taken up arms during the Troubles have done so by claiming they are victims defending their communities: 'Without the status of victim-hood their violence becomes politically inexplicable and morally indefensible' (Smyth 1998: 39). Victimhood is thus a powerful yet paradoxical injunction. Powerful because, 'once claimed, it can provide the moral basis for redress, retaliation and even revenge in order to right any given wrong – real or imagined'. Paradoxical because 'in order to harness that power, one must first admit weakness'. Victims must appear powerless compared to their persecutors; victimhood is a passive state – 'the result of bad things happening to people who are unable to prevent it' (Younge 2004).

With the stock value of victimhood steadily rising during the post-Agreement dispensation, nationalists and unionist groups enroll in what Buruma (1999) has called an 'Olympics of suffering', in which competitors compete for 'superior status for their particular psychic suffering'. Victims can thus sometimes be manipulated by political organizations who target victims for their own ideological ends. Research (Morrissey and Smyth 2002) has found, as Hamber (2006b: 133) notes, 'a continued hijacking of the so-called victim issue, both in terms of individuals and in terms of defining one "community" or the other as the "real" victim'.

Despite the immense political capital to be gained from purchasing 'victimhood', victims can enshrine a polarized symbolic meaning in divided societies. On one level, victims can become 'moral beacons' for future reconciliation. Society's identification with the suffering of individuals affords an opportunity to break down the sense of 'otherness' which is attributed to members of rival ethnic groups. On another level, those who have suffered are a stark reminder of the 'eroded interpretations' of each other which 'justified' actions aimed at inflicting terrible suffering. They are permanent reminders of malevolence, warning the living in divided societies of the eternal grievous capability of the enemy and the need for ever vigilance (Hamber 2006a).

It could be argued that the victims' issue represent the grand theme of post-Agreement politics in Northern Ireland, offering either the hope of a shared future and reconciliation or the despair of enmities maintained in perpetuity. The role of the British state has been to encourage the formation of a victims sector, including furnishing resources, social and welfare initiatives and encouraging the formation of victims' groups, as part of its commitment to peace-building (Nagle 2009d). This emplacement of victims within the welfare state represents the removal of notions of grieving and suffering from the private to the public sphere. However, such rational 'administrative planning', as Habermas (1988: 72) defines it, 'produces unintended, unsettling and publicizing effects'. Thus the uprooting of notions of suffering from the private to the public sphere facilitates new opportunities for ethno-national mobilization by placing it into a political framework through the discourse of communicative action. Furthermore, because the administrative system appears unreceptive to forms of public opinion, 'the system frustrates the very same projects that it sets in motion, amplifying the intensity of these projects and their tendency to follow "alternative" and "contentious" routes' (Crossley 2002: 162). It is important, here, to show how the exponential growth of victims' groups in Northern Ireland since 1998 is a microcosm of how contesting claims of victimhood defines ethno-national group politics. Many victims' groups have rallied and mobilized on the basis of protesting against aspects of British state policy in dealing with victims. Some of these victims' groups have also managed to form alliances and networks with non-victims' groups as they have mobilized on a civil rights agenda by claiming a whole ethno-national group can be defined as 'victims'. Some victims' groups have therefore become embroiled in much wider political debates beyond issues concerning the delivery of services to groups. This politicization of victims' groups can be seen best in the way some victims' groups are aligned with nationalism or unionism.

Nationalist victims groups

Many nationalist victims' groups predate 1997, the point in which the British state took a more interventionist stance regarding the victims' sector. The notion of victimhood appeared more apposite for nationalism rather than unionism because they were the minority group in the state and they had historically suffered from some forms of inequality.

However, the major dynamic for the mobilization of these groups during the 1990s was to highlight and uncover the level of collusion between the British state and loyalist paramilitaries in the deaths of nationalists. For instance, the website of Relatives for Justice (2009) notes: 'The issues of accountability, truth and justice are paramount for all those affected by State and State sponsored violence'.

A number of other nationalist victims' groups have emerged since 1997 to draw attention to specific cases of British state involvement in the killings of nationalists. These groups include the Ardoyne Commemoration Project, the Bloody Sunday Trust and Firinne/Truth. The range of work and services provided by these groups are extensive and wide-ranging. While some groups place emphasis on advocacy work – particularly promoting measures and initiatives designed to bring the British state to account for its accused role in killings – other groups have prioritized forms of 'truth-telling', in which victims provide testimonies of their suffering. Occasionally, there have also been public demonstrations of nationalist victims' groups, such as the 'March for Truth' that took place in Belfast in August 2007. Featuring a number of victims' groups, the parade sought to illuminate collaboration between the British state and loyalist paramilitaries. A rally to culminate the protest included Gerry Adams, the President of Sinn Féin, who stated:

> The objective of this march and rally is to draw attention to collusion and British state violence, a policy which resulted in many thousands of victims who were killed or injured or bereaved, and the administrative and institutional cover-up by the British government and its state agencies. (*An Phbolacht* 9 August 2007)

Unionist victims' groups

Prior to 1997 very few unionist victims' groups were recorded. The situation rapidly changed during 1998 and 2000 as at least ten unionist victims' groups were quickly formed. Whereas nationalist victims' groups almost exclusively focus on nationalist victims of state violence, unionist victims' groups almost wholly deal with victims of republican violence. The factors which have contributed to their mobilization are multifaceted and complex.

One reason for this complexity is because, as Donnan and Simpson (2007) note, unionism has historically been more defined by confidence and democratic majorityism rather than victimhood. Certainly, unionism historically evoked an image of a confident democratic majority secure in their political identity within the union (Finlay 2001). In more recent years, a discernible countertrend has been identified. This trend points to a new unionist encapsulation. Unionists are now more likely to be portrayed and portray their own experience, as Finlay (2001: 3) notes, as that of 'defeat and associated emotions... More than one author has claimed to detect self-pity and a predilection for victimhood'.

There are a number of factors which contribute to this transformation of identity. First, there has always been a residual propensity for unionists to see themselves as a minority. Although unionists were a substantial majority in Northern Ireland, able to use this numerical constituency to dominate the polity, overall on the island of Ireland they are a substantial minority and often fearful of what some view as an irredentist Irish Republic who once claimed political sovereignty over Northern Ireland. Furthermore, many of the victims' groups are located in isolated rural parts of Northern Ireland near the Irish border. It is here where unionists are the distinct minority and where they feel the most vulnerable since they were subjected to republican sectarian attacks (Donnan and Simpson 2007).

Unionist confidence has most clearly been eroded during the Northern Ireland peace process, especially in the aftermath of the signing of the GFA in 1998. The power sharing agreement moves the polity from being unionist majoritarian or controlled from Westminster, the seat of the British parliament. Of equal problem for many unionists is that the Agreement is seen as ushering in legislation which discriminates unionists by favouring nationalists. Informed by a multicultural framework, the Agreement has sought to redress a number of imbalances and grievances identified by nationalists. Labelled the 'equality agenda' by nationalists, unionists have alternatively identified the Agreement as an anti-unionist agenda (see Mac Ginty and du Tois 2007). To prove their point, unionists have pointed to what they believe is anti-unionist legislation, which curbs, for instance, the 'right to march' for some Orange Order parades, and outlines sweeping reform of the police. The reform of the police service, a force which was historically almost wholly Protestant, has featured new symbolic insignias and recruitment quotas. These quotas, designed to redress the imbalance of Catholics in the force, have been framed by unionist politicians as blatant discrimination against Protestants. Further to this, unionist politicians have argued that more reforms have been granted to Irish republicans in exchange for embracing the political path. Such concessions, state unionist politicians, range from the release of prisoners convicted of paramilitary offences, amnesties for so-called on-the-run paramilitaries and the downscaling of the British military presence in the north.

For unionist victims of republican violence the lack of appropriate justice which has characterized the post-Agreement phase has made composite their sense of disenfranchisement from the peace process. Although a small minority of unionists originally supported the Agreement, this was quickly turned into a substantial minority (see Mac Ginty and du Toit 2007: 23–27), which is reflected in surveys. As we can see in Figure 6.1, during 1999–2003 when both Catholics and Protestants were asked 'Has the Good Friday Agreement Benefited Nationalists more than Unionists', Protestant respondents have increasingly and overwhelmingly stated that the GFA has benefited nationalists. Contrariwise, a much lower, though growing, percentage of Catholics agreed that the GFA has benefited nationalists.

In response to perceived grievances, unionists have sought to construct intragroup alliances and networks to protest against aspects of the Agreement. In this context, unionist victims' groups have come to stand for the current status of contemporary unionism as a whole. Many unionist victims' groups identify the actions of the British state during the peace process as exacerbating their suffering; in response they have protested against specific aspects of British state policy in Northern Ireland, which, in zero-sum fashion, they believe favours

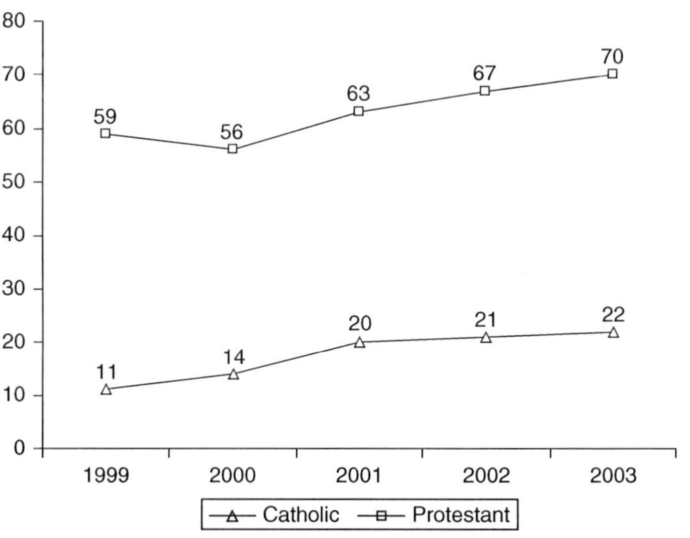

Figure 6.1   'Who has benefited the most from the GFA?' (%)

Source: Northern Ireland Life and Times Survey 1999–2003, Module: Political Attitudes, Variable: BENFCHNG.

Irish nationalists, thereby discriminating against unionists. The 1998 Agreement, especially, is identified as key to the emergence of the unionist victims sector as a protest movement. As one unionist victims' group, West Tyrone Voice, state:

> like other pro-British innocent victims' groups, [West Tyrone Voice] has its genesis in the latter months of 1998, in the wake of the early and accelerated release of terrorist prisoners in accord with the provisions of the Belfast Agreement 1998. Victims realised that there was nothing in this Agreement for them, felt keenly the injustice of such early release of terrorists back on to the streets, and came together to 'voice' their concerns. (West Tyrone Voice 2008: 1)

Significantly, many victims' groups managed to create networks with other unionist groups, especially political parties and the Orange Order to protest about a range of grievances. This network was forged by a number of groups. These groups constructed a particular frame which emphasized that not only are unionist victims of the Troubles adversely affected by the policies of the British state, but also that all unionists are discriminated against in the post-Agreement political dispensation. In many ways, the unionist victims' mobilization has been articulated by participants as a civil rights movement. An example of this broad based victims' movement occurred in 1999, when a committee composed of victims' groups, Protestant clergy, political parties and cultural organizations mobilized. Calling themselves the Northern Ireland Victims of Terrorism Association (NIVTA), they announced to the media their intention to embark upon a 117-mile trek across Northern Ireland. Titled the 'Long March', the march, as the organizers made clear, was a demonstration of 'human rights' for what they perceived to be a victimized Protestant unionist community in Northern Ireland. A unionist politician, who acted as a spokesperson, stated:

> We want to show who are the real victims in Northern Ireland. We aim to highlight that Protestants have legitimate grievances which have been ignored.…This is about the right to live free from intimidation, abuse and discrimination. (*Belfast Telegraph* 26 May 1999)

Despite managing to coalesce together a number of disparate unionist concerns, these mobilizations have rarely achieved unity for long or attracted sufficient levels of support. The movement been characterized by splits and by criticism from many former members. For instance, a unionist politician, Fraser Agnew, who had taken part in the Long March, stated that it 'was like emotional blackmail…I believe innocent victims are being exploited for political ends' *(Belfast Telegraph* 25 September 1999). A related problem for the movement is that the status of victimhood is politically contingent. For example, while one unionist political party – the DUP – were once happy to support the victims' movement as a means to vehemently oppose unionists sharing political power with republicans, they have now engaged in something of a *volte-face* by going into partnership with republicans in a new power sharing executive in 2007. The integration of hard-line unionists in power sharing is to some extent based on a resurgence of unionist confidence. Ian Paisley, then the leader of uncompromising unionism, spoke of republicans being defeated and humiliated. This self-confidence stems from a new framing of the peace process as one that ends with the defeat of republicans and the consolidation of the UK union. Such positive unionist engagement with the devolved government does not allow space for a self-encapsulation based on marginalization and victimhood.

While this change of heart is partly due to the fact that political parties strategically manipulate victims' groups for their own political exigencies, it is also to do with wider political and cultural notions of victimhood prevalent in conflict transitional societies. Although during times of political uncertainty victims' suffering are a pertinent reminder of the wrongs meted out by adversarial groups, when political élites decide that many of the issues relating to victims are finished, there is an expectation that victims will oblige by 'moving on'. The persistence of victims' groups to raise politically inexpedient issues can open them to accusations of being 'dinosaurs' or only concerned with gaining 'blood money' (see Hamber 2006b).

Healing through Remembering

The protracted and often virulent debates over which group should rightfully claim victimhood has stymied the opportunity for a shared mechanism to deal with the past. Addressing this precise problem, there have been some other initiatives – located at the level of civil society rather than the state – that have strived to deal with the past in an inclusive way to help forge a 'shared society'. The most prominent of these initiatives concerns the 'Healing through Remembering' project.

The Healing through Remembering project has its roots in the visit of Alex Boraine, Deputy Chair of the South African Truth and Reconciliation Commission to Northern Ireland in 1999. Boraine was invited by a number of groups aiming to learn lessons from South Africa. The South African Truth and Reconciliation Commission had aimed to build 'a historic bridge between the past of a deeply divided society characterised by strife, conflict, untold suffering and injustice, and a future founded on the recognition of human rights, democracy and peaceful co-existence and development opportunities for all South Africans' (cited in Healing through Remembering 2000: 4). A report – entitled *All Truth Is Bitter* (Healing through Remembering 2000) – was produced in response to Boraine's visit. The report recommended a wide-ranging consultancy surrounding Northern Ireland to debate ways of examining the past and remembering so as to build a better future.

Taking up the suggestions of *All Truth Is Bitter*, in 2001 the Healing through Remembering project was formed with the vision of securing 'acknowledgement of the events connected with the conflict in and about Northern Ireland, and in so doing, individually and collectively to have contributed to an understanding of, and the healing of, the wounds of society' (Healing through Remembering 2008: 4). To help address these aims the project prompted a public consultation process to help identify the possible mechanisms which are required to remember the past in an inclusive manner. One Healing through Remembering initiative, initiated in 2006, was to consult with the public on what form a Living Memorial Museum should take. The result of the consultative process called for a museum to 'disseminate information and provide educational opportunities ensuring lessons are learned for the future' (Healing through Remembering 2007). By hosting the varying historical perspectives of different groups on the conflict in Northern Ireland the proposed museum hopes to 'strengthen our communal forms of remembering, and increase respect and tolerance for all' (Healing through Remembering 2007).

Back to the future

The issue of how to deal with the legacy of Northern Ireland's decisive and violent past remains unresolved. Despite the effort of some to build the 'common ground', so that sufficient consensus could be forged among all groups in Northern Ireland for a unified memorial or approach to the past, the subject remains highly divisive. Drawing a line under the past – subjecting it to the 'violence of amnesia' – is also impracticable and unhelpful. Individuals and groups simply do not forget; instead 'Buried memories fester in the unconscious minds of communities in conflict, only to emerge later in even more distorted and virulent forms to poison minds and relationships' (Consultative Group on the Past 2009: 52). The question, therefore, is: Can conflict transitional societies engage with 'legacy issues' in ways which do not contribute towards division and acrimony? For the remainder of this chapter we explore what a commemorative process might contribute to peace-building in divided societies by assessing two dimensions: *Healing* and *Pedagogy*.

Healing

Although societal healing is often made an activating feature of any mechanism to 'deal with the past', it is erroneous to state that society can be jointly traumatized. Indeed, 'Nations do not have collective psyches which can be healed, nor do whole nations suffer post-traumatic stress disorder and to assert otherwise is to psychologize an abstract entity which exists primarily in the minds of nation-building politicians' (Hamber and Wilson 2002: 36). This perspective is particularly acute in Northern Ireland, where the demography of the conflict was unevenly distributed. Some localities and communities were almost wholly immune from the ravages of violence while others were immersed on an almost daily basis. The danger of trauma theory, then, is that it 'implicates us all in an undifferentiated world of hurt' thus obscuring real differences in experience (Gray and Oliver 2004: 10).

While societies do not exist in traumatized states, can it be argued that the themes of trauma, mourning and melancholia shape the collective experience of groups? These narratives, as Volkan (1997) argues, are often present in groups embroiled in ethnic conflict. The experience of losing territory, people and prestige for ethnic groups can leave them in a stage of melancholia – that is, the affected party continues to identify with the lost object. The ego of the melancholic feels ambivalence or hostility towards the lost object and refuses to acknowledge that the object has been lost. Trapped in a cycle of narcissistic loathing, the melancholic is incapable of becoming free from the lost object. The cycle of narcissistic loathing is performed in repetitive, looping commemorative acts.

Such melancholia is a common experience for ethno-national groups in times of conflict transition. It seems apparent in how both unionists and nationalists have framed the peace process and how the issue of victims and commemoration hangs forebodingly over society. For unionists, as we have seen, the post-Agreement dispensation has, more often than not, been portrayed by its leaders as one where unionists have lost ground to nationalists. It has been said that they have lost the 'right to march', in the form of Orange Order parades; they have increasingly lost control of the political institutions of the state and they have lost territory. Nationalists, on the other hand, have also had to abandon the realistic hope of a united Ireland in the short-to-medium term and reconcile their place in the British state, including recognizing its policing and judicial authority. Commemorative practice, thus, can be an expression of melancholia, articulating and constantly iterating a sense of loss. This is augmented by those aspects that feature the *tremendum horrendum* of history. The presence of victims and victims' groups, as we have seen, come to stand as permanent reminders of this group loss.

While melancholic commemoration is unhealthy and can lead to the sustenance of ethno-national conflict, can healthy mourning be achieved instead? Here, 'the non-melancholic mourner tests the reality of loss and ultimately disengages from the departed' (Winter 1995: 113). Though the individual and group go through mourning, it is a fixed journey which reaches a definite conclusion. When completed, the individual and group can begin to move on. For Winter (1995), as noted earlier, the task is to find commemorative solutions which facilitate healthy mourning.

The celebratory rendering of the therapeutic dimensions of commemorative practice is also plagued with flaws. Such an approach presumes a typical process of grieving. Winter and Sivan has subsequently acknowledged this point by noting 'the ambiguity of the healing effects' (1999: 32). They note that: 'mourning is an essential part of the story of remembrance of war, but there is much evidence that it is problematic to consider remembrance as the work of mourning, leading to healing, reconciliation and separation of the living from the lost loved-one' (Winter and Sivan 1999: 32). Clearly, grieving and mourning is not universally experienced in a uniform fashion, nor is there one standardized, panacea-inducing and identikit form of commemoration which can engender melancholia.

In fact, the point may not be to resolve melancholia, because this is not possible. Walter Benjamin pleaded that the point of remembrance is not to contain the blows of trauma, but to compel 'society to face squarely what had happened and confront its deepest sources rather than let the wounds scar over' (Jay 1999: 235). Benjamin defended repetitive, never-worked-through remembrance. Benjamin pleaded for forms of commemoration which refused to countenance mourning.

Pedagogy

The pedagogic aspect of commemoration signals the practical synthesis of the questions what should be taught and why with considerations as to how that teaching should take place. As a pedagogical form, commemoration incorporates a set of evaluations which structure what memories should inform our social imagination as well as a detailed, structured set of operations for presenting and engaging historical representations intended to provoke and sediment affect and meaning which can contribute towards peace-building. In other words, we should look towards shared commemorative forms which might allow citizens to critically consider how to change the conditions which contribute to conflict in Northern Ireland. This requires forms of commemoration which are not merely aesthetically abstract, as they are in the case of the 'Symbolic Memorial' on the site of Oklahoma City bombing. Commemorative practice can, instead, provide an educational function. Commemorations, such as holocaust commemorations, not only urge us to remember the dead, but it must also leave such an effect on its victims that their story must be told to prevent future repetition. As one Northern Irish commentator states: a 'monument to tragedies of the past may prevent those of the future' (Garland 2009). In Northern Ireland, 'We need something that attempts to explain the past and that will remind us never again to allow conditions to develop that could drive us back' (Garland 2009).

Applying a pedagogic or educational aspect to any proposed commemoration in Northern Ireland is challenging. This challenge derives from the fact that not only is the past highly contested by political communities in Northern Ireland but that it is also constantly being used as a form of social memory to justify current ideological expediencies. Using memory to assist with understanding the socio-political context of conflict presents real problems when there is little consensus at present regarding the past. In Northern Ireland there is not a relatively simple dichotomy between the 'good' and the 'bad', a wholly repressive and coercive state and those minority groups who were denied their memories.

In one sense this is indicative of a more universal trend. The very number of groups demanding that their own historical narrative be included within the remit of official and state-sanctioned commemoration ensures, as Hass (1998) has suggested, that it is increasingly difficult in mass democratic societies to construct a unified public memory of conflict. One reason for this is that minority groups, who were once and even continue to be persecuted by the majority, have established their identities by reconstructing their pasts, which in turn is often challenged by other groups.

Commemorative practice is rarely, if ever, consensual and without any form of conflict over its essential meaning. For example, the memory of the Vietnam War in Maya Lin's Veterans Memorial, which challenges nationalistic and militaristic symbolism, was repudiated by the political right who sponsored a monument to face, somewhat provocatively, Lin's memorial. 'The Three Fighting Men' is a strong, highly masculine and heroic figurative image of American soldiers. More than just providing different versions of recent US military interventions, these particular forms can touch off a range of emotional reactions. Whereas the traditional imagery of the fighting man encourages a pose of respectful passivity among viewers, the open form of Maya Lin's Wall encourages an active relationship to the dead, such as bringing to the wall objects which symbolize personal loss.

Any proposed commemorative template in Northern Ireland has to countenance the fact that political communities may wish to present particularistic versions of their own history. For example, groups representing state security personnel killed during the conflict may desire commemorations, which portray their loved ones in traditional ennobling, and heroic poses defending the state. Many families of civilians killed by loyalists, security forces or republican paramilitaries may also find it hard to countenance commemorations which make no distinction between their lost ones and the people responsible for their deaths.

The issue of 'dealing with the past' in divided societies may not, therefore, be best reached by encouraging a shared or cohesive representation of the past. However, because social memory is inherently constructed for current political projects, it can be made more malleable for various narratives which are more conducive to conflict management. The modes of remembrance in commemorative forms, practices and other spaces of memory, like murals and commemorative rituals can be, with encouragement, made less antagonistic and constitutive of immutable conflict between groups. The task at present, consequently, may not be to create a shared commemorative template which equally embraces all groups; a more fruitful direction may be to try and reframe some of the commemorative practices used by ethno-national groups so that they don't appear as threatening and that they are less apt to act as harbingers of violence and unalterable group differences.

One particular project which has been quite successful in recent years is Belfast City Council's 'Re-Imagining Communities' project.

In this project 'sectarian murals, emblems, flags and graffiti will be replaced by positive images that reflect the community's culture, as well as highlight and promote the social regeneration taking place in communities today' (Belfast City Council 2008a). One area in which the 'Re-imagining' project has been applied to is the Lower Shankill, a unionist district of northwest Belfast.

During the Troubles, the Lower Shankill and neighbouring districts were located in the conflict's cauldron. Circa 20 per cent of all deaths during the Troubles occurred within a square mile of the Shankill (Shirlow and Murtagh 2006). During the late 1980s and early 1990s, one of the most ruthless loyalist paramilitary units, the Ulster Defence Association (UDA)/Ulster Freedom Fighters (UFF), held control of the area where they launched numerous attacks on neighbouring nationalist areas as well as on members of their own group. To signify their command of the Lower Shankill a number of murals were painted in the area. Some murals simply acted to inform strangers that they were entering into an area controlled by the UDA/UFF and consequently depicted hooded paramilitary gunmen. Other murals, in typical 'time collapse' fashion, evoked historical incidents which were meant to remind those in the present of the constant, unchanging danger of Irish Catholic nationalism. For instance, one mural featured a scene from the seventeenth century in which the native Catholic Irish are butchering Protestant settlers. A caption in the mural states: 'The persecution of the Protestant people by the Church of Rome 1600. The ethnic cleansing still goes on today'. Another mural illustrated a scene from the Siege of Derry, which, as we discussed earlier in the chapter, is often remembered by unionists for providing a perennial situation in which they are under siege from nationalists.

The 're-imagining communities' project has successfully worked with local leaders and groups in the Lower Shankill district to have the murals painted over with new 'positive' and alternative images. These new images depict more benign representations of the local 'community' less rooted in antagonistic politics characterized by a perpetual, never-ending, binary relationship with the nationalist 'other'. The new images seek to portray the local district's proud industrial roots, its cultural heritage and famous characters. The paramilitary mural which acted as the gateway to the Lower Shankill has been repainted with an image which explains the history of the district. The mural depicting 'ethnic cleansing' against Protestants in the seventeenth century has been replaced with a complex illustration of a house where in each room a different social issue was represented in a caption, like 'sustainable employment for all'; 'the right to a proper education'; 'regeneration and not gentrification'. A number of other murals have also undergone similar redesigns.

While these repainted murals do not generally try to fashion a shared nationalist/unionist narrative, their contribution to the task of peace-building should not be underestimated. By providing more thoughtful representations of the local area, a new narrative can be forged which steers away from one which stressed endless violence and conflict between nationalists and unionists. One of the major reasons underlying the success of the 'Re-imagining Communities' project is that it has not simply strived to eradicate murals in the area, or enforced a particular narrative of harmonious cross-community relations; this would be unrealistic and would lack salience in an area renowned for its experience of extreme sectarian violence and a very high degree of residential segregation. The success of the initiative can be attributed to a sensitivity regarding representing local unionist historical and social identities by ensuring they are articulated in a positive non-belligerent fashion. As Smithey (2009) notes, the integrity of such projects lie in how they 'reorient loyalist worldviews and narratives in ways that could improve the environment for communal relations work and continued political projects towards a shared democratic future'. They solve identity problems, in so far as the new murals allow groups to maintain in-group solidarity and ontological security through these practices; at the same time 'they also lower the salience of sectarian and ethnopolitical boundaries that have helped fuel conflict in Ireland' (Smithey 2009: 93).

Conclusion

In this chapter we have examined some of the debates and initiatives concerned with 'dealing with the past' in Northern Ireland, especially those which propose that 'healthy remembering' can help with the task of building a 'shared society'. We have argued that the idea of 'societal healing' to augment peace-building is highly ambiguous. Societies do not contain collective psyches which can be repaired in the same way as those belonging to individuals. Moreover, in divided societies social memory is constructed so as to maintain ethno-national boundaries by providing a static view of historical relations between groups founded on extreme acrimony. Where intercommunal conflict and violence has occurred ethno-national identities are strengthened through commemorative practices. Memory is thus dialectically implicated in terms of its capacity to both cause and result from violence. Considering the divisive and bitter politicized debates generated by the issue of victims and remembrance in post-Agreement Northern Ireland, it does not seem feasible, for the moment at least, to try and foster shared mechanisms for commemorating the past. Despite this, because social memories can be readapted for different purposes, it is possible that commemorative practices can be reframed so that they foster narratives which are not mired in the politics of antipathy. This project does not mean trying to eradicate group based differences in the performance of memory; a more profitable initiative might be, as the 'Re-imagining Communities' project in the Lower Shankill district in Belfast has successfully done, to instil more benign alternative group based memories which promote social issues and a positive local identity.

7
Neoliberalism and Shared Consumers

Potemkin village

There is an apocryphal story that during a visit by Catherine the Great to view her newly acquired lands in the Crimea she was delighted to see beautiful villages lined along the banks of the river Dnieper. Little did she know, the vision was a hollow façade built by her Minister Potemkin to obscure the desolate tundra. Trite as the comparison seems, it is tempting to conclude that tourists visiting contemporary Belfast city centre are endowed with a variation of the 'Potemkin Village' (see Nagle 2009e).

Certainly, tourists see little signs of the violent legacy of the civil conflict in the city centre today; it is here where the conflict seems to have been successfully transformed and ameliorated through inward investment, the arrival of 'cathedrals of consumption' and inner-city regeneration. In a 2004 speech, Mitchell Reiss (2004), then the US Special Envoy to Northern Ireland, welcomed the appearance of what he called a 'new peace' in Belfast, adding that 'in a sure sign of the region's up-and-coming status, Starbuck's coffee has already opened two shops and has plans for four more'. The showcase of this new peaceful Belfast arrived in March 2008 with the opening of Victoria Square, a £400 million shopping centre replete with '800,000 sq. feet of shops and arcades selling Creme de la Mer face creams and Joseph trouser suits – and extremely expensive handbags' (Addley 2008). Such urban regeneration has been packaged by some as providing scope 'to reposition the city as a neutral, modernising place that has left its parochial sectarianism behind' (see Murtagh 2008: 3). Belfast City Council (2008b) has claimed: '[a] strong brand for Belfast, representing the city, will find it easier to attract people, visitors, investment and events, sell its products and services'.

Yet it could be said that such attempts to 'normalize' the city centre by making it into a commercial shared space for Catholic and Protestant consumers represents a Potemkin Village, a façade to subvert and mask the 'injustices of segregation and socio-spatial exclusion' (Shirlow 2006: 101) which are hidden from the tourist gaze. Practically, all contemporary metropolises contain a roughly similar 'mask' strategies of economic redevelopment, including adaptive commercial reuse, designating areas of the city as artistic quarters, and forms of historical preservation – which cover continuing disinvestment and increasing social inequality (Harvey 1988: 168). In exposing the purpose of the mask, many critical theorists have attributed its ownership to the 'neoliberal project' (see Harvey 1988, Smith 2002, Swyngedouw 1996). The salient question, thus, is to what extent are regeneration and other economic growth strategies in Belfast and Northern Ireland neoliberal? This chapter, accordingly, assesses whether neoliberal policies are being promoted as the central *modus operandi,* above other forms of peace-building, to transform the conflict and create a shared identity by generating free-market solutions to the problems inherent to a divided society. The chapter also assesses to what extent can neoliberalism weaken the basis of competing ethno-national encapsulations and even contribute to a 'shared society'.

Rather than arguing that contemporary Northern Ireland is witnessing the complete 'rollout' of a homogeneous neoliberal format, packaged as a unified ideology and set of practices, this chapter takes heed of Wendy Larner's (2003: 509) admonishment: 'little attention is paid to the different variants of neoliberalism, to the hybrid nature of contemporary policies and programmes, or to the multiple and contradictory aspects of neoliberal spaces, techniques, and subjects'. As a place characterized by profoundly embedded patterns of sectarian separation, operating at multiple scales, Northern Ireland's capacity to embrace neoliberalism is contradicted by the enormous cost of segregation to the public purse, estimated as circa £1.5 billion per year (Deloitte and Touche 2007). Despite wishing to advance neoliberalism, the British state and the regional government are unable to wash their hands from underwriting wide swathes of social reproduction, from housing to welfare to transportation infrastructure. The capacity of any neoliberal project to flourish in Northern Ireland is consequently problematic and contradictory, forced to steer an uncomfortable hybrid 'Third Way' partnership with welfarist policies. Furthermore, while aspects of neoliberalism are increasingly advocated by Northern Ireland's major political parties – both Irish nationalist and British unionist – this is not to say this is representative of a an emerging post-ethnic shared identity. The rhetoric of neoliberalism provides instead a matrix for nationalists and unionists to compete for their share of resources; both groups also provide discrepant meanings of what economic liberalism means for their respective constituencies.

Disaster capitalism?

In order to examine these issues, it is necessary first to provide an outline of what is neoliberalism. From there, the chapter examines the extent that Northern Ireland is currently driven by the logic of neoliberalism, with the devolved regional Northern Ireland Executive government, effectively acting as the consummate agent of an unfettered free-market. And if Northern Ireland deserves the epithet of 'neoliberal', is it transforming ethno-national identities and notions of statehood upon which such identities lie?

Neoliberalism seems to be everywhere. If neoliberalism was once characterized as a 'monolithic project emanating from the "ideological heartlands" of the United States and the United Kingdom' (see Larner 2003: 509), it has now emerged in societies undergoing reconstruction after sustained ethnic conflict. For example, the Kosovo Trust Agency and its successor, the Privatisation Agency Kosovo, promote low taxation, inward foreign investment and the privatization of the public sector to help build stability in the region. For critics, the presence of neoliberalism in such societies is a form of 'disaster capitalism', which uses desperation and fear to constitute privatization strategies and land grabs before the locals are able to effectively resist (Horgan 2007, Klein 2008). In the immediate aftermath of the US occupation in 2003, the underpinning strategy for post-war reconstruction outlined by the Coalition Provisional Authority (CPA) was to implant a successful neoliberal economy in the Middle East by luring in foreign (almost exclusively US owned) multinational investment. To facilitate this, the CPA decreed the privatization of 200 state-owned Iraqi firms, the reduction of corporate tax from 40 to 15 per cent, and permission for foreign companies to own 100 per cent of privatized Iraqi assets, including the right to 'transfer abroad without delay all funds associated with its foreign investment, including shares or profits and dividends' (Coalition Provisional Authority 2003). All of this was passed without seeking consent from the Iraqi people, thus acting to ignite grievances and filling the ranks of a growing insurgency seeking to exploit ethnic conflict, especially since little was done by the CPA to deal with basic problems, like water sanitization, unemployment, security and electricity. Many Iraqis viewed the privatization of the nation's industry into the hands of foreign contractors as little less than colonization (see Harvey 2005: 6, Chandrasekaran 2007, Klein 2008: 345). Even where the locals are allowed to partake in privatization strategies – like Bosnia – the new economic freedoms have been hijacked by war élites to the detriment of pre-existing systems of social welfare, pensions and healthcare (Richmond and Franks 2009: 33).

Neoliberalism has also been accused of surfacing in conflict transitional Northern Ireland. Hillyard et al. (2005: 47) claim to identify 'an almost religious belief in the conflict-solving powers of neoliberalism'. Horgan (2006) and O'Hearn (2008) conclude that neoliberal policies have been foisted upon the regional devolved power sharing Northern Ireland government by the UK state, one of 'the most adherent in Western Europe to neoliberal principles of privatization, fiscal conservatism, and low social welfare' (2008: 115). Wilford and Wilson (2008: 7) note that 'the private-sector-oriented, economic focus' of the regional power sharing Northern Ireland Executive government has 'a distinctly neoliberal tenor'. Similarly, Murtagh (2008: 20) agrees that the 'new Executive…dispensed the neoliberal medicine for a dysfunctional economy, too reliant on subvention, state jobs and complacency'. Others (Hodgett and Johnson 2001) have even traced the roots of the neoliberal project in Northern Ireland back to the 1980s, seeing it as part of counter-insurgency efforts to regenerate Belfast through building partnerships between the state, business and the community sector.

Neoliberalism

To begin examining whether Northern Ireland has taken a neoliberal turn as part of peace-building, it is necessary first to ask what precisely is neoliberalism? In mapping out the historical roots and contemporary character of neoliberalism, Neil Smith (2002: 429) notes that from the eighteenth century onwards economic liberalism pivoted on two crucial assumptions:

> That the free and democratic exercise of individual self-interest led to the optimal collective social good; and that the market knows best: that is, private property is the foundation of this self-interest, and free market exchange is its ideal vehicle.

In other words, neoliberal theory 'proposes that human well-being can best be advanced by liberating individual entrepreneurial freedoms and skills within an institutional framework characterized by strong private property rights, free markets, and free trade' (Harvey 2005: 2). The role of the state is to provide a structure conducive to such practices, meaning that it should not interfere in the market because it does not possess enough information to second-guess market prices and due to the fact that powerful interest groups will distort state interventions for their own benefit (Harvey 2005: 2).

Although this 'possessive individualism' remained at the core of liberal democratic states, during the twentieth century there was at least an attempt by social democrats to regulate the excesses of the market. These forms of regulation included the construction of Keynesian monetary policies, the formation of trade unions, a strong welfare state and a vibrant civil society. As such, a historical compromise between capital and labour was achieved to dampen business cycles and to ensure reasonably full employment. This 'embedded liberalism' (Harvey 2005: 11) was not simply granted by a benevolent state but the result of class struggle (Smith 2002).

In more recent decades, however, many liberal democratic states have all but abandoned their regulatory role. Significantly, the original axioms of economic liberalism have returned with vengeance and are being reformulated in line with current political exigencies. Although critics contest the varieties of neoliberalism (see Campbell and Pedersen 2001), there is a broad consensus that it entails principles favouring free-market solutions to social problems. Part and parcel with this project is the promotion of a lean welfare state, deregulation, low taxation and flexible labour markets (Fuller and Geddes 2008: 255). In many neoliberal states, there has been an attack on the trade unions, a restriction on municipal authorities which hindered competitive flexibility, the roll back of the welfare state, the privatization of public services, huge tax reductions, the sponsorship of entrepreneurialism, and the creation of a propitious business environment to allow a major inflow of foreign investment (Harvey 2005: 23).

In some instances, like the 'New Labour' project in the UK, lip service is paid to compensating for the implications of competitive individualism. New Labour has initiated a number of policies aimed at tackling social exclusion, community cohesion and neighbourhood renewal. In one sense this may indicate a desire to at least recognize and deal with the systemic nature of social problems. Underlying these sentiments, however, is the dominance of neoliberal thinking. Rather than trying to navigate a 'third way' between free-market economics and state-led social justice, the dominant strands of New Labour's social inclusion policies are that 'integration into the labour market must be the principal solution, and the welfare state must be reoriented to enable the excluded to grasp the "opportunities for all" offered by the labour market, rather than providing a refuge from it' (Fuller and Geddes 2008: 259). In this synopsis, the emphasis is placed on equality of opportunity rather than on equality of outcome. Redistribution, accordingly, is framed as the redistribution of opportunities rather than as the redistribution of traditional tax and benefits policies.

Importantly, the neoliberal enterprise requires a linkage between modernization and the rescaling of the state. This rescaling includes a move away from centralized and bureaucratic forms of governance (Purcell 2003), to those featuring 'various forms of manageralism, privatisation policies and thus the consolidation of the "mixed market"' (Fuller and Geddes 2008: 252) in local public service provision, along with more networked governance arrangements involving both hierarchy and market.

Purcell (2003: 568), in particular, argues that this 'rolling out' of neoliberalism is profoundly eroding 'the national scale as the privileged scale at which economic and political activity are organized'. As a consequence, Purcell (2003: 568) continues, citizenship is being reoriented away from the nation as the predominant community. Recent shifts, he argues, in the organization of capital accumulation have deprivileged the national scale. The intensification of the transnationalization of production and finance since the 1970s has expanded the scale at which investment, production and information flows are functionally integrated. The smooth performance of neoliberalism requires the free mobility of capital across all sectors and regions, and any attempts to curb this (such as tariffs) have to be (theoretically) removed (Harvey 2005: 66).

It is not only at a global scale that the discreteness of the nation state is being reformulated; but also in an interlinked way the nation state is simultaneously being downscaled to local and regional scales. Local and regional economies are increasingly prioritized as crucial nodes in the world's economic geography. The process of devolution, as states hand over forms of political and economic power at substate regional scale, is geared towards creating competitive regional spaces through institutional state forms which fit more closely the scalar structure of the changing economic geography of the area. Erik Swyngedouw (1996), for instance, has shown how the process of devolution in Belgium is part of urban/regional restructuring efforts to produce globally competitive spaces. Examining the dismantling of heavy industry in the Flemish province of Limburg, Swyngedouw examines the subsequent programme of urban regional redevelopment which largely concentrates on creating large-scale tourist projects. Such projects rely on constructing a branded localism, designed to draw on 'indigenous identities and histories' (Murtagh 2008).

'Open for business': 'Northern Ireland PLC'

To what degree, if any, is neoliberalism being advanced in Northern Ireland, especially to augment the transition from conflict to sustainable peace? As a starting point, it is noted that the virtues of free-market enterprise, urban regeneration, private finance initiatives to bolster public services and inward investment by global multinationals have become hegemonic in Northern Ireland: all the major political parties largely subscribe to these neoliberal values. These values are manifest in a number of specific proposals and initiatives.

First, all of the major political parties have called for the reduction of corporate tax from 28 per cent to 12 per cent – equivalent to the Republic of Ireland – to help generate high-value Foreign Direct Investment (FDI). The idea was first mooted by Sir George Quigley, head of the Industrial Task Force, and then research by the Economic Research Institute of Northern Ireland (Hewitt 2007) claimed that the reduction would create over 184,000 new jobs by 2030 and recover an initial loss of £150 million in reduced corporation tax within six years. It has been estimated that in 2007 global foreign investment totalled $947 billion, of which Northern Ireland received almost £1 billion compared to the $27 billion received by the Republic of Ireland. Moreover, while 24 of the Fortune top 100 North American companies have investments in the Republic, Northern Ireland can only claim a small handful. Nevertheless, the proposal was rejected by the UK government who claimed that such a move would unfairly favour Northern Ireland compared to other UK regions.

Despite the cross-party devolved Northern Ireland government failing in its bid to reduce corporate tax, the commitment to FDI remains strong. In April 2008, the leaders of the Northern Ireland Executive announced that as much as $760 million of US public investment was to be ploughed into Northern Ireland, half through the mechanism of the 'Emerald Investment Development Fund'.[34] The apotheosis of neoliberalism's influence in Belfast followed in May 2008 as a delegation of 100 US corporate leaders, headed by Michael Bloomberg, the Mayor of New York City, visited the city for an investment conference. After comparing the proposed redevelopment of Belfast's Titanic Quarter to the ongoing redevelopment of Manhattan's Far West Side, Bloomberg spoke of how Belfast could become one 'of the most competitive financial hubs in the world'. In order to display Northern Ireland's readiness to the world's business community after years of violence and lack of inward investment, even professed socialists, such as Irish Republican leader Martin McGuinness (2008), have stated that Northern Ireland is 'open for business and ready to meet the challenges ahead'; some politicians have even rebranded the north as 'Northern Ireland PLC'.

A further area in which Northern Ireland's economy has been identified for growth is inner-city regeneration, especially the 'Cathedral', 'Laganside' and 'Titanic' Quarters, areas the authorities call 'character zones', which they hope will facilitate 'cultural reanimation' and the 'local economy' (Belfast City Council 2004). Plans for the Titanic Quarter, a 185 acre site located on de-industrialized shipyards, feature over 5000 apartments, 180,000 sq metres of 'business, education, office and research and development floor space together with hotels, restaurants, cafes, bars and other leisure uses'. Investors claim the project will create over 20,000 new jobs over fifteen years (Titanic Quarter 2009). The portioning of selected parts of Belfast into 'cultural quarters' is reminiscent of 'urban cloning' seen in other cities across Europe, an almost identikit regeneration scheme which draw on a sanitized version of local identity. Belfast's official niche is not so much mired in 'dark tourism' to reflect the legacy of conflict; the place promotion of the city relies more on evoking the city's industrial heritage, especially as the place where the Titanic was built (Murtagh 2008).

Another neoliberal sphere is the Strategic Investment Board (SIB), which was introduced in 2002 as part of the Reinvestment and Reform Initiative (RRI). Modelled on the Kosovo Trust Agency (Horgan 2007), the purpose of the SIB aims to build partnerships between the public and private sectors to help 'accelerate the delivery of major public infrastructure projects'. These partnerships include major works at over one hundred schools; the building of a new central library in Belfast; the building of new hospitals; and 'the commencement of a major mixed-use regeneration scheme in the North East Quarter of Belfast city centre by 2011 leveraging in significant private sector investment' (Strategic Investment Board 2009). These Public-Private Partnerships (PPP) are one way of drawing in private investment to progress some of the large capital projects and the government then repay their private partners – the investors – usually over a period of 25–30 years. In such arrangements, the state takes most of the risks while the private sector takes most of the profits (Harvey 2005: 77). Alongside this is the Private Finance Initiative (PFI), a specific form of PPP, which refers to a strictly defined legal contract for involving private companies in the construction and provision of major public sector infrastructure projects and associated services. Under PPP/PFIs, a capital project such as a school or a hospital is designed, built, financed and operated by a private sector company in possession of a contract that typically lasts 25–30 years. By the end of 2003, Northern Ireland had 31 PPP projects with an average worth of £11 million each; and now PPP is an option only for larger projects with a capital value of more than £20 million. Indeed, eight of the latest projects in procurement have an average value of £110 million each, the largest of which is £260 million for the construction of a hospital (Horgan 2006).

Building a better (shared) economic future?

Although inward foreign investment, urban regeneration and private–public finance partnerships have become particularly dominant modes of organizing economies in most western states, they have taken on a particular character in conflict transitional Northern Ireland. That is, these practices and policies have become the central plank of governance and its obligation to peace-building. This commitment was outlined in the devolved regional Northern Ireland power sharing Executive's 'Building a Better Future: Draft Programme for Government 2008–2011'. In this 'business friendly' document, the Northern Ireland Executive stated that:

> Growing the economy is our top priority. This is vital if we are to provide the wealth and resources required to build the peaceful, prosperous, fair and healthy society we all want to see. (OFMDFM 2007: 2)

As part of these aims, the Northern Ireland government has stated its desire 'to halve the private sector productivity gap with the UK average by 2015'; to secure 'inward investment commitments promising over 6,500 new jobs by 2011 … 70% of new FDI projects secured to locate within 10 miles of an area of economic disadvantage' (OFMDFM 2007).

Notably, at the same time that 'Building a Better Future' was being launched, a report previously commissioned by the Northern Ireland Executive government revealed 'Research into the Financial Cost of the Northern Ireland Divide' (Deloitte and Touche 2007). Comparing 'the extent to which the NI public expenditure allocation differs from that of comparable regions', the report concluded that Northern Ireland 'spends an additional £1.5 billion per annum on its public services'. The research argued that 'the costs of the deeply entrenched communal divide in NI are visible at all levels of society'. In particular:

> The divide has…led to duplication or even multiplication of service delivery for the communities as they live side by side but do not integrate or share easily. (Deloitte and Touche 2007: 6)

The main political parties in Northern Ireland, however, decided to eschew the conclusions of the 'Research into the Financial Cost of the Northern Ireland Divide'. In choosing to practically ignore or deride the results of the research, the auspices of 'Better Future' made it clear that economic growth precipitates the amelioration of a 'divided society' rather than the elimination of sectarianism and segregation as a prelude to prosperity.

New consensus or constructive ambiguity?

One of the most prominent aspects of 'Better Future' is the degree to which the main political parties, both nationalist and unionist, have embraced the principles of free-market economics as a remedy for a divided society. It is significant because the alignment between nationalist and unionist parties is exceedingly rare in a milieu where the parties' principal affiliations to their respective national identities ordinarily override the potential for cross-cleavage alliances. Indeed, an article in *Spiegel Online* in 2008 noted: 'both sides [unionists and nationalists] seem to be willing to put aside their differences, at least in the business sphere'. A Belfast business leader confirmed that 'the economy is the one area where we can build true consensus' (Capell 2008). A visible symbol of such consensus came with the joint appearance of the once warring factions of republicanism and unionism, now wiling partners in political power sharing, led by First Minister Ian Paisley and Deputy First Minister Martin McGuinness, to announce that US public investment was to be ploughed into Northern Ireland.

The further significance of the 'new consensus' on free-market economics is the presence of Sinn Féin. Sinn Féin's willingness to court US money was particularly notable because it represented a *volte-face* from its historical position when they told US supporters not to invest in what republicans considered 'a failed statelet' characterized by economic stagnation and ethnic disadvantage (McDonald 2008). Sinn

Féin's socialist ethos has indeed been subjected to severe maladaption. Sinn Féin's socioeconomic strategy from 1979 to 1986 was contained within the hybrid Christian and Socialist ethos of 'Eire Nua' ('New Ireland'), 'a broad outline based upon a 32-county agrarian economy within a federal structure' (Tonge 2006: 39). On one level, to create an 'Economic Resistance Movement', Sinn Féin instructed followers to 'buy Irish' (Sinn Féin 1979). On another level, militant republicans bombed businesses and financial districts across Northern Ireland to cripple the economy. In fact, the IRA even abducted and killed business leaders, including the English-born manager of a US-owned business in Derry (Adshead and Tonge 2009: 183). The logic underlying the economic war was that by seeking to incur upon the British state an exorbitant economic price on maintaining Northern Ireland they would be left with no option other than withdrawal.

Although Sinn Féin still labels itself as 'a left republican party', its relationship to the principles of inward foreign direct investment, lower corporate tax and PPPs range from approval to resigned *realpolitik*. While it has actively campaigned for lower corporate tax to stimulate inward foreign investment, its policy position on PPPs appears to be one of clear 'opposition' and proposes instead that 'it is Sinn Féin policy that the protective role of the state, in providing public services of a high quality, must be restored and expanded for the good of all residents of the island of Ireland' (Sinn Féin 2008). However, in Northern Ireland Assembly debates, a Sinn Féin politician stated: '[Sinn Féin is] not in favour of either the PFI or the PPP approach to provision of public-sector facilities, but we are faced with economic realities... We are faced with a future that contains PFI and PPP arrangements, but we must ensure that they are properly managed' (O'Dowd 2008). Sinn Féin ministers in the Executive have supported PFI projects in education, regional development and health. Sinn Féin's growing acceptance of the 'realities' of the free-market has provided fuel for unionist opponents to claim that they 'can detect a nascent conversion to Thatcherite principles' (Weir 2007), and that 'once, republicans were committed to bombing businesses and stopping economic growth in the Province; now, it is hoped that they are committed to building economic growth' (Moutray 2007).

In the context of a deeply divided society like Northern Ireland neo-liberalism might be viewed as particularly propitious. As we noted in Chapter 2, without the glue of a shared pan-ethnic identity to sustain society-wide economic redistribution, divided societies are noted for low economic growth and poor public services. Promoting free-market solutions, therefore, removes the problem of an overburdened welfare state in which public goods are multiplied for the respective groups. This also helps with conflict management in so far as conflicts over distributive issues, with their potential to exacerbate ethnic divisions, are limited. In a corollary, the smooth performance of neoliberalism requires that individuals do not associate with organizations which stymie the progress of capital accumulation. Ethnic groups competing for their share of public resources therefore provide an unnecessary restriction on the freedom of possessive individualism. Such a perspective was essentially outlined by Michael Bloomberg, the mayor of New York City, who stated when he visited Belfast that 'in the interests of peace and prosperity' the 'visible signs of segregation and sectarianism needed to be dismantled...the sooner the physical barriers come down too – the sooner the floodgates of private investment will open (*International Herald Tribune* 8 May 2008).

A vigorous round of privatization and market competition would also potentially reduce the fear that the state favours one group over the other. This is particularly the case in 'ethnocratic regimes', where there is a 'conspicuous ethnic logic of capital, which tends to stratify groups through uneven processes of capital mobility, immigration and economic globalization' (Yiftachel and Ghanem 2004: 650). In order to disproportionately distribute resources to one group at the expense of the other, rigid forms of socioeconomic stratification are maintained, despite countervailing market forces. Characteristically, the ethnocratic state promotes mechanisms that include:

the cultural division of labor...the flow of international and domestic capital, which tends to favor the more educated groups, the uneven pattern of urban and industrial development, the typically skewed distribution of governmental assistance and incentives. (Yiftachel and Ghanem 2004: 655)

Since the power of neoliberalism usurps the authority of the state, and it promises to deliver equality of opportunity, it might be proposed that the free-market is greater qualified to facilitate social equality than the British state, which has been accused of historically favouring unionists. Certainly, one of the accusations made by nationalists is that the state economically privileged unionists, with most of the key industrial jobs (such as engineering and shipbuilding) reserved for them and concentrated in unionist heartlands (Farrell 1976). Similarly, the same allegation has been applied to the allocation of public services, like executive level civil service jobs and the location of universities (see

O'Hearn 2008). A recent report by the Portland Trust (2007: 13) has gone as far to argue that the public sector in Northern Ireland increased the 'persistence of violence', because 'when narrowly directed by partisan administrators to their own constituents, it entrenched division and became yet another point of grievance'.

In a slightly different way, McGarry and O'Leary (1995: 295–96) concluded that Northern Ireland's economic reliance on the British tax payers' subvention and the dominance of the public sector in employment ensured that the region's middle classes were quarantined from carrying the costs of the conflict, and may have even have benefited from it. This provided a disincentive for public sector professionals to contribute towards reaching a comprehensive peace settlement. If this class was forced to shoulder the economic burden of the conflict, they would be more favourably disposed to pursuing peace.

It would be mistaken, however, to view contemporary cross-cleavage concord on the virtues of the free-market as representing a radical departure from the traditional rhetoric of 'consolidation' or 'transition' articulated respectively by nationalism and unionism. As with the logic of constructive ambiguity discussed in Chapter 2, nationalists and unionists articulate incongruous interpretations of what neoliberalism represents.

For unionism, inward foreign investment represents an opportunity to create wealth, to foster a picture of economic success, normalization and therefore the best *modus operandi* for *consolidating* the UK union. For nationalists, alternatively, like Sinn Féin, the same process is read as promulgating a *transition* to a united Ireland by extending all-Ireland economic cooperation and eliding inequalities experienced by nationalists which originate from the fiscal mismanagement of Northern Ireland by the British state. For instance, when in 2008 Gerry Adams, President of Sinn Féin, welcomed the announcement of a major investment of New York's pension fund into the north's infrastructure, he commented: 'Sinn Fein's endeavours to secure inward investment are geared towards improving the economic condition of those who have been disadvantaged by patterns of historic discrimination' (*Irish Independent* 12 April 2008). Also, Sinn Féin's campaign for the harmonization of corporate tax rates across the whole of Ireland is framed as providing a rationale for an all-Ireland political system. For them, the cost of duplicating services, outlined in the 'Research into the Financial Cost of the Northern Ireland', is caused by the partition of Ireland: 'partition is wasteful and inefficient and duplicates government and public-service structures; it imposes an unnecessary administrative burden on those wishing to do business in both jurisdictions' (McCann 2008). For unionists, on the other hand, a lower corporation tax to stimulate inward foreign investment provides an opportunity to regenerate Northern Ireland's economy after decades of paramilitary violence. Similarly, although both republicans and unionists both support urban regeneration schemes to promote tourism, discrepant readings are proffered as to how Belfast should be packaged for tourists. While republicans argue that there is a niche for 'political tourism' because 'more visitors would rather see attractions that relate to the Troubles than those that relate to the Titanic Quarter' (Maskey 2008), unionists decry this 'terror tourism' replete with imagery of 'bombs blowing people to bits and destroying our towns and cities and of the numerous murders and shootings…Northern Ireland needs a positive image' (McCree 2008).

Lessons from Northern Ireland

Despite discrepant ethno-national readings being proffered about neoliberalism, on a broader scale is there any scope for arguing that the free-market has the potential to ameliorate endemic patterns of ethnonational segregation, sectarianism, poverty and social exclusion which underpin violence? Moreover, can inward foreign investment and economic growth provide opportunities for shared non-sectarian identities to eventually take root in opposition to the destructive antagonism of competing ethno-nationalisms?

As mentioned earlier, on a global scale some theorists argue that neoliberalism is fundamentally undermining and rescaling the basis upon which national citizenship is constructed (Purcell 2003). Such is the influence of neoliberalism, it is said citizenship is undergoing a process of reorientation to ensure that the nation is no longer the primary community which defines political identity and political loyalty. Stripped loose from their one symbiotic relationship with the nation state, cities and devolved regions are increasingly important functional hubs in the world's economic geography. Citizenship is being re-territorialized such that the nation state's territorial sovereignty has been thrown open to question and contestation.

Taking this view, Purcell (2003) argues that the rescaling of the nation state due to neoliberalism should be seen as providing potential to furnish new conceptions of identity unfettered by its subordination to the nation state. For Purcell, the re-territorializing of state power not only challenges national sovereignty but it also allows new progressive and multiple forms of post-national citizenship, including a greater focus on human rights and other transnational notions of rights and responsibilities (2003: 565). Political issues, like the economy, migration and environment, rather than restricted to the domain of the local, must profoundly link with the transnational level, which requires activists to 'think globally, act locally'. Certainly, the combination of local and global scales of economic production has led some theorists to speak of processes of 'glocalisation' (Swyngedouw 1996), as the old model of economic activity coordinated and contained at national state scale is deteriorating. As Smith concedes: 'in strictly economic terms, the power of most states organized at the national scale is eroding' (Smith 2002: 433).

Some sources have argued that the benefits of being linked to the global free-market provide a distinct palliative to the problem of 'ancient' ethno-national hostilities. A report by the Portland Trust (2007), which hopes to fruitfully export to the Middle East the lessons gained from the Northern Ireland peace process, argues that 'the overarching economic lesson from Northern Ireland is this: economic progress is crucial to the political forces that favour peace' (2007: 4). For them, private sector growth supported by substantial foreign direct investment, from the US in particular, has been a key driver of peace in the region (2007: 5). The report continues:

> The importance of economics in conflict resolution is that it sets aside the question of motive, of grievance, of historical rights and wrongs, and focuses instead on the question of economic opportunity: what conditions – economic conditions in particular – have made the conflict possible? For if these conditions can be removed, progress to end the conflict might be made, just as surely as if the motives had been removed. (Portland Trust 2007: 5)

Rather than defining the conflict in terms of competing ethno-national aspirations, the Portland Trust (2007: 7) argue that 'Economic disparity between Catholics and Protestants was a principal aggravating factor in touching off and sustaining violence in Northern Ireland'. By highlighting the economy as the major impetus for improving community relations, by closing the differential between Catholics and Protestants, thereby increasing the prospects for integration, the report portrays economic progress as a 'moral, rational and political project in which material prosperity will overwrite tribal allegiances' (Murtagh 2008: 4). There is some basis for this argument. Increasing prosperity can bring about so-called post-material values within society. The creation of wealth reduces material values based on a hierarchy of needs, including religion and nationalism, and instead instils post-material values rooted in secularism and cosmopolitanism.

In another analysis, the expansion of global capitalism is the variable which explains why some societies are peaceful and successful and why others are riven by conflict and murder:

> Show me where globalization is thick with network connectivity, financial transactions, liberal media flows, and collective security, and I will show you regions featuring stable governments, rising standards of living, and more deaths by suicide than murder…But show me where globalization is thinning or just plain absent, and I will show you regions plagued by politically repressive regimes, widespread poverty and disease, routine mass murder, and – most important – the chronic conflicts that incubate the next generation of global terrorists. (Barnett 2003)

In a corollary, conflict management has been promoted by many international organizations as involving the peaceful integration of conflict regions into free-market capitalism, including supporting indigenous free-market entrepreneurs to produce wealth, thereby reducing the polarizing strategies of ethno-national entrepreneurs. For instance, the CPA in Iraq invested $20 million for 'catch-up business training' to 'develop and train a cadre of entrepreneurs in business fundamentals and concepts that were missing in the former Iraqi regime' (cited in Chandrasekaran 2007: 170). Here, the World Bank, International Monetary Fund and international businesses often play significant roles in shaping peacemaking and post-conflict reconstruction programmes (Mac Ginty 2009: 693). If advocates of neoliberalism argue that state-controlled foreign aid perpetuates a culture of dependency, resource conflict and endemic poverty in war-torn areas, then opening up such societies to the opportunities afforded by the global free-market can allow individuals to pursue their own goals free from the binds of communal affiliation. Such a perspective was outlined by one British politician who served in Northern Ireland. He claimed that an ethno-national leader in Belfast resisted 'economic growth' since 'he would lose control of his community…if people had jobs they would become independent' (cited in Bean 2008: 24).

Yet such a benign representation of globalism as a palliative for ethnic conflict obscures its nostrums. Many of today's conflicts are 'wars of globalization', in which a 'backlash against globalization provides the core organizing principle' (Kilcullen 2009: 8). Globalism has created a system of haves and haves-not, and, paradoxically, global media makes the have-nots increasingly aware of what they lack thus exacerbating localized anger and grievances. Globalism has also been identified as causing a cultural and political backlash against Western influences, especially when it is framed as corroding deeply held social, cultural and religious identities.

Moreover, rather than neoliberalism signalling the decline of the nation, the rhetoric of nationalism provides a key discourse which allows neoliberalism to deal with its internal contradictions. While neoliberalism promotes a concept of social relations which frees the individual from communal affiliations, the anarchy of unbridled competitive individualism can lead to a system of complete social breakdown and anomie. Such centrifugal forces need to be counterbalanced by centripetal motions. Harvey (2005: 85) argues that the 'neoliberal state needs nationalism of a certain sort to survive', since such sentiments can act as an 'antidote to the loss of former bonds of social solidarity'. States also mobilize nationalism to endow them an advantage in a competitive global market by making economic performance into something approximating a sporting competition (Harvey 2005).

Although it is not this chapter's intention to argue that neoliberalism is inherently bad, it is another thing to question whether current strategies are working in Northern Ireland regarding either engendering economic success or for transforming ethno-national division. First, it needs to be noted that rather than looking like a neoliberal success story, some commentators have unfavourably compared Northern Ireland's economy to 'the old communist regimes in eastern Europe' (Ruddock 2006). Public spending represents 63 per cent of the North's gross domestic product. Economic output is approximately 20 per cent below the British average; the level of economic inactivity stands at an unsustainable 26 per cent. Northern Ireland's fiscal deficit is around £7 billion, which is made up by a subvention from the Westminster Government. This is almost double the figure for Scotland, another devolved region. Northern Ireland continues to experience the lowest private sector productivity of the nine UK regions, to only 92.5 per cent of the UK average. The public sector still accounts for a significant proportion of employee jobs (31 per cent) and Northern Ireland has the lowest private sector wage of all UK regions (Hutchinson and Byrne 2007).

Moreover, there is little proof that neoliberal policies are particularly successful. For instance, PFIs and PPPs in Northern Ireland have largely proven to be poor value for money. PFI and PPP contracts have escalated in scale and cost, leading to an affordability gap that is met from other parts of the public sector and by reductions in services and capacity. PFI and PPP is accused of reducing standards of pay, conditions and employment prospects, representing a huge increase in the privatization of economic and social life, including the determination of public services by, in many instances, unaccountable commercial criteria, rather than social need. Equally problematic is the impact of inward foreign investment: the success of Transnational Corporations (TNC) in Northern Ireland, especially those based in 'knowledge-based manufacturing and services', is limited, with employment and investment falling in this sector (O'Hearn 2008). Invest Northern Ireland – the organization charged with generating FDI – has been branded a failure after only attracting 10 foreign firms to invest in Northern Ireland between 1999–2003 (Adshead and Tonge 2009: 189), and most FDI investment is in lower value added sectors such as shared services, retail and call centres. As of the time of writing (March 2010), none of the money promised by New York City's Emerald Fund has been invested in Northern Ireland after failed attempts to raise revenue. Nor is the North showing real signs of economic prosperity. Over 30 per cent of those aged between 16 and 60 lack paid work; 22 per cent of the workforce are low paid; nearly 25 per cent of households are unable to afford adequate home heating; nearly 100,000 children and 50,000 pensioners are living in income poverty; and there are 3000 premature deaths each year because of disadvantage and poverty (Hillyard et al. 2005, Horgan 2006).

The gentrification of 'murder mile' or lebensraum?

To explore further the role of 'economics in peacemaking', as the Portland Trust (2007) put it, the chapter provides some background information on how the private sector, especially FDI, was advanced as key players driving the peace process. From there, it looks at urban regeneration in Belfast, in both the city centre and outlying working-class districts historically most affected by segregation, violent conflict and poverty.

Since the late 1980s, economic growth and peace have come to be seen as mutually reinforcing. In this analysis, the stagnant Northern Irish economy, characterized not only by zero growth and a bloated public sector, but also by a marked difference between levels of Protestant and Catholic employment had to be addressed in order for peace to take root. To deal with this, in 1986, Britain and the Republic of Ireland established the International Fund for Ireland (IFI), aimed at promoting economic advancement in Northern Ireland. To date, the IFI has generated £383 million from foreign donors. As part of the strategy to make the private sector a major generator of peace, the idea of a peace dividend was encouraged. The first major ceasefire, in 1994, appeared to precipitate such a dividend. Tourism grew, unemployment lessened and over £30 million of new investment ventures were announced in its immediate aftermath. The private sector, furthermore, took a more vocal role in encouraging a peace settlement. Prior to the1998 Agreement, leading businesses formed the Group of 7 (G7), which was charged with advocating to the wider public the economic benefits of power sharing. At the same time, levels of FDI peaked in 1997, a year before the Agreement, by generating £530 million (Portland Trust 2007).

Another strand to the emphasis on growing the private sector was as part of counter-insurgency strategies. Reviewing the consequence of the IRA's bombing campaign against Belfast city centre as part of its economic war, the then Secretary of State for Northern Ireland, Richard Needham (1998: 166), claimed that 'by the early 1980s the city was in trauma'. Under the aegis of Needham a plan was engineered to commercially regenerate the city centre. Needham (1998: 1) summed up this approach as 'the third arm of the British government's strategy to resolve the Northern Ireland conflict … the economic and social war against violence'. The plan 'was to isolate the terrorists by proving it was they … in Belfast who were the villains, delaying progress and strangling investment' (1998: 167). Under the rubric of 'Making Belfast Work', a programme to build relationships between the state, business and the community sector, the state built private housing in the city centre in a professed attempt to lure 'yuppies' (1998: 167); they constructed a huge new shopping complex, 'Castlecourt' and commercially redeveloped Belfast's riverfront, the 'Laganside, in a model borrowed from London's Docklands and Boston's Waterfront. It was through these forms of regeneration that the state believed they would not only illuminate the 'terrorists' responsible for an economically moribund city, but that the creation of a commercially vibrant city centre would facilitate 'safe areas where both communities could mix and match' (1998: 168). By imagining the city centre as a shared space of consumption, the state hoped to 'build a shared sense of civic pride, security and enjoyment among people whose attitudes, shaped by separated experience, may well be mutually antagonistic … radiating a sense of citizenship outward to a divided population' (Hadaway 2001). Simply put, the logic was that if the state could present a picture of 'normality' the citizens of the city would willingly subscribe to this model and act accordingly.

In line with the 'Potemkin Village' – the construction of a façade which masks, but does little or nothing to tackle poverty and sectarianism – a number of anxious commentators (Neil 2004, Shirlow 2006, Shirlow and Murtagh 2006, Murtagh 2008) have critiqued the regeneration of the city centre as little more than putting 'lipstick on a gorilla', an 'ultimately cosmetic approach' which failed at a deeper level to engage with 'cultural and identity meanings' in a space which could be naively seen as neutral. (Neil 2004: 193). Indeed, 'having an interest in the city as a shopper...is not the same as an emotional stake where one's cultural identity is acknowledged under the common umbrella of citizen' (2004: 193). Moreover, while the regeneration of the city centre provides an image of a normalized, 'post-conflict city', the 'ever present reproduction of bigotry is a more enduring, if officially masked, understanding of the burdens that affect this place' (Shirlow 2006). As noted in Chapter 3, away from the confines of the city centre is a city which remains stratified in terms of ethno-national segregation and by socio-economic indicators.

The disparity between the city centre and outlying working-class 'sink estates' (Murtagh 2008) demonstrates that 'the fate of the city lies somewhere between the uniformity of corporate globalization and the continual balkanising of social and cultural life' (Shirlow 2006: 100). While commentators have sought to expose the 'veneer' (Shirlow 2006) of the city centre, by demonstrating the interdependent levels of segregation, violence and poverty which afflict working-class districts, little attention has been paid to emerging forms of urban regeneration which are beginning to permeate these districts. Murtagh (2008), for example, has looked at new mixed housing developments which have developed in the high-value end of the housing market, especially in the south of the city. Here, Murtagh (2008: 3) notes that processes of gentrification in middle-class south Belfast have the capacity 'to reduce the relevance of traditional binary identities' while producing 'new forms of segregation centred on tenure and class'. In other words, while gentrification in middle-class south Belfast attracts affluent Catholics and Protestants less tied to ethno-national identities, these 'neutral spaces' are characterized as forms of 'urban bubbling' (Murtagh 2008); they provide a sanctuary for people who share economic positions, and are happily segregated from those less affluent, irrespective of ethnicity.

While urban regeneration in Northern Ireland has largely been concentrated on the inner-city or disused industrial sites, which are now re-imagined as heritage sites and cultural quarters, it has now started to colonize outlying working-class districts. This is important. Currently, the two largest political parties in the Northern Ireland power sharing executive – the DUP and Sinn Féin – draw the bulk of their support from the working-class, particularly those who live in districts which experience the highest levels of poverty, immobility, sectarian violence and ethno-national segregation. These two parties are also the main drivers of the Northern Ireland Executive's new plan of action which promotes economic growth as the fundamental basis for sustainable peace. Their positive disposition towards urban regeneration cannot be viewed as an attempt to widen the gap between the middle- and working-classes, since this would threaten their electoral base. These political parties have prioritized economic growth because they assert it will fundamentally improve economic opportunities for their disadvantaged 'communities'. One particular place to assess the impact of urban regeneration strategies on outlying working-class districts of Belfast is with 'new urbanism', particularly that of gentrification as a global urban strategy.

Neil Smith (2002) describes how the gentrification of inner-city areas has moved from a rather discrete process to one in which ambitions for urban renaissance are globally hegemonic. Whereas private-market gentrification was once an almost 'serendipitous', unplanned process confined to a few of the largest urban centres, it is now scrupulously planned by corporate, government and corporate-governmental partnerships. As gentrification exhausts the inner-city, when land becomes overdeveloped or too expensive to regenerate, 'districts further out become caught in the momentum for gentrification' (Smith 2002: 442). Alongside attempts to regenerate the inner-city of Belfast, like the Titanic Quarter, gentrification has begun to permeate working-class nationalist and unionist districts outside of the city centre. An example of this 'outlying' gentrification can be witnessed in seemingly unexpected places, like the district of Ardoyne in north Belfast.

Located in Ardoyne is an old linen mill built in the nineteenth century called Brookfield. The mill closed in the 1960s, and soon after the outbreak of civil violence in Northern Ireland at the end of the 1960s the mill was requisitioned by the British army to act as a base. For many local nationalists in Ardoyne the old mill contained two different narratives. On the one hand, the mill represented the local community's traditional identification with industrial labour; indeed, Ardoyne was built in response to the need to provide labour for the mill. On the other hand, the mill reflected nationalist Ardoyne's experience during the Troubles; in particular, locals viewed the mill as a place where British army detained and tortured nationalists (communication with authors). Notably, also, Ardoyne was located at the centre of the conflict in Northern Ireland. Situated in what is gruesomely known to locals as 'murder mile', Ardoyne and neighbouring areas hosted a disproportionate number of deaths during the conflict (Shirlow and Murtagh 2006). It is also a deeply segregated area. Typical of north Belfast – often described as a patchwork quilt of nationalist and unionist districts lying uneasily side by side – there are a number of 'peace walls' which separate the two groups. Ardoyne is also assessed by all socioeconomic indicators to be one of the poorest districts in Northern Ireland.

The spread of neo-gentrification to Ardoyne reveals the zero-sum and inherently fractious basis of an uneasy peace. For instance, some proposed redevelopments in Ardoyne and other parts of Belfast have caused animosity, especially when the developments are located near or at so-called interfaces. Claims by one community to land for regeneration are seen by the other as attempts at territorial expansionism at their expense.

An example of this was a plan to develop the Brookfield Mill in Ardoyne. Plans for the proposed development in 2006 included converting the mill into 170 modern apartments plus a row of shops. The plans for the modern apartments were extensive and they were branded as 'Manhattan style loft-living'. Due to rapid house price rises at that period, it was presumed, in line with similar developments in the area, that middle-class Catholics, mostly from outside the district, as well as investors would be interested in buying apartments. Another reason for these developments is a substantial housing shortage in some nationalist areas, especially north Belfast.

Although the mill is located at a relatively uninhabited edge of Ardoyne, it also borders the working-class unionist district of the Shankill. Nationalist politicians in the area claimed that the redevelopment offered a chance to relieve the demand for housing in the area. For local unionists politicians and 'community workers' the proposed development augured a concerted attempt by nationalists to encroach upon unionist territory. Indeed, one unionist politician, Nigel Dodds, viewed what he perceived to be nationalist expansionism in north Belfast as comparable to Hitler's ethnic cleansing policy of 'lebensraum' (*Irish News* 29 June 2000). In a meeting organized to block the proposed redevelopment in 2006, a local unionist politician, Nelson McCausland, stated: 'all nationalist areas are trying to bring back professionals in a bid to develop and expand their communities, basically this is part of a longer-term programme building up and expanding Ardoyne'. Another politician, Councillor Billy Patterson, argued: 'we have to hit back at this very disturbing proposal and stand side by side and fight this side by side'. A community worker noted: 'for years Protestants have stood idly by and let nationalists develop their areas, but if they put up a reasonable and logical fight and make things clear and concise there is no reason why this cannot be stopped' (see Emerson 2006). Notably, such zero-sum politics are not limited to unionists; there have been analogous objections articulated by nationalists to a proposed redevelopment in a unionist district in another part of north Belfast. Despite neo-urbanism migrating from the city centre and the more affluent parts of the city to working-class districts, which have historically bore the brunt of violence and segregation, this does not mean the process represents a break from how nationalists and unionists seek to maintain territory. Neo-urbanism thus becomes enmeshed in the politics of 'territoriality' (Sack 1986) described in Chapter 3.

Exposing the façade?

Notably, as the chapter has explored, there appears to be a consensus cutting across the ethno-national cleavage that the free-market can engender economic prosperity; some have even seen it as contributing towards sustainable peace (Portland Trust 2007). In opposition to this perspective, others have pointed to how the same processes provide a mask or a 'Potemkin Village' to obscure the poverty and sectarianism hidden behind. If the latter proposition holds water, to what extent have there been attempts to expose the 'mask'?

There was, for instance, some initial resistance to the advancement of PPPs in Northern Ireland. The original impetus for PPPs in Northern Ireland came from the UK treasury, who stressed that not all of the capital projects required to repair the infrastructural deficit in the region could be undertaken with public money (Horgan 2006). As such, the Northern Ireland government was forced to embrace neoliberal policies to generate revenue (O'Hearn 2008). Trade unions opposed PFI/PPPs by calling for an alternative which could keep affected workers in the public sector. There was even some political resistance to PPPs. From this, an interdepartmental working group was established in the Assembly and a report issued for consultation. The report advocated limited use of PFI/PPPs, with a social partnership approach which would involve trade unions and the voluntary sector in decisions about which projects should involve the private sector (Horgan 2006). There have also been some visible signs of disquiet with gentrification in north Belfast; a wall in the area bore graffiti stating: 'We need social housing, not yuppie housing', and as we saw in Chapter 6, some new murals in working-class districts demand 'regeneration and not gentrification'.

While there has been some degree of opposition to neoliberal policies in Northern Ireland, as we have seen, there is an uneasy consensus for such policies. One reason for this is because the Northern Ireland Executive is under immense strain to generate revenue streams, especially as the British Exchequer is promising to vastly reduce the subvention granted to the region. There is also an important historical aspect which may explain cross-community support for neoliberal policies: economic arguments have long been utilized by nationalists and unionists to try and persuade the other side the merits of their ethno-national projects. Economic arguments are therefore important means through which ethno-national entrepreneurs seek to recruit members of the opposing group as well as means to bolster their claims for self-determination.

For instance, as early as the late eighteenth century Irish republicans argued that a fundamental *raison d'être* of a united Ireland was to allow its citizens to engage in free trade. Inspired by the mercantilists largely responsible for the American War of Independence, the United Irishmen and women, who desired the unification of Irish of all creeds, outlined their core principles and rationale for a united Ireland:

That the weight of English influence in the Government of this country is so great as to require a cordial union among all the people of Ireland, to maintain that balance which is essential to the preservation of our liberties and the extension of our commerce. (Cited in McCann 2006)

Their desire to unite 'Irishmen of all persuasion' in common cause for Irish independence floundered when it ignited violent sectarian conflict (Bew 2007).

For unionists, alternatively, the process of fostering closer economic integration with the rest of the Union, thereby maintaining access to the global trade networks of the British Empire, served their interests best. Mobilizing to counter the movement for Irish Home Rule in the late nineteenth and early twentieth centuries, unionists argued that a prosperous, industrial city like Belfast was inextricably connected to the economic triangle containing the ports of Liverpool and Glasgow rather than Dublin and the rest of Ireland. They feared that any form of political independence for Ireland would dangerously harm their economic interests. In their Covenant of 1912, a document to express opposition to a devolved Irish parliament, the unionist leadership stated that 'Home Rule would be disastrous to the material well-being of Ulster' (cited in Kautt 1999: 127).

Rising economic standards have also been identified as conducive to persuading members of the rival ethno-national group to come to their senses. For instance, during the 1960s the liberal unionist government of Northern Ireland, headed by Prime Minister Terence O'Neill, hoped that their plan to modernize Northern Ireland's failing post-war economy could kick-start a consumer society and raise living standards across Northern Ireland. An appealing by-product of economic growth, the unionist government hoped, was that it would entice Catholics into accepting the benefits of the union. As McAllister (1979: 279) notes: 'O'Neill's message was that material values were worth more than non-material ones and that both religious groups could gain new benefits without undermining each other'. Unfortunately for O'Neill, his failed attempts at a Fordist-type rationalization of the economy inadvertently raised and then deflated Catholic expectations that pervasive inequalities would be addressed (Bew et al 2002); hard-line unionists, alternatively, feared that attempts at reformism would inevitably weaken local unionist hegemony. All of this conspired to provide more grist for the mill of ethno-national conflict and division as sectarian violence erupted in the late 1960s. Rather than melting, as O'Neill hoped, ethno-national boundaries solidified. After being forced to resign from the leadership of Northern Ireland, O'Neill infamously provided an excuse for his conciliatory actions towards Catholics:

> It is frightfully hard to explain to Protestants that if you give Roman Catholics a good job and a good house they will live like Protestants because they will see neighbours with cars and television sets; they will refuse to have eighteen children. (*Belfast Telegraph* 5 May 1969)

Another form of *integrationist* economics is often found in the logic of Irish nationalism. Again the premise is based upon the rationale that members of the opposing ethno-national group could be persuaded to jump ship and join their faction if they believed their material interests would be better served. This approach is subtly different, however, in that it often assumes that unionists are in fact really Irish nationalists and that it is only a form of false-consciousness manufactured by ethno-national entrepreneurs which prohibited them from grasping their true identity as Irish men and women. Nationalists argued that the partition of Ireland and the formation of Northern Ireland were ostensibly based upon sectarian head-counting to ensure that Northern Ireland preserved a two-thirds unionist majority. Economics, in the scenario of a divided society, was one strategy used by the unionist élites to consolidate their tenuous hold on power, nationalists pleaded. Nationalists argued that the core *modus operandi* of unionist élites to maintain hegemony was to make a 'traditional' appeal to sectarian privilege, to 'buy off' the Protestant working-class by ensuring that working-class Protestants, in theory, were led to believe that the pick of industrial jobs were reserved for them (see Farrell 1976). Economic arguments for a unified Ireland could thus be deployed to lift the scales from the eyes of unionists and help them see that their greatest concerns would primarily be secured as Irish men and women.

Problematically for Irish nationalists, the economic inducement for unionists to join a united Ireland were severely curtailed by the economic performance of the Irish Republic's economy, which was characterized by prolonged periods of chronic stagnation and recession resulting in successive huge waves of outward migration. In lieu of a persuasive economic motivation, nationalists were forced to use cultural or ideological arguments to attract unionists. These arguments included pointing out the shared culture and origins which existed between the two groups or by illuminating that the British state had fostered animosity among the groups to exercise *divide et imperia* (see McGarry and O'Leary 1995).

Since the mid-1990s, however, nationalists have been able to increasingly utilize economic arguments to support their claim for a united Ireland. A major factor underpinning this was the development of the 'Celtic Tiger', a phase of economic growth which has transformed the image of the Irish Republic from one of the poorest nations in the EU to one of the wealthiest in the western world and a model for a range of small countries in Europe. This growth has been fuelled by a range of factors, including low corporate tax rates to stimulate inward foreign investment, EU subsidies and an unfettered access to the export markets of the single union, and the Republic's decades long investment in higher education to provide a highly skilled and qualified workforce. The Republic's integration in the EU has also helped it reduce its reliance on the UK for trade.

Accordingly, Irish nationalist discourse has changed as nationalists employ an array of statistics to illuminate how the Celtic Tiger should convince unionists of joining a united Ireland. Gerry Adams, the leader of Sinn Féin, who once subscribed to the tenets of *Eire Nua*, has argued for the benefits of an all-Ireland Celtic Tiger to convince unionists of Irish independence:

> What price the Union now? When there used to be a shipbuilding industry and a linen industry there might have been some value in having a connection with the Union, when it was an empire. If there is a Celtic Tiger, why should it stop at the border? Why cannot it come into East Belfast? Is anyone telling me the loyalist people of East Belfast are not going to accept jobs and the economic dividends that would come out of the Celtic Tiger if there is a 32 County Celtic Tiger? (Sharrock 2007)

Conculsions: neoliberalism in an era of global recession

This chapter has examined a number of related issues. It has assessed the claim by a number of commentators that Northern Ireland has taken a neoliberal turn. In answer, the chapter has shown that rather than the complete 'rollout' of neoliberalism, it has developed in a hybrid form, partnered on the one hand by the over reliance of the North's economy on state subsidies, and on the other, by the dominance of ethno-national based politics and economic redistribution. The zero-sum debates regarding the development of the Brookfield Mill demonstrate that processes of neoliberalism – specifically neo-gentrification – are currently being readapted in line with ethno-national projects which involve resource competition and the politics of territoriality. Despite some optimism, even from the power sharing government, that an unfettered free-market could deliver sustainable peace and a 'Better Future', there is little sign that this process is transforming deep-rooted problems of poverty and segregated living which afflict the poorest districts of Northern Ireland or the nature of sectarian conflict. This should not be surprising given the long-term historical dynamics of social segregation which stretch back to the nineteenth century. Forms of social exclusion are also intensifying, which often results in chronic civil disturbances such as riots or overt manifestations of sectarianism, which in turn lead to a further strengthening of segregation. It is also noted that despite a growing consensus between nationalists and unionists that internal foreign direct investment and urban regeneration are to be welcomed, they submit mutually exclusive interpretations of whether these processes will either deliver a united Ireland or the ultimate consolidation of Northern Ireland's position in the UK. Moreover, the impact of the global financial downturn in 2008 – which has even been seen by some neoliberal supporters as the moment 'the dream of global free-market capitalism died' (Wolf 2008) – threatens the idea that Northern Ireland can, as politicians boast, become a 'PLC', an attractive option for multinational companies. Heralded as the symbol of Belfast's nascent conversion to a successful post-conflict society, Victoria Square, the huge shopping complex mentioned at the beginning of the chapter which opened in 2008 had within a year recorded a footfall of 2 million less than initial projections and the closure of some shopping units (BBC 2009c). Somewhat worryingly, moreover, despite the spectre of global recession, there appears little chance of the north's politicians questioning their commitment to wedding the economy to FDI; far from it, it is seen by some as a golden opportunity. The First Minister of the Northern Ireland Executive, Peter Robinson, has stated: 'the current financial climate presents Northern Ireland with an opportunity, because people are looking at reducing costs and at becoming leaner and more efficient'. Northern Ireland is thus imagined as an affordable investment opportunity governed by low wages relative to competitors.

Conclusion: The Narcissism of Minor Differences?

In some of his writings, Sigmund Freud (for example, 2004) argued that the smaller the real differences between two peoples, the larger it is bound to loom in their imagination, a phenomenon he called the 'narcissism of minor differences'. In fact, Freud noted, conflict often occurred between individuals and groups who appeared highly similar even to the point of being *doppelgangers* or identical twins. Freud, however, stopped short from arguing that the existence of close resemblances between groups was more likely to induce conflict compared to when a large physiological or cultural chasm was present. Nevertheless, the idea of the narcissism of minor differences has been resurrected in recent decades by commentators seeking to comprehend the seeming surfeit of ethnic conflicts which have emerged particularly since the collapse of the Berlin Wall in 1989. Many of these conflicts, as we noted at the beginning of Chapter 1, seem to be fought between groups who share so much and who often appear indistinguishable for outsiders.

For a number of commentators, it is the mimetic cultural similarity between groups which is responsible for the most vicious ethnic violence (Blok 1998, Harrison 2002, Ignatieff 1993, 1998, Volkan 1997). Ignatieff (1993: 244) continues this theme: 'nationalism is the most violent where the group you are defining yourself against most closely resembles you…hatred between brothers is more ferocious than hatred between strangers'. Similarly, Blok (1998: 33) argues 'the fiercest struggles often take place between individuals, groups, communities, that differ very little'. Blok (1998) goes as far as to argue that is precisely when hierarchies and differences between groups are threatened and biodegradable that interethnic conflict and violence are likely to occur. For example, extreme violence used by Hutu against Tutsi, according to Blok, results from a 'gradual dissolution of hierarchical interdependencies and the differences connected with them' (1998: 48).

What, then, can cause ethnic distinctions to melt? One reason identified for expediting a backlash of violent ethnic chauvinism is the homogenizing and disorientating forces of globalism:

Globalism scours away distinctions at the surface of identities and forces us back into an ever more assertive defence of inner differences – language, mentality, myth, and fantasy – that escape the surface scouring. As it brings us closer together, makes us all neighbours, destroys the old boundaries of identity marked out by the national or regional consumption styles, we react by clinging to the margins of difference that remain. (Ignatieff 1998: 58)

Contemporary social identity, states Blok, is therefore 'based on subtle distinctions that are emphasized, defended, and reinforced against what is closest because that is what poses the greatest threat' (1998: 48). Conversely, Blok continues, the presence of hierarchy and great differences helps facilitate lasting stability and peace.

Taking the logic of the narcissism of minor differences to its logical conclusion, it would appear that the idea of encouraging closely related ethnic groups to share or integrate more closely would not lead to greater peaceful coexistence but would instead ignite intense conflict. Conflict regulation, in this conspectus, would appear to work best when it helps groups maintain their differences, as opposing groups 'do not wish to acknowledge any degree of similarity, for that concession would diminish the distinctions between them' (Volkan 1997: 108). Such a perspective is often evoked by those (Caspersen 2004) who quote Robert Frost's (1914) line that 'good fences make good neighbours'. It also resonates with Schopenhauer's allegory of the frozen porcupines. In this fable, the porcupines, which huddled together for warmth on a bitterly cold day pricked one another and were forced to disperse. After a number of attempts to get closer, the porcupines discovered that a comfortable relationship involved maintaining a little distance from one another. The lesson is that it is only when we discover a moderate distance that life becomes tolerable; our mutual needs can be reasonably satisfied and, as far as possible, we can avoid pricking one another (Aughey 2002).

Are we to take it from this that the task of those involved in conflict regulation is not to bring together the porcupines of rival ethnic groups but to accept the salience of ethnic divisions in divided societies and accordingly ensure that each group is treated with equality? Does it mean that conflict regulators have to resign themselves to the existence of social segregation in almost all spheres of social life, such as separate housing, schools and political parties? We can begin to answer this by addressing Blok's argument that the diminishment of hierarchies and distinctions between groups is a causal variable of horrific violence. This is not so. The argument is somewhat ahistorical, profoundly culturalist; it essentializes differences and removes the instrumental and material bases of ethno-national conflict from the picture. The more similar or different groups and their cultures appear is not in itself a *casus belli*. As we have continually stressed, when groups have incompatible claims to territory and resources, and relationships exist in a structure of inequality, then ethnic differences can be made salient and made to interact with wider political processes.

On a different level, the narcissism of minor differences thesis has a further paradox which supports the idea that conflict can occur when differences are put under erasure. This paradox stems from the realization that it is not just the case that groups wish to preserve their differences in order to maintain their sense of identity; it is also often true that rival ethnic groups hold narratives which claim that the other is the same as them. In this narrative, one or both groups believe that the other is in fact a lost relative which has unfortunately become separated or somehow distorted from recognizing their fraternal relationship with the other group. These ethno-national groups, especially, often possess deeply embedded narratives that their destiny is to assimilate the other group, to make them the same. For instance, in the context of the conflict in Ireland, nationalists often argue that unionists are really Irish people and they fail to see this because they have been manipulated by their élites to think otherwise. As Curtis (2007: 104) points out, nationalists have often believed that unionist élites 'divided the Protestants of Ulster from realizing they shared a common cultural heritage with their fellow Irish Nationalists'. Similarly, Serbs often argue that Bosnian Muslims and Catholic Croats who speak the štokavian dialect are really Serbs and therefore 'the most natural target for assimilation' (Banac 1994: 144). Groups often view many of their cultural and political identities as universal rather than particular and thus believe that sharing entails the rival group submitting to their will. This desire to assimilate other groups viewed as inherently similar does not suggest a more peaceful system to mitigate conflict between ethno-national groups; such assimilative strategies can typically result in strong forms of resistance from those earmarked for assimilation and an even further hardening of boundaries.

In this way, it seems fair to say that conflict often occurs when one group tries to obliterate the differences of the other group through attempts at assimilation. This may point to the fact that while it is probably important to allow groups the right to maintain their distinctions for fear of getting too close, the markers of difference do not have to be the focus of antagonism, nor should differences justify the claim that the groups should be left alone in their own autonomous living spaces. What matters is not the presence of ethnic differences militating against sharing; these are sometimes arbitrary, they can also change and are often de-emphasized as markers of social relations. What does matter is the extent to which superordinate goals can be constituted within divided societies so that social segregation is lessened and the multiplication of public services is diminished.

Conflict regulators often approach this issue from the wrong direction. As Stansfield (2006) notes in regards to the attitudes of both the US government and many western academics in the run-up to the war in Iraq: a primary error 'was the implicit belief that most people in the world are post-ethnic individualists... The continuing hold of ethnic and sectarian allegiances was underestimated'. Such assumptions often lead to nostrums that a shared identity and society can be achieved by creating centripetal institutions and even cultural forms which disavow the salience of ethnic affiliation. As we have continually stressed throughout this book: it is highly unlikely that ethnic groups in divided societies will abandon their identities or surrender their national goals for new shared ones. Despite the fact that ethnic identities are often constructed does not equate to a situation where they can just as easily be deconstructed. Peace-builders probably have to take with utmost seriousness the continuing existence of divisions and the fact they cannot be easily wished away – at least for the short-to-medium term. These identities are rarely completed ameliorated by economic redistributive policies or by integrationist institutions which seek to relegate them wholly to the private sphere. The point is not to try and make individuals into what we want them to be – cosmopolitan subjects holding plural non-ethnic identities – but to allow them to flourish without advancing identities which are antagonistic and constitutive of violence.

However, this starting point is not as terminally bleak as it seemed at first glance. Recognizing and working with divisions can provide a scenario in which hostile expressions of difference, which give rise to violence, can be harmlessly defused. When group identities are at their most secure they can be made more benign; in counterpoint, when they are threatened, as Blok (1998) and others reiterate, they can often be the focus for the most virulent strains of ethnic chauvinism. Security can be characterized in terms of groups having their national identities officially recognized in the public sphere of the polity, both through the exercise of power sharing as well as in symbolic cultural expressions. Security also occurs when groups begin to trust each other's intentions, allowing cooperation to thrive. Security is equally characterized by the presence of economic equality between groups. Although ethnonational conflict is often zero-sum in nature, based as it is on irreconcilable claims over the same territory, it is amenable to accommodation when purposeful institutions are designed to facilitate the recognition of national identities (O'Neill 2007). When exogenous actors play a supporting role to peace, rather than simply promoting irredentist policies, this further reinforces group security (Kerr 2006).

Critics may argue that this is a dangerous game. As Sartori (1997: 72) warns: 'if you reward divisions…you increase and eventually heighten divisions and divisiveness'. Academics can even pay lip service to group conflict by lazily reducing it to dichotomous ethnic differences when multiple factors and identities may be at play. A perfect example of the moral hazard arising from accommodating centrifugal forces can be seen in present day Bosnia where a decentralized political system has led to ethnic partition at all levels of the state, allowing ethnic extremists to thrive and the threat of war to return (McMahon and Western 2009).

We naturally do not wish to promote such a state of affairs. It is unrealistic that under conditions of contemporary globalism to believe that groups can be siphoned off into their own autonomous silos bereft of any contact (Bose 2007). In many divided societies the groups live by cheek by jowl in the same villages, towns and cities, and there are also always a proportion of citizens who simply do not wish to be pigeonholed by a singular conception of communal identity. A benign apartheid is therefore an impracticable solution. In places like Northern Ireland, Aughey (2009) states, 'a failed incivility can become a tentative civility such that even if people may not choose to live together they are compelled to live together'.

This means that while it is correct that groups should be endowed with strong rights to protect their national identities, a counterbalancing motion needs to be applied to ensure that the polity makes decisions made on the basis of the common good and not in support of particularized interests. This may mean, for instance, when it comes to governance, group based vetoes should be limited where practical and more emphasis placed on mechanisms to facilitate collective decisions by government. Similarly, the idea that public services should be multiplied to ensure that groups have one of each when this is not cost-effective should be eschewed. It is also important that, as far as possible, liberal values are encouraged so that individuals are not wholly constrained by the communal behemoth they are perceived as belonging to. Individual citizens should be allowed to freely vote for parties which belong outside of their ethnic bloc.

However, these preferences are purely normative and may not be a reasonable match with the specific exigencies of many divided societies. These divided societies have often been blighted by a protracted violent conflict or even a civil war. In order for groups to abandon their militaristic objectives a *quid pro quo* system of rights is required that guarantees their permanent place in government. In divided societies like Bosnia, Cyprus and Lebanon, liberal democratic values are sometimes eschewed for the sake of accommodating so-called warring groups. Citizens may have to vote from an ethnically based electoral roll rather than from a common roll and the élite political representatives of each bloc may be reserved positions and resources proportional to their numbers in public life. While it is best that groups, as we noted in Chapter 2, are self-determined rather than pre-determined, such ideal-type scenarios are not always realistically achievable. In fact, if it leads to the exclusion of minorities from power sharing it could lead to hardliners within the group opting to return to violent tactics. Indeed, peace agreements have a very uneven record, with 50 per cent of them failing within five years of their signing, returning the region to conflict. This all suggests that there is no identikit form or single palliative for dealing with the problems of a divided society and the specific circumstances of each place needs to be carefully addressed.

In this book, we have critically engaged with the concept of a shared society to replace one that has been violently divided by competing ethno-national aspirations. In order to facilitate sustainable peace a number of initiatives are often launched in such societies to promote the premise of a 'shared society'. A shared society can refer to mechanisms which allow both ethno-national groups to transcend various forms of segregation and divisive violent sectarianism to constitute a civic engagement based upon cross-community cooperation. Examples of schemes to promote a 'shared society' include the intensification of processes of democratization, including governmental power sharing mechanisms and modes of deliberative democracy, shared cross-community cultural initiatives, like festivals and symbols, the construction of shared spaces, and shared approaches to dealing with the past. There are other important factors which some analysts have identified as important in entrenching peace and creating shared identities. Some analysts have asked to what extent can economics – especially 'peace dividends', inward foreign investment and the wedding of divided regional economies to global forces – weaken the basis of ethno-national identities?

In this book, we have argued that it is unlikely that groups in divided societies will become post-ethnic and integrate to foster a shared identity in society. Ethnic divisions, though they may often be constructed, are not so easily reconstructed. While social identities are malleable and open to change, this is only within limits. When ethno-national groups do talk about integration with rival group, it is usually made to rhyme with assimilation. Centripetal institutions designed to encourage moderation and even integration rarely work and can even lead to the fortification of social divisions. Exogenous processes – such as the intensification of globalism, neoliberalism and the institutions of the EU – do not seem to provide the raw material to furnish a post-ethnic world. In the context of Northern Ireland, there may be some grounds for hope at a more localized endogenous scale, since there is some survey evidence of a growing appeal for a common regional identity. Nevertheless, this is only tentative since the demand for integrated education and integrated residential districts is as limited as the support for political parties which promote a shared regional identity. Neither is there a majority public will in Northern Ireland for shared forms to commemorate and deal with the past in order to engender a shared future. The promotion of acculturation – the creation of shared values – cannot be expected to end conflict either. Ethno-national groups, as McGarry and O'Leary (1995: 357) note, can maintain themselves in the face of increasing secularization and linguistic homogenization. We can remove the cultural markers which differentiate the groups only to find that they can (re)create shibboleths to retain ethno-national divisions. Perhaps the best hope, as Wilson notes (2009c), is that 'ethnic conflicts tend over time to burn themselves out, despite the efforts of ethno-political entrepreneurs to stoke the fires, as the quotidian concerns of ordinary citizens take over'. Notably the media called the 2007 elections in Northern Ireland 'lacklustre', a reflection of the fact that party political clashes were increasingly fought over bread-and-butter issues rather than those of the 'pork barrel' variety (see McEvoy 2008: 170, cf. Moloney 2008). This does not mean, however, that voters were any more likely to vote outside their communal blocs.

In this light, we have argued that although it is important to accept the reality of the strength of divisions in divided societies, and that it is a quixotic undertaking to try and redirect ethno-national identities; it is possible, though, to make them more benign and less threatening. The belligerent sharp edge of ethno-national identities, which are often used as instruments to expedite extreme violence, can be smoothened. Expressed through cultural practices, in particular, ethno-national identities can be reframed so as not to appear provocative to rival groups. While differences remain between groups, the antagonistic ways in which groups articulate ethno-national identities can be de-emphasized to even allow progressive relations between the groups to flourish. As part of this dynamic, it is important that there is mutual acknowledgement of the other's identities even if this does not mean there has to be agreement and consensus between the groups. Conflict remains, but it is channelled through democratic institutions and the public sphere of dialogue to ensure that peace prevails.

Notes

1. Enloe (2000: 142) also found that 34 per cent of all Sarajevo's marriages were multiethnic in 1990.
2. In a similar way, Fearon and Laitin (2000) note that groups can emphasize 'scripts' and narratives which become models for specific behaviours, including intergroup violence. For example, the Hutu reconstruction of the colonial myth of Tutsi foreignness creates scripts of proper or heroic action which invite young men to re-enact them in violent forms.
3. We wish to note that these three categories largely derive from the work of McGarry and O'Leary (2004, 2009).
4. In 2008, Sammy Wilson, a politician in Northern Ireland, stated that local workers in Northern Ireland should be given preference for jobs over migrant workers.
5. The Opsahl Report (Pollak 1993: 180–85) noted a number of submissions from individuals and groups calling for either an independent or autonomous Northern Irish state.
6. This 'civic unionist' argument has recently gained strong political backing with the partnership of the UUP and the Conservative Party. In a speech, the leader of the Conservative Party, David Cameron, called for a 'deep commitment to the union…built around shared belonging, shared past and a shared destiny' (Cameron 2008). Other examples of assimilationist thinking can be read in some of the submissions to the Opshal Report (see Pollak 1993: 187–95).
7. For instance, the Police Service of Northern Ireland (PSNI) has a 'positive discrimination' policy of recruiting 50 per cent of its officers from a Catholic background and 50 per cent from a non-Catholic background.
8. The Agreement is also often called the Belfast Agreement. However, for the sake of consistency, we will call it the Agreement.
9. Much of the proceeding analysis is taken from Clancy (2010).
10. These include: a small size, leaving the government with relatively fewer administrative and international relations burdens and possibly leaving domestic élites feeling more insecure about external threats and thus more inclined to cooperate; distinct cleavages, thus inviting fewer occasions for conflict; common external threats; overarching national loyalties; a history of élite accommodation; relative isolation of the segmented communities; socioeconomic equality; and a multiple balance of power between the segments (Lijphart 1977).
11. Strand Two of the Agreement makes provisions for North-South and all-Island institutions, such as the North-South Ministerial Council and other areas of common concern, like agriculture and tourism. Strand Three covers East-West institutions, especially the formation of the British-Irish Council.
12. 'The d'Hondt rule means that parties get the right to nominate Ministers according to their respective strength in seats' (O'Leary 1999: 71).

13. In an Executive formed through a voluntary power sharing coalition parties would be expected to create an agreed programme for government, based on collective responsibility, which it is hoped would encourage better cooperation among parties working for the common good rather than for communal interests.
14. In an attempt to defeat the IRA in 1971 the Northern Ireland government introduced a policy of internment to indefinitely detain suspected terrorists.
15. The 82nd anniversary of the signing of the Ulster League and Covenant.
16. However, it is difficult to determine adequately how far segregation is worsening because of major gaps in census data on religion from 1971 to 2001 (Anderson and Shuttleworth 1994: 76).
17. It is estimated that between August 1969 and February 1973 over 60,000 people in Belfast, 10 per cent of the city's population, were forced to move because of violence (Bew and Gillespie 1999: 18).
18. The residents of these interface districts are not only poorer than the rest of the citizenry, but also suffer greater ill-health and have less access to leisure facilities and other public services. It is also recorded that 90 per cent of killings during the Troubles occurred within 1000 metres of an interface (see Shirlow and Murtagh 2006: 81–100).
19. Remembrance Sunday and the Battle of the Somme Commemoration.
20. Unionists claimed that Sinn Féin made representations through the Anglo-Irish secretariat and that it was discussed by the Irish government in Dublin, who asked the British state to put pressure on the security forces to grant permission for the march (see Sullivan 1993: 6).
21. 'Tories' was a term for capitalists.
22. We are grateful to Aidan McGarry, who conducted this interview.
23. Catholic Bishops rejected the proposal on the basis that any change in the law would lead to the degeneration of public morality resulting in a situation in which the most vulnerable people in society – especially the young – would be endangered. A similar objection was raised by the Presbyterian Church in Ireland.
24. Dudgeon's complaint to the European Commission contained a number of strands, the most important of which was that the law making homosexual acts between consenting male adults criminal offences in Northern Ireland, and that the police investigation pursuant thereto constituted an interference with his right to respect for private live, in breach of Article 8 of the European Convention. The ECHR then declared Dudgeon's complaints admissible to the European Court of Human Rights, where it was lodged with the registry of the Court on 18 July 1980.
25. Including the Northern Irish Gay Rights Association, Lesbian Line, Gay and Lesbian Youth Northern Ireland, the Queer Space Project, the Coalition on Sexual Orientation and the Rainbow Project.
26. Especially unionist Orange Order and nationalist Easter Rising parades (see Chapter 6).
27. Gagnon (2004) uses the term 'demobilize' to describe how respective ethno-national leaders in the former Yugoslavia used coercion to render mute those forces who dissented against their violent nationalisms.
28. The street, the Garvaghy Road, became the site for one of the longest running parade disputes in Northern Ireland. The conflict is between the local

Orange Order, who wish to parade down the Garvaghy Road to their place of worship at Drumcree, and the nationalist residents, who wish to stop the march coming through their street (Bryan 2000).
29. The origins of the flag of St Patrick are disputed but it has variously been incorporated into both nationalist and unionist insignias and is therefore largely acceptable as a common symbol.
30. For instance, Conor Maskey, a nationalist organizer of the St Patrick's Day parade wrote to a newspaper to complain that 'Belfast City Council does not ban emblems or try to impose a dress code in other events they organise...They should not try to do so for next year's St Patrick's Day celebrations' (*Irish News* 10 November 2005).
31. In 2007, it was calculated that in Northern Ireland there were 2691 parades categorized as unionist, representing 70 per cent of all parades. During the same period, the number of nationalist parades was 203, representing 5 per cent of the overall total (Parades Commission 2008).
32. Particularly Pat Finucane, Rosemary Nelson, Billy Wright and the Bloody Sunday Tribunal.
33. The Consultative Group on the Past was co-chaired by Denis Bradley, who was vice chairman of the Policing Board, and former Archbishop of Armagh, The Right Reverend Lord Eames.
34. It is expected that about $80m will be used to finance projects in Northern Ireland which target energy, waste management, water, property and ports.

Bibliography

Addley, E. (2008) 'The New Divide', *The Guardian,* 12 April.

Adshead, M. and J. Tonge (2009) *Politics in Ireland: Convergence and Divergence in a Two-Polity Island* (Basingstoke: Palgrave Macmillan).

Alibhai-Brown, Y. (2000) *After Multiculturalism* (London: Foreign Policy Centre).

Allister, J. (2009) 'Allister Answers Alex Kane's Article', *TUV*, www.jimallister. org/default.asp?blogID=1768, date accessed 25 November 2009.

Almond, G.A. (1956) 'Comparative Political Studies', *Journal of Politics,* XVIII, 391–409.

Alonso, R. (2007) *The IRA and Armed Struggle* (London: Routledge).

Amin, A. and N. Thrift (2002) 'Guest Editorial: Cities and Ethnicities', *Ethnicities,* 2(3), 291–300.

Anderson-Gold, S. (2001) *Cosmopolitanism and Human Rights* (Aberystwyth: University of Wales).

Anderson, J. and I. Shuttleworth (1994) 'Sectarian Readings of Sectarianism: Interpreting the Northern Ireland Census', *The Irish Review,* 16(1), 74–93.

Andeweg, R.B. (2000) 'Consociational Democracy', *Annual Review of Political Science,* 3, 509–36.

Ashplant, T.G., G. Dawson and M. Roper (2000) 'The Politics of War Memory and Commemoration: Contexts, Structures and Dynamics', in T.G. Ashplant, G. Dawson and M. Roper (eds) *The Politics of War Memory and Commemoration* (London: Routledge), pp. 3–86.

Aughey, A. (1989) *Under Siege: Ulster Unionism and the Anglo-Irish Agreement* (London and New York: Hurst and Co.).

—— (2002) 'Three Fables of Britishness', unpublished manuscript.

—— (2005) *The Politics of Northern Ireland: Beyond the Belfast Agreement* (London: Routledge).

—— (2009) 'Wild Catastrophism to Mild Moderation in Northern Ireland', *openDemocracy,* http://opendemocracy.net/blog/ourkingdom-theme/arthur-aughey/2009/05/07/wild-catastrophism-to-mild-moderation-in-northern-ireland, date accessed 25 October 2009.

Bakhtin, M. (1998) 'Carnival and the Carnivalesque', in J. Storey (ed.) *Cultural Theory and Popular Culture: A Reader* (London: Prentice Hall), pp. 338–50.

Banac, I. (1994) 'Bosnian Muslims: From Religious Community to Socialist Nationhood and Post-Communist Statehood, 1918–1992', in M. Pinson (ed.) *The Muslims of Bosnia-Herzegovina* (Harvard, MA: Harvard University Press).

Barnett, T.P.M. (2003) 'The Pentagon's New Map: It Explains Why We're Going to War. And Why We'll Keep Going to War', *Esquire,* www.thomaspmbarnett. com/published/pentagonsnewmap.htm, date accessed 25 October 2009.

Barth, F. (1969) *Ethnic Groups and Boundaries: The Social Organization of Cultural Difference* (Oslo: Universitetsforlaget).

Barton, K.C. (2005) 'History and Identity in Pluralist Democracies: Reflections on Research in the U.S. and Northern Ireland', *Canadian Social Studies,*

39(2), http://www.quasar.ualberta.ca/css/Css_39_2/ARBarton_pluralist_democracies.htm

Barry, B. (2001) *Culture and Equality* (Cambridge: Polity).

Baumann, G. (1996) *Contesting Culture: Discourses of Identity in Multi-Ethnic London* (Cambridge: Cambridge University Press).

BBC (1995) *The Death of Yugoslavia*, TV Documentary Series.

—— (2002) 'Belfast's Divisions "Even Greater"', http://news.bbc.co.uk/1/hi/northern_ireland/1742276.stm, date accessed 25 October 2009.

—— (2007) 'Group to Deal with Troubled Past', http://news.bbc.co.uk/1/hi/northern_ireland/6229190.stm, date accessed 25 October 2009.

—— (2009a) 'Little Change from Stormont Rule', http://news.bbc.co.uk/1/hi/northern_ireland/northern_ireland_politics/8278584.stm, date accessed 25 October 2009.

—— (2009b) 'No Tory Police Funding Guarantee', http://news.bbc.co.uk/1/hi/northern_ireland/8257938.stm, date accessed 25 October 2009.

—— (2009c) 'Further Blow for Victoria Square', http://news.bbc.co.uk/1/hi/northern_ireland/8111478.stm, date accessed 25 October 2009.

Bean, K. (2008) *The New Politics of Sinn Féin* (Liverpool: Liverpool University Press).

Beat Initiative (2005) 'Flyer' (Belfast: Beat Initiative).

Belfast City Council (2004) 'Sharing Belfast's Public Space', *The Development Brief: Newsletter*, 22, 1–4.

—— (2005) *Your City: Your Space* (Belfast: Belfast City Council).

—— (2006) 'Belfast Marks Year of Celebrations with a City Hall Party', www.belfastcity.gov.uk/news/news.asp?id=686, date accessed 25 October 2009.

—— (2008a) 'Re-Imaging Communities Project', www.belfastcity.gov.uk/re-image/, date accessed 25 October 2009.

—— (2008b) 'Belfast Brand', www.belfastcity.gov.uk/brand/, date accessed 25 October 2009.

Belfast Newsletter (2009) 'Twisted Logic Flaws Report on Troubles', www.newsletter.co.uk/editorial/Twisted-logic-flaws-report-on.4925710.jp, date accessed 25 October 2009.

Bell, J.B. (1993) *The Irish Troubles: A Generation of Violence, 1967–92* (Dublin: Gill and MacMillan).

Bell, C. (2003) 'Dealing with the Past in Northern Ireland', *Fordham International Law Journal*, 26(4), 1095–147.

Belloni, R. (2008) 'Civil Society in War-to-Democracy Transitions', in A.K. Jarstad and T.D. Sisk (eds) *From War to Democracy: Dilemmas of Peacebuilding* (Cambridge: Cambridge University Press), pp. 182–210.

Benford, R. (1987) *Framing Activity, Meaning, and Social Movement Participation: The Nuclear Disarmament Movement*, PhD thesis (Austin: University of Texas).

Benford, R. and D. Snow (2000) 'Framing Processes and Social Movements: An Overview and Assessment', *Annual Review of Sociology*, 26, 611–39.

Benhabib, S. (2002) *The Claims of Culture* (Princeton, NJ: Princeton University Press).

Ben-Porat, G. (2006) *Global Liberalism, Local Populism: Peace and Conflict in Israel/Palestine and Northern Ireland* (Syracuse, NY: Syracuse University Press).

Bew, P. (2007) *Ireland: The Politics of Enmity 1789–2006* (Oxford: Oxford University Press).

Bew, P. and H. Patterson (1985) *The British State and the Ulster Crisis: From Wilson to Thatcher* (London: Verso).

Bew, P. and G. Gillespie (1999) *A Chronology of the Troubles, 1968–1999* (Dublin: Gill and Macmillian).

Bew, P., P. Gibbon and H. Patterson (2002) *Northern Ireland 1921/2001: Political Forces and Social Classes* (London: Serif).

Biggar, N. (2003) *Burying the Past: Making Peace and Doing Justice after Civil Conflict* (Georgetown, Washington DC: Georgetown University Press).

Blok, A. (1998) 'The Narcissism of Minor Differences', *European Journal of Social Theory*, 1(1), 33–56.

—— (2000) 'The Enigma of Senseless Violence', in G. Aijmer and J. Abbink (eds) *Meanings of Violence: A Cross Cultural Perspective* (Oxford: Berg), pp. 23–38.

Bloomfield, K. (1998) *We Will Remember Them: Report of the Northern Ireland Victims Commissioner* (Northern Ireland Office: Belfast).

Bose, S. (2007) *Contested Lands* (Harvard, MA: Harvard University Press).

Boyle, F. (1993) 'Nationalist City Centre March Looks Set for Approval', *Irish News*, 7 August.

Bourke, K. (2005) 'Gay Community to Stage Annual Parade', *Irish News*, 6 August.

Brass, P. (1991) *Ethnicity and Nationalism: Theory and Comparison* (London: Sage).

Breen, R. and B.C. Hayes (1996) 'Religious Mobility in the United Kingdom', *Journal of the Royal Statistical Society*, Series A 159, 493–504.

Breen, R. and P. Devine (1999) 'Segmentation and the Social Structure', in P. Mitchell and R. Wilford (eds) *Politics in Northern Ireland* (Boulder, CO: Westview Press), pp. 52–65.

Browne, D. (2003) *Irish Echo Online*, February, 7(6), 19–25.

Brubaker, R. (2002) 'Ethnicity Without Groups', *Archives Europeennes de Sociologie*, 43(2), 163–89.

Bryan, D. (2000) *Orange Parades: The Politics of Ritual, Tradition and Control* (London: Pluto).

Burton, F. (1978) *The Politics of Legitimacy: Struggles in a Belfast Community* (London: Routledge and Kegan Paul).

Buruma, I. (1999) 'The Joys and Perils of Victimhood', *New York Review of Books*, 8 April.

Byrne, S. (2000) 'Conflict and Group Identity: Lessons from Northern Ireland', *MCS: Conciliation Quarterly*, Winter, 6–8.

Cameron, D. (2008) 'A New Political Force in Northern Ireland', www.conserva-tives.com/News/Speeches/2008/12/David_Cameron_A_new_political_force_in_Northern_Ireland.aspx, date accessed 25 October 2009.

Campbell, J. and O. Pedersen (2001) *The Rise of Neoliberalism and Institutional Analysis* (Princeton, NJ and Oxford: Princeton University Press).

Capell, K. (2008) 'The New Celtic Tiger: Belfast is Open for Business,' *Spiegel Online*, www.spiegel.de/international/business/0,1518,563841,00.html, date accessed 25 October 2009.

Caspersen, N. (2004) 'Good Fences Make Good Neighbours? A Comparison of Conflict-Regulation Strategies in Postwar Bosnia', *Journal of Peace Research*, 41(5), 569–88.

Chandrasekaran, R. (2007) *Imperial Life in the Emerald City: Inside Baghdad's Green Zone* (London: Bloomsbury).

Chrisafis, C. (2005) 'Katrina "Sent by God to Punish Gays"', *The Guardian*, 19 November.

Cimet, A. (2002) 'Symbolic Violence and Language: Mexico and Its Uses of Symbols', in J.J. Climo, Jacob and M.G. Cattell (eds) *Social Memory and History: Anthropological Perspectives* (Walnut Creek, CA: Altamira), pp. 143–60.

Clancy, M.A.C. (2007) The United States and Post-Agreement Northern Ireland, 2001–6, *Irish Studies in International Affairs*, 18, 155–73.

—— (2010) *Peace without Consensus: Power Sharing Politics in Northern Ireland* (Farnham and Burlington VT: Ashgate Press).

Coalition Provisional Authority (2003) 'Order 39: Foreign Investment' (Baghdad: CPA).

Coakley, J. (2009a) 'Implementing Consociation in Northern Ireland', in R. Taylor (ed.) *Consociational Theory: McGarry and O'Leary and the Northern Ireland Conflict* (London: Routledge), pp. 122–43.

—— (2009b) 'The Political Consequences of the Electoral System in Northern Ireland', *Irish Political Studies*, 24(3), 253–84.

Cochrane, F. (2006) 'Two Cheers for the NGOs: Civil Society and the Good Friday Agreement', in M. Cox, A. Guelke and F. Stephen (eds) *A Farewell to Arms? From Long War to Long Peace in Northern Ireland* (Manchester: Manchester University Press), pp. 253–67.

Cohen, A.P. (1985) *The Symbolic Construction of Community* (London: Tavistock).

Cohen, S. (2007) 'Winning While Losing: The Apprentice Boys of Derry Walk their Beat', *Political Geography*, 26(8), 951–67.

Collin, M. (2007) *The Time of the Rebels: Youth Resistance Movements and 21st Century Revolutions* (London: Serpent's Tail).

Community Development Review Group (1991) *Community Development in Northern Ireland: A Perspective for the Nineties* (Belfast: Community Development Review Group).

Connerton, P. (1989) *How Societies Remember* (Cambridge: Cambridge University Press).

Connor, W. (1994) *Ethnonationalism: The Quest for Understanding* (Princeton, NJ: Princeton University Press).

Conrad, K. (2001) 'Queer Treasons: Homosexuality and Irish National Identity', *Cultural Studies*, 15(1), 124–37.

Consultative Group on the Past (2009) *The Report of the Consultative Group on the Past* (OFMDFM: Belfast).

Cornell, S. and D. Hartmann (1998) *Ethnicity and Race: Making Identities in a Changing World* (Thousand Oaks, CA: Pine Forge Press).

Coulter, C. and M. Murray (2009) 'Introduction', in C. Coulter and M. Murray (eds) *Northern Ireland after the Troubles: A Society in Transition* (Manchester: Manchester University Press), pp. 1–28.

Council of Europe (1995) *Framework Convention on the Protection of National Minorities* (Strasbourg: Council of Europe).

Cradden, T. (1994) 'The Trade Union Movement in Northern Ireland', in D. Nevin (ed.) *Trade Union Century* (Dublin: Mercier Press), pp. 66–84.

Cronin, M. and D. Adair (2002). *The Wearing of the Green: A History of St Patrick's Day* (London: Routledge).

Crossley, N. (2002) *Making Sense of Social Movements* (Buckingham: Open University Press).

Curtis, K. (2007) 'P.S. O'Hegarty and the Ulster Question', *Irish Political Studies*, 22(1), 103–20.

Darby, J. (1993) 'Submission to the Opsahl Inquiry', in A. Pollak (ed.) *A Citizens' Inquiry, The Opsahl Report on Northern Ireland* (Dublin: Lilliput Press), pp. 4–5.

Day, G. (2006) *Community and Everyday Life* (London: Routledge).

Della Porta, D. and M. Diani (2006) *Social Movements: An Introduction* (Oxford – Malden, MA: Blackwell).

Deloitte and Touche (2007) *Research into the Financial Cost of the Northern Ireland Divide* (Belfast: Deloitte and Touche).

Deng, F.M. (1995) *War of Visions: Conflict of Identities in the Sudan* (Washington, DC: Brookings Institution).

Diani, M. (2000) 'Simmel to Rokkan and Beyond: Elements for a Network Theory of (New) Social Movements', *European Journal of Social Theory*, 3(4), 387–406.

Dixon, P. (2002) 'Political Skills or Lying and Manipulation? The Choreography of the Northern Ireland Peace Process', *Political Studies*, 50(4), 725–41.

(2005) 'Why the Good Friday Agreement is not Consociationalism', *Political Quarterly*, 76(3), 357–67.

Donnan, H. and K. Simpson (2007) 'Silence and Violence among Northern Ireland Border Protestants', *Ethnos*, 72(1), 5–28.

Doss, E. (2002) 'Death, Art and Memory in the Public Sphere: The Visual and Material Culture of Grief in Contemporary America', *Mortality*, 7(1), 63–82.

Dryzek, J.S. (2005) 'Deliberative Democracy in Divided Societies: Alternatives to Agonism and Analgesia', *Political Theory*, 33(2), 218–42.

Dryzek, J. and P. Dunleavy (2009) *Theories of the Democratic State* (Basingstoke: Palgrave Macmillan).

Duffy, J. (2000) *Patrick: In His Own Words* (Dublin: Veritas).

DUP (2009) 'Sinn Fein Failing to Deliver a Shared Future', www.dup.org.uk/articles.asp?ArticleNewsID=1269, date accessed 25 October 2009

Edwards, M. (2004) *Civil Society* (London: Polity).

Emerson, N. (2006) 'One Thing Worse Than the "Devil You Know"', *Irish News*, 12 October.

—— (2009) 'SF in Identity Crisis that Dare not Speak its Name', *Irish News*, 15 October, www.irishnews.com/articles/540/606/2009/10/15/630117_39704743 2690SFiniden.htm, date accessed 25 October 2009.

Enloe, C. (2000) *Does Khaki Become You? The Militarization of Women's Lives* (London: Pandora Press).

EU (2007) *Regional Policy: United Kingdom, Ireland* (Brussels: European Union).

Evans, E.E. (2005) [1973] *The Personality of Ireland: Habitat, Heritage and History* (Cambridge: Cambridge University Press).

Farrell, M. (1976) *Northern Ireland: The Orange State* (London: Pluto).

Farry, S. (2009) 'Consociationalism and the Creation of a Shared Future for Northern Ireland', in R. Taylor (ed.) *Consociational Theory: McGarry and O'Leary and the Northern Ireland Conflict* (London: Routledge), pp. 165–79.

Fearon, D. and J. Laitin (1996) 'Explaining Interethnic Cooperation', *American Political Science Review*, 90(4), 715–35.

—— (2000) 'Violence and the Social Construction of Ethnic Identity', *International Organization*, 54(4), 845–77.

Feldman, A. (1991) *Formations of Violence: The Narrative of the Body and Political Terror in Northern Ireland* (Chicago, IL: University of Chicago).

Finlay, A. (2001) 'Defeatism and the Northern Protestant "Identity"', *The Global Review of Ethnopolitics*, 1(2), 3–20.

Finlay, A. (2006) 'Anthropology Misapplied? The Culture Concept and the Peace Process in Ireland', *Anthropology in Action*, 13(1–2), 1–10.

Forter, G. (2003) 'Against Melancholia: Contemporary Mourning Theory, Fitzgerald's *The Great Gatsby*, and the Politics of Unfinished Grief', *Differences*, 14(2), 1.

Foster, R.F. (1988) *Modern Ireland 1600–1972* (London: Allen Lane).

Fraser, N. (2000) 'Rethinking Recognition', *New Left Review*, 3, 107–20.

Freud, S. (2004) *Civilization and its Discontents*, revised edition (London Penguin).

Friedland, R. and R. Hecht (1998) 'The Bodies of Nations: A Comparative Study of Religious Violence in Jerusalem and Ayodhya', *History of Religions*, 38(2), 101–49.

Frost, R. (1914) 'Mending Wall', in *North of Boston*, http://www.gutenberg.org/etext/3026, date accessed 20 March 2010.

Fuller, C. and M. Geddes (2008) 'Urban Governance under Neoliberalism: New Labour and the Restructuring of State-Space', *Antipode*, 40(2), 252–82.

Gaffikin, F., M. McEldowney, G. Raffery and K. Sterrett (2008) *Public Space for a Shared Belfast* (Belfast: Belfast City Council).

Gagnon, V.P., Jr (2004) *The Myth of Ethnic War: Serbia and Croatia in the 1990s* (Ithaca, NY: Cornell University Press).

Garland, R. (2009) 'Monument to Tragedies of Past May Prevent Those of the Future', *Irish News*, 16 November.

Geertz, C. (1973) *The Interpretation of Cultures* (New York: Basic Books).

Gillis, J. (1994) 'Memory and Identity: The History of a Relationship', in J. Gillis (ed.) *Commemorations: The Politics of National Identity* (Princeton: Princeton University Press), pp. 3–27.

Glenny, M. (1992) *The Fall of Yugoslavia* (London: Penguin).

Globalise Resistance (2002) www.resist.org.uk/reports/archive/mayday/belfast.htm, date accessed 12 May 2007

—— (2007) 'What Globalise Resistance Stands For', www.resist.org.uk/?q=node/4, Date Accessed 25 October 2009.

Goldstock, R. (2004) *Organised Crime in Northern Ireland: A Report for the Secretary of State and Government Response* (Belfast: OFMDFM).

Gordon, D. (2010) 'United Ireland Poll: We Are Not at Peace with Ourselves', *Belfast Telegraph*, http://www.belfasttelegraph.co.uk/news/local-national/united-ireland-poll-we-are-not-at-peace-with-ourselves-14721125.html, date accessed 16 March 2010.

Gourevitch, P. (1998) *We Wish to Inform You That Tomorrow We Will Be Killed with Our Families: Stories from Rwanda* (New York: Picador).

Graham, B. and C. Nash (2006) 'A Shared Future: Territoriality, Pluralism and Public Policy in Northern Ireland', *Political Geography*, 25(3), 253–78.

Gray, P. and K. Oliver (2004) 'Introduction', in P. Gray and K. Oliver (eds) *The Memory of Catastrophe* (Manchester: Manchester University Press), pp. 1–18.

Gurr, T. (2000) *Peoples versus States: Minorities at Risk in the New Century* (Washington, DC: United States Institute of Peace).

Haagerup, N.J. (1984) 'Report Drawn up on Behalf of the Political Affairs Committee on the Situation in Northern Ireland', *European Parliament Working Document*, 1–1526/83, Strasbourg.

Habermas, J. (1988) *Theory and Practice* (Boston, MA: Beacon).

Habyarimana, J., M. Humphreys, D. Posner and J. Weinstein (2008) 'Better Institutions, Not Partition', *Foreign Affairs*, 87(4), 138–41.

Hadaway, P. (2001) 'Cohesion in Contested Spaces', *Architects Journal*, November, 38–40.

Hall, S. (2000) 'Conclusion: The Multi-Cultural Question', in B. Hesse (ed.) *Un/settled Multiculturalisms: Diasporas, Entanglements, Transruptions* (Zed Books: London), pp. 209–41.

—— (2002) 'Political Belonging in a World of Multiple Identities', in S. Vertovec and R. Cohen (eds) *Conceiving Cosmopolitanism: Theory, Context, and Practice* (Oxford: Oxford University Press), pp. 25–31.

Hall, M. (2007) *Is There a Shared Ulster Heritage* (Belfast: Ireland Publications).

Halpern, S. (1986) 'The Disorderly Universe of Consociational Democracy', *West European Politics*, 9(2), 181–97.

Hamber, B. (2001) 'Healing Through Remembering? The Search for Truth and Justice', *Scope: Social Affairs Magazine*, www.brandonhamber.com/publications/art_scope.htm, date accessed 25 October 2009.

—— (2006a) 'Narrowing the Micro and the Macro: A Psychological Perspective on Reparations in Societies in Transition', in P. DeGreiff (ed.) *The Handbook of Reparations* (Oxford: Oxford University Press), pp. 560–88.

—— (2006b) 'Flying Flags of Fear: The Role of Fear in the Process of Political Transition', *Journal of Human Rights*, 5(1), 127–42.

Hamber, B. and R.A. Wilson (2002) 'Symbolic Closure Through Memory, Reparation and Revenge in Post-Conflict Societies', *Journal of Human Rights*, 1(1), 35–53.

Hammel, E. (1997) 'Ethnicity and Politics: Yugoslav Lessons for Home', *Anthropology Today*, 13(3), 5–9.

Harrison, S. (2002) 'The Politics of Resemblance: Ethnicity, Trademarks, Head-Hunting', *The Journal of the Royal Anthropological Institute*, 8(2), 211–32.

Harvey, D. (1988) 'Voodoo Cities', *New Statesman and Society*, 1, 30 September, 33–35.

—— (2003) 'The Right to the City', *International Journal of Urban and Regional Research*, 27(4), 939–41.

Harvey, D. (2005) '*A Breif History of Neoliberalism*' (Oxford: Oxford University Press).

Hass, K. (1998) *Carried to the Wall: American Memory and the Vietnam Veterans Memorial* (Berkeley, CA: University of California).

Hayden, T. (1999) 'Foreword', in M. O'Muilleoir (ed.) *Belfast's Dome of Delight: City Hall Politics, 1981–2000* (Belfast: Beyond the Pale), pp. i–ix.

Hayes, B., I. McAllister and L. Dowds (2007) 'Integrated Education, Intergroup Relations, and Political Identities in Northern Ireland', *Social Problems*, 54(4), 454–82.

Hayes, M. (1972) *Community Relations and the Role of the Community Relations Commission in Northern Ireland* (Belfast: Runnymede Trust).

Hayward, K. (2006) 'Reiterating National Identities: The European Union Conception of Conflict Resolution in Northern Ireland', *Cooperation and Conflict* 41(3), 261–84.

Healing through Remembering (2000) *All Truth is Bitter* (Belfast: Healing Through Remembering).

—— (2007)'Living Memorial Museum–Overview',http://healingthroughremembering.info/index.php/living_memorial_museum/, date accessed 25 October 2007.

Healing through Remembering (2008) *Submission to Consultative Group on the Past* (Belfast: Healing through Remembering).

Heaney, S. (1995) 'Crediting Poetry', in T. Frängsmyr (ed.) *The Nobel Prizes 1995* (Stockholm: Nobel Foundation).

Hechter, M. (1992) 'The Dynamics of Secession', *Acta Sociologica*, 35(4), 267–83.

—— (2000) *Containing Nationalism* (Oxford: Oxford University Press).

Held, D. (1995) *Democracy and the Global Order: From the Modern State to Cosmopolitan Governance* (Cambridge: Polity).

—— (2002) 'Culture and Political Community: National, Global, and Cosmopolitan', in S. Vertovec and R. Cohen (eds) *Conceiving Cosmopolitanism: Theory, Context, and Practice* (Oxford: Oxford University Press), pp. 48–60.

Hetherington, K. (1998) *Expressions of Identity: Space, Performance and Politics* (London: Sage).

Hewitt, V. (2007) 'Differential Corporation Tax in Northern Ireland: Analysis and Policy', *Northern Ireland Economic Bulletin*, 11(4), 36–43.

Higson, R. (2008) 'Anti-Consociationalism and the Good Friday Agreement: A Rejoinder', *Journal of Peace, Conflict and Development*, 12, May, 1–17.

Hillyard, P., W. Rolston and M. Tomlinson (2005) *Poverty and Conflict: The International Evidence* (Dublin: Combat Poverty Agency/Institute of Public Administration).

Hodgett, S. and D. Johnson (2001) 'Troubles, Partnerships and Possibilities: A Study of the Making Belfast Work Development Initiative in Northern Ireland', *Public Administration and Development*, 21(4), 321–32.

Horgan, G. (2006) 'Devolution, Direct Rule and Neoliberal Reconstruction in Northern Ireland', *Critical Social Policy*, 26(3), 656–68.

—— (2007) 'Northern Ireland: The Privatisation of Peace', *International Socialism*, 114–15.

Horowitz, D. (2000a) 'Constitutional Design: An Oxymoron?' in I. Shapiro and S. Macedo (eds) *Designing Democratic Institutions* (New York: New York University Press), pp. 253–84.

—— (2000b) *Ethnic Groups in Conflict* (Berkeley, CA: University of California Press).

—— (2001) 'The Northern Ireland Agreement: Clear, Consociational, and Risky', in J. McGarry (ed.), *Northern Ireland and the Divided World: Post-Agreement Northern Ireland in Comparative Perspective* (Oxford: Oxford University Press), pp. 89–108.

—— (2002) 'The Primordialists', in D. Conversi (ed.) *Ethnonationalism in the Contemporary World: Walker Connor and the Theory of Nationalism* (London: Routledge), pp. 72–82.

—— (2006) 'Strategy Takes a Holiday: Fraenkel and Grofman on the Alternative Vote', *Comparative Political Studies*, 39(5), 652–62.

—— (2008) 'Conciliatory Institutions and Constitutional Processes in Post-Conflict States', *William and Mary Law Review*, 49(4), 1213–48.

Howe, S. (2000) *Ireland and Empire: Colonial Legacies in Irish History and Culture* (Oxford: Oxford University Press).

Humphrey, C. and J. Laidlaw (1994) *The Archetypal Actions of Ritual: A Theory of Ritual Illustrated by the Jain Rite of Worship* (Oxford: Oxford University Press).

Hutchinson, G. and T. Byrne (2007) 'Northern Ireland Economy: Latest Position and Future Prospects', *The Northern Ireland Economic Bulletin*, 1, 7–19.

Ignatieff, M. (1993) *Blood and Belonging: Journeys into the New Nationalism* (New York: Farrar, Straus, Giroux).

—— (1998) *The Warrior's Honour: Ethnic War and Modern Conscience* (New York: Metropolitan Books).

Institute of Irish Studies (2006) *St Patrick's Day Outdoor Event: 2006 Monitoring Report* (Belfast: Queen's University of Belfast).

Isaacs, H.R. (1977) *The Idols of the Tribe* (New York: Harper and Row).

Jacoby, T. (2008) *Understanding Conflict and Violence: Theoretical and Interdisciplinary Approaches* (London: Routledge).

Jarman, N. (1997) *Material Conflicts: Parades and Visual Displays in Northern Ireland* (Oxford: Berg).

Jarstad, A.K. (2008) 'Power Sharing: Former Enemies in Joint Government', in A.K. Jarstad and T.D. Sisk (eds) *From War to Democracy: Dilemmas of Peacebuilding* (Cambridge: Cambridge University Press), pp. 105–33.

Jasper, J.M. (1997) *The Art of Moral Protest: Culture, Biography, and Creativity in Social Movements* (Chicago, IL: University of Chicago Press).

Jay, M. (1999) 'Walter Benjamin and the Refusal to Mourn', in J. Winter and E. Sivan (eds) *War and Remembrance in the Twentieth Century* (Cambridge: Cambridge University Press), pp. 221–39.

Jenkins, R. (2004) *Social Identity* (London: Routledge).

Johnson, N. (2007) 'Foreword', in J. Beunderman and H. Lownsbrough (eds) *Equally Spaced: Public Space and Interaction Between Diverse Communities* (London: Demos), pp. 2–4.

Kaufman, S.J. (2001) *Modern Hatreds: The Symbolic Politics of Ethnic War* (Ithaca, NY and London: Cornell University Press).

Kautt, W.H. (1999) *The Anglo-Irish War, 1916–1921: A People's War* (Westport, CT: Praeger).

Kearney, R. (1997) *Postnationalist Ireland: Politics, Culture and Society* (London: Routledge).

Kerr, M. (2006) *Imposing Power-Sharing: Conflict and Coexistence in Northern Ireland and Lebanon* (Dublin: Irish Academic Press).

—— (2009) 'A Culture of Power Sharing', in R. Taylor (ed.) *Consociational Theory: McGarry and O'Leary and the Northern Ireland Conflict* (London: Routledge), pp. 206–20.

Kertzer, D. (1989) *Ritual, Politics and Power* (Yale, CT: Yale University Press).

Kilcullen, D. (2009) *The Accidental Guerilla: Fighting Small Wars in the Midst of a Big One* (London and New York: Hurst and Company).

Kitchin, R. (2002) 'Sexing the City: The Sexual Production of Non-heterosexual Space in Belfast, Manchester and San Francisco', *City*, 6(2), 205–18.

Kitchin, R. and K. Lysaght (2004) 'Discursive Formations of Sexual Citizenship: Sexuality, Religion and Nationalism in Belfast, Northern Ireland', *Gender, Place and Culture*, 11(1), 83–10.

Klein, N. (2008) *The Shock Doctrine* (London: Penguin).

Kukathas, C. (1995) 'Are There Any Cultural Rights?' in W. Kymlicka (ed.) *The Rights of Minority Cultures* (Oxford: Oxford University Press), pp. 228–56.

Kundnani, A. (2002) 'The Death of Multiculturalism', *Institute of Race Relations*, www.irr.org.uk/2002/april/ak000001.html, date accessed 25 October 2009.

Kymlicka, W. (1989) *Liberalism, Community and Culture* (Oxford: Clarendon Press).

Kymlicka, W. (1995) *Multicultural Citizenship: A Liberal Theory of Minority Rights* (Oxford: Oxford University Press).

—— (2001) *Politics in the Vernacular: Nationalism, Multiculturalism, Citizenship* (Oxford: Oxford University Press).

—— (2007) *Multicultural Odyssey* (Oxford: Oxford University Press).

Laitin, D.D. (2007) *Nations, States and Violence* (Oxford: Oxford University Press).

Lake, D.A. (1995) *Ethnic Conflict and International Intervention*, Institute on Global Conflict and Cooperation Policy Brief no. 3 (La Jolla, CA: University of California).

Lamont. M. and S. Aksartova (2002) 'Ordinary Cosmopolitanisms: Strategies for Bridging Racial Boundaries among Working-Class Men', *Theory, Culture & Society*, 19(4), 1–25.

Larner, W. (2003) 'Neoliberalism?' *Environment and Planning D: Society and Space*, 21(5), 509–12.

Lederach, J-P. (1997) *Building Peace: Sustainable Reconciliation in Divided Societies* (Washington DC: USIP Press).

Leersen, J. (2001) 'Monument and Trauma: Varieties of Remembrance', in I. McBride (ed.) *History and Memory in Modern Ireland* (Cambridge: Cambridge University Press), pp. 204–22.

Lefebvre, H. (1976) *The Survival of Capitalism* (New York: St Martin's Press).

—— (1978) *Les Contradictions de l'état Moderne, la Dialectique de l'état*, Vol. 4 of 4 (Paris: UGE, Collection 10/18).

—— (1991) *The Production of Space* (Oxford: Blackwell).

—— (1996) 'The Right to the City', in E. Kofman and E. Lebas (eds) *Writing on Cities* (Oxford: Blackwell), pp 63–181.

Lier, D.C. and K. Stokke (2006) 'Maximum Working Class Unity? Challenges to Local Social Movement Unionism in Cape Town', *Antipode*, 38(4), 802–24.

Lijphart, A. (1969) 'Consociational Democracy', *World Politics*, 21(2), 207–25.

—— (1975a) *The Politics of Accommodation: Pluralism and Democracy in the Netherlands* (Berkeley, CA: University of California Press).

—— (1975b) 'The Northern Ireland Problem: Cases, Theories, and Solutions', *British Journal of Political Science*, 5(1), 83–106.

—— (1977) *Democracy in Plural Societies: A Comparative Exploration* (New Haven, CT: Yale University Press).

—— (1985) *Power-sharing in South Africa* (Berkeley, CA: University of California Press).

—— (1999) *Patterns of Democracy: Government Forms and Performances in Thirty-Six Countries* (New Haven, CT and London: Yale University Press).

Little, A. (2004) *Democracy and Northern Ireland* (Basingstoke: Palgrave Macmillan).

Lownsbrough, H. and J. Beunderman (2007) *Equally Spaced: Public Space and Interaction between Diverse Communities* (London: Demos).

Lulofs, R.S. and D. D Cahn (2000) *Conflict: From Theory to Action* (Boston, MA: Allen and Bacon).

Lustick, I. (1979) 'Stability in Deeply Divided Countries: Consociationalism versus Control', *World Politics*, 31(3), 325–44.

—— (1993) *Unsettled States, Disputed Lands: Britain and Ireland, France and Algeria, Israel and the West Bank-Gaza* (Ithaca, NY: Cornell University Press).

Lustick, I. (1997) 'Lijphart, Lakatos and Consociationalism', *World Politics* 50(1), 88–117.

MacDonagh, O. (1983) *States of Mind: A Study of Anglo-Irish Conflict, 1780–1980* (London: Unwin Hyman).

Mac Ginty, R. (2009) 'The Liberal Peace at Home and Abroad: Northern Ireland and Liberal Internationalism', *British Journal of Politics and International Relations*, 11, 690–708.

Mac Ginty, R. and P. du Toit (2007) 'A Disparity of Esteem: Relative Group Status in Northern Ireland after the Belfast Agreement', *Political Psychology*, 28(1), 13–31.

Maginness, A. (2009) 'Agreement is Not a Conflict Substitution Process', *North Belfast News*, http://www.belfastmedia.com/columnists_article.php?ID=875, date accessed 2 December 2009.

Maskey, P. (2008) 'Private Members Business: Tourism', *Northern Ireland Assembly*, 19 February.

May, S. (1999) 'Critical Multiculturalism and Cultural Difference: Avoiding Essentialism', in S. May (ed.) *Critical Multiculturalism* (Abingdon: Routledge), pp. 11–42.

McAllister, I. (1979) 'The Modern Development of the Northern Ireland Party System', *Parliamentary Affairs*, 32(3), 279–316.

McBride, I. (2001) 'Introduction: Memory and National Identity in Modern Ireland', in I. McBride (ed.) *History and Memory in Modern Ireland* (Cambridge: Cambridge University Press), pp. 1–42.

McCann, E. (2006) 'What Wolfe Tone and the Ian Paisley of '69 Have in Common', *Belfast Telegraph*, 7 December.

—— (2009a) 'Why There Will be no Votes in Visteon at the Euro Polls Today', *Belfast Telegraph*, 4 June.

—— (2009b) 'How Fight against Water Charges could Erode Sectarian Rivalries', *Belfast Telegraph*, 10 September.

McCann, J. (2008) 'Private Members Business: Varney Review', *Northern Ireland Assembly*, 31 March.

McCausland, N. (2006) *Patrick: Apostle of Ulster* (Belfast: St. Patrick's Day Heritage Association).

—— (2007) 'Private Members Business: Republican Parade', *Northern Ireland Assembly*, 25 September.

McCormack, B. and Bridget (2000) *Perceptions of St Patrick in Eighteenth Century Ireland* (Dublin: Four Courts Press).

McCree, L. (2008) 'Private Members Business: Tourism', *Northern Ireland Assembly*, 19 February.

McCulloch, A. (2009) *Seeking Stability amid Deep Division: Consociationalism and Centripetalism in Comparative Perspective*, PhD thesis (Ontario: Queen's University Kingston).

McDonald, H. (2008) 'US Invests in Ulster Future after Old Foes Change Tune', *The Guardian*, 12 April.

McEvoy, J. (2008) *The Politics of Northern Ireland* (Edinburgh: Edinburgh University Press).

McGarry, J. (1998) ' "Orphans of Secession": National Pluralism in Secessionist Regions and Post-Secession States', in M. Moore (ed.) *National Self-Determination and Secession* (Oxford: Oxford University Press), pp. 215–32.

McGarry, J. and B. O'Leary (1995) *Explaining Northern Ireland: Broken Images* (London: Wiley-Blackwell).

—— (2004) *The Northern Ireland Conflict: Consociational Engagements* (Oxford: Oxford University Press).

—— (2006) 'Consociational Theory, Northern Ireland's Conflict, and its Agreement. Part 2: What Critics of Consociation Can Learn from Northern Ireland', *Government and Opposition*, 41(2), 249–77.

—— (2009) 'Power Shared after the Deaths of Thousands', in R. Taylor (ed.) *Consociational Theory: McGarry and O'Leary and the Northern Ireland Conflict* (London: Routledge), pp. 15–84.

McGhee, D. (2005) *Intolerant Britain? Hate, Citizenship and Difference* (Maidenhead: Open University Press).

—— (2008) *The End of Multiculturalism: Terrorism, Integration and Human Rights* (Maidenhead: Open University Press).

McGuinness, M. (2008) 'Executive Committee Business: Programme for Government and Investment Strategy for Northern Ireland', *Northern Ireland Assembly*, 28 January.

McIntosh, G. (2006) *Belfast City Hall: One Hundred Years* (Belfast: Blackstaff Press).

McKittrick, D. (2004) 'Ulster to Tackle Segregation with Mixed Housing Estates', *The Independent*, www.independent.co.uk/news/uk/this-britain/ulster-to-tackle-segregation-with-mixed-housing-estates-559075.html, date accessed 20 November.

McMahon, P.C. and J. Western (2009) 'The Death of Dayton: How to Stop Bosnia from Falling Apart', *Foreign Affairs*, online version, 88(5).

Melucci, A. (1996) *Challenging Codes: Collective Action in the Information Age* (Cambridge: Cambridge University Press).

Miller, D. (1999) 'Group Identities, National Identities and Democratic Politics', in J. Horton and S. Mendus (eds) *Toleration, Identity and Difference* (Basingstoke: Palgrave Macmillan), pp. 103–25.

Mitchell, A. (2010) *Lost in Transformation: Peace and Radical Change in Northern Ireland* (Basingstoke: Palgrave Macmillan)

Mitchell, C. and J. Tilley (2004) 'The Moral Minority: Evangelical Protestants in Northern Ireland and their Political Behaviour', *Political Studies*, 52(4), 585–602.

Mitchell, P. (2001) 'Transcending an Ethnic Party System? The Impact of a Consociational Governance on Electoral Dynamics and the Party System', in R. Wilford (ed.) *Aspects of the Belfast Agreement* (Oxford: Oxford University Press), pp. 28–48.

Mitchell, P. and G. Evans (2009) 'Ethnic Party Competition and the Dynamics of Power Sharing in Northern Ireland', in R. Taylor (ed.) *Consociational Theory: McGarry and O'Leary and the Northern Ireland Conflict* (London: Routledge), pp. 146–64.

Mitscherlich, A. and M. Mitscherlich (1975) *The Inability to Mourn: Principles of Collective Behaviour* (New York: Grove Press).

Modood, T. (2007) *Multiculturalism* (Cambridge: Polity).

Moloney, E. (2008) *Paisley: From Demagogue to Democrat?* (Dublin: Poolbeg).

Moriarty, G. (2009) 'Eames Says £12,000 is a Way to Tell Families "Sorry for your Troubles"', *Irish Times*, www.irishtimes.com/newspaper/ireland/2009/0129/1232923372178.html?via=rel, date accessed 25 October 2009.

Morrissey, M. and F. Gaffikin (2006) 'Planning for Peace in Contested Space', *International Journal of Urban and Regional Research*, 30(4), 873–93.

Morrissey, M. and M. Smyth (2002) *Northern Ireland and the Good Friday Agreement: Victims, Grievance and Blame* (London: Pluto).

Mouffe, C. (2000) *The Democratic Paradox* (London: Verso).

Moutray, S. (2007) 'Committee Business: Draft Programme for Government and the Draft Investment Strategy', *Northern Ireland Assembly*, 26 November.

Muldoon, O., N. McNamara, P. Devine and K. Trew (2008) 'Beyond Gross Divisions: National and Religious Identity Combinations', *ARK*, www.ark. ac.uk/publications/updates/update58.pdf, date accessed 25 October 2009.

Muller, J.Z. (2008) 'Us and Them: The Enduring Power of Ethnic Nationalism', *Foreign Affairs*, online edition, 87(2).

Murphy, D. (1978) *A Place Apart* (Penguin: London).

Murtagh, B. (2008) 'New Spaces and Old in "Post-conflict" Belfast', *Divided Cities/Contested States*, Working Chapter No. 5 (Belfast: Queen's University of Belfast).

Nagle, J. (2005a) ' "Everybody is Irish on St. Paddy's": Ambivalence and Alterity at London's St. Patrick's Day', *Identities: Global Studies in Power and Culture*, 12(4), 563–83.

—— (2005b) *A Research Report into People's Attitudes Into St Patrick's Day 2004* (Belfast: Institute of Irish Studies, Queen's University of Belfast).

—— (2006) 'Belfast St. Patrick's Day Celebrations and the Act of Forgetting: Trying to Create Cross-Community Identities', *Anthropology in Action*, 13(1–2), 32–43.

—— (2008a) 'Multiculturalism's Double-Bind: Creating Inclusivity, Difference and Cross-Community Alliances in the London-Irish', *Ethnicities*, 8(2), 177–98.

—— (2008b) 'From "Ban-the-Bomb" to "Ban-the-Increase": 1960s Street Politics in Pre-Civil Rights Belfast', *Irish Political Studies*, 23(1), 41–58.

—— (2008c) 'Challenging Ethno-National Division: New Social Movements in Belfast', *Social Movement Studies,* 7(3), 305–18.

—— (2009a) *Multiculturalism's Double-Bind: Creating Inclusivity, Cosmopolitanism and Difference* (Farnham and Burlington, VT: Ashgate Press).

—— (2009b) 'Sites of Social Centrality and Segregation: Lefebvre in Belfast, a "Divided City" ', *Antipode*, 41(2), 326–47.

—— (2009c) 'Belfast City Centre: From Ethnocracy to Liberal Multiculturalism?' *Political Geography*, 28(2), 132–41.

—— (2009d) 'The Ulster Unionist Victims' Movement: Political Opportunities and Cultural Framing', *Irish Journal of Sociology*, 17(1), 19–37.

—— (2009e) 'Potemkin Village: Neoliberalism and Peace-Building in Northern Ireland', *Ethnopolitics*, 8(2), 173–90.

Needham, R. (1998) *Battling for Peace* (Belfast: Blackstaff Press).

Neeson, S. (1999) 'Address to the Centre for Reform', *Alliance Party*, www.allianceparty.org/speeches/000034/address_to_the_centre_for_reform.html, date accessed 25 November 2009.

Neil, W.J.V. (2004) *Urban Planning and Cultural Identity* (London: Routledge).

Nic Craith, M. (2002). *Plural Identities, Singular Narratives: The Case of Northern Ireland* (New York: Berghahn).

NIO (1998) *Agreement Reached in the Multi-Party Negotiations* (Belfast: HMSO).

Nordlinger, E. (1972) *Conflict Regulation in Divided Societies* (Cambridge: Center for International Affairs, Harvard University, Occasional Papers in International Affairs).

Noutcheva, G., N. Tocci, B. Coppieters, T. Kovziridze, M. Emerson, M. Huysseune (2004) 'Europeanization and Secessionist Conflicts: Concepts and Theories', *Journal of Politics and Minority Issues in Europe*, 5(1), 1–35.

O'Dowd, J. (2008) 'Private Members Business: Private Finance Initiatives', *Northern Ireland Assembly*, 15 April.

O'Dowd, L. (2009) 'Debating the Agreement: Beyond a Communalist Dynamic', in R. Taylor (ed.) *Consociational Theory: McGarry and O'Leary and the Northern Ireland Conflict* (London: Routledge), pp. 295–308.

O'Dowd, L., B. Rolston and M. Tomlison (1980) *Northern Ireland: Between Civil Rights and War* (London: CSE Books).

O'Dowd, N. (2009) 'Bearing Pain Equally', *Irish Central*, www.irishcentral. com/news/col/NOdowd/Editorial-Bearing-Pain-Equally-Col3297.html, date accessed 25 October 2009.

OFMDFM (2003) *A Shared Future: Consultation Paper* (Belfast: Community Relations Unit, OFMDFM).

—— (2005) *A Shared Future* (Belfast: Community Relations Unit, OFMDFM).

—— (2007) *Building a Better Future: Draft Programme for Government 2008 -2011* (Belfast: OFMDFM).

O'Hearn, D. (2008) 'How Has Peace Changed the Northern Irish Political Economy?' *Ethnopolitics*, 7(1), 101–18.

O'Leary, B. (1999) 'The Nature of the British/Irish Agreement', *New Left Review*, 233, January/February, 66–96.

—— (2001) 'The Character of the 1998 Agreement: Results and Prospects', in R. Wilford (ed.) *Aspects of the Belfast Agreement* (Oxford: Oxford University Press), 49–83.

—— (2005) 'Debating Consociational Politics: Normative and Explanatory Arguments', in S. Noel Jr (ed.) *From Power Sharing to Democracy: Post-Conflict Institutions in Ethnically Divided Societies* (Montreal: McGill-Queen's Press), pp. 3–43.

—— (2006) 'Foreword: The Realism of Power-Sharing', in M. Kerr *Imposing Power-Sharing: Conflict and Coexistence in Northern Ireland and Lebanon* (Dublin: Irish Academic Press), pp. xvii-xxxv.

Olzak, S. (2006) *The Global Dynamics of Racial and Ethnic Mobilization* (Stanford, CA: Stanford University Press).

Ó Muilleoir, M. (1998). 'Glorious Green Gridlock', *Andersontown News*, 21 March.

O'Neill, S. (2001) 'Mutual Recognition and the Accommodation of National Diversity: Constitutional Justice in Northern Ireland', in A-G. Gagnon and J. Tully (eds) *Multinational Democracies* (Cambridge University Press), pp. 221–41.

—— (2007) 'Critical Theory and Ethno-National Conflict: Assessing Northern Ireland's Peace Process as a Model of Conflict Resolution', *Irish Political Studies*, 22(4), 411–31.

Parades Commission (2005) *Public Processions and Related Public Meetings* (Belfast: Parades Commission).

—— (2008) *Public Processions and Related Public Meetings* (Belfast: Parades Commission).

Parekh, B. (2006) *Rethinking Multiculturalism: Cultural Diversity and Political Theory* (Basingstoke: Palgrave Macmillan).

Portland Trust (2007) *Economics in Peacemaking: Lessons from Northern Ireland* (London: The Portland Trust).

Pollak, A. (1993) *A Citizens' Inquiry: The Opsahl Report on Northern Ireland* (Dublin: The Lilliput Press).

Porter, N. (1996) *Rethinking Unionism: An Alternative Vision for Northern Ireland* (Belfast: Blackstaff Press).

Purdie, B. (1990) *Politics in the Street: The Origins of the Civil Rights Movement in Northern Ireland* (Belfast: Blackstaff).

Purcell, M. (2003) 'Citizenship and the Right to the Global City: Reimagining the Capitalist World Order', *International Journal of Urban and Regional Research*, 27(3), 564–90.

Queerspace (2007) 'About', www.queerspace.org.uk, date accessed 12 May 2007.

Ramsay, R. (2009) *Ringside Seats: An Insider's View of the Crisis in Northern Ireland* (Dublin: Irish Academic Press).

Rawls, J. (1971) *A Theory of Justice* (Cambridge, MA: Harvard University Press).

Relatives for Justice (2009) 'About Us', www.relativesforjustice.com/, date accessed 25 October 2009.

Reilly, B. (2001) *Democracy in Divided Societies: Electoral Engineering for Conflict Management* (Cambridge: Cambridge University Press).

—— (2004) 'Electoral Systems and Conflict Management: Comparing STV and AV Systems', *ESRC Devolution & Constitutional Change Programme*, www.devolution.ac.uk/pdfdata/Reilly_Electoral_Systems_and_conflict_management.pdf, date accessed 29 October 2009.

Reilly, B. and A.W. Reynolds (1997) *The International IDEA Handbook of Electoral System Design* (Stockholm: IDEA).

Reiss, M.B. (2004) 'Northern Ireland: American Principles and the Peace Process', Speech by Mitchell B. Reiss to the National Committee on American Foreign Policy, 30 September 2004, www.state.gov/s/p/rem/36749.htm, date accessed 2 November 2005.

Richmond, O. and J. Franks (2009) 'Between Partition and Pluralism: The Bosnia Jigsaw and an "Ambivalent Peace"', *Journal of Southeast Europe and Black Sea Studies*, 9(1), 17–38.

Ricoeur, P. (1988) *Time and Narrative. Vol. 3* (Chicago and London: The University of Chicago Press).

Robertson, R. (1992) *Globalization: Social Theory and Global Culture* (London: Sage).

Rothchild, D. and P.G Roeder (2005a) 'Dilemmas of State-Building in Divided Societies', in P.G. Roeder and D. Rotchild (eds) *Sustainable Peace: Power and Democracy After Civil Wars* (Ithaca, NY and London: Cornell University Press), pp. 1–25.

—— (2005b) 'Power Sharing as an Impediment to Peace and Democracy', in P.G. Roeder and D. Rotchild (eds) *Sustainable Peace: Power and Democracy After Civil Wars* (Ithaca, NY and London: Cornell University Press), pp. 29–50.

Rose, G. (1993) *Feminism and Geography* (Oxford: Polity).

Rose, R. (1971) *Governing Without Consensus: An Irish Perspective* (London: Faber and Faber).

Ross, M.H. (2007) *Cultural Contestation in Ethnic Conflict* (Cambridge: Cambridge University Press).

Ruane, J. and J. Todd (1996) *The Dynamics of Conflict in Northern Ireland: Power, Conflict, and Emancipation* (Cambridge: Cambridge University Press).

—— (2003) (eds) *After the Good Friday Agreement: Analysing Political Change in Northern Ireland* (Dublin: University College Dublin Press).

RTE (2009) 'Clinton Uses NI as Example of Resolution', www.rte.ie/news/2009/0924/north.html, date accessed 25 October 2009.

Ruddock, A. (2006) 'Northern Ireland – Where is the Bright New Future?' *Management Today*, www.managementtoday.co.uk/news/542849/, date accessed 25October 2009.

Sack, R. (1986) *Human Territoriality: Its Theory and History* (Cambridge: Cambridge University Press).

Santino, J. (2001) *Signs of War and Peace: Social Conflict and the use of Public Symbols in Northern Ireland* (Basingstoke: Palgrave Macmillan).

Sartori, G. (1997) *Comparative Constitutional Engineering: An Inquiry into Structures, Incentives and Outcomes* (Basingstoke: Palgrave Macmillan).

Sassen, S. (2001) *The Global City: New York, London, Tokyo* (Princeton, NJ: Princeton University Press).

Schubotz, D. and G. Robinson (2006) 'Cross-Community Integration and Mixing: Does it Make a Difference?' *ARK Research Update*, 43, www.ark.ac.uk/publications/updates/update43.pdf, date accessed 25 October 2009.

Sell, L. (2002) *Slobodan Milosevic and the Destruction of Yugoslavia* (Durham, NC: Duke University Press).

Sennett, R. (2005) 'Bulletin 1', *Urban Age*, Summer, 1–3.

Sewell, William, H., Jr (2001) 'Space in Contentious Politics', in R.R. Aminzade (ed.) *Silence and Voice in the Study of Contentious Politics* (Cambridge: Cambridge University Press), pp. 51–81.

Sharrock, D. (2007) 'Why Even Paisley May Favour a Ride on the Celtic Tiger', *Times Online*, www.timesonline.co.uk/tol/news/politics/article1577342.ece?print=yes&randnum=1151003209000, date accessed 25 October 2009.

Shills, E. (1957) 'Primordial, Personal, Sacred and Civil Ties: Some Particular Observations on the Relationships of Sociological Research and Theory', *The British Journal of Sociology*, 8(2), 130–45.

Shirlow, P. (2003) ' "Who Fears to Speak": Fear, Mobility and Ethno-Sectarianism in the Two "Ardoynes" ', *Ethnopolitics*, (3), 76–92.

(2006) 'Belfast: The "Post-Conflict" City', *Space and Polity*, 10(2), 99–107.

Shirlow, P. and B. Murtagh (2006) *Belfast: Segregation, Violence and the City* (London: Pluto Press).

Silber, L. and A. Little (1995) *The Death of Yugoslavia* (London: Penguin BBC).

Sinn Féin (1979) *Éire Nua: The Sinn Féin Policy. The Social, Economic and Political Dimensions* (Dublin: Sinn Féin).

—— (2008) 'Private Finance Initiative', www.sinnfein.ie/policies/document/151, date accessed 25 October 2009.

—— (2009) *Sinn Féin's Response to the Consultation Document 'A Shared Future'* (Belfast: Sinn Féin).

Sisk, T.D. (1995) *Democratization in South Africa: The Elusive Social Contract* (Princeton, NJ: Princeton University Press).

Smith, A.D. (1991) *National Identity* (London: Penguin).

(1999) *Myths and Memories of the* Nation (Oxford: Oxford University Press).

Smith, M.L.R. (1999) 'The Intellectual Internment of a Conflict: The Forgotten War in Northern Ireland', *International Affairs*, 75(1), 77–97.

Smith, N. (2002) 'New Globalism, New Urbanism: Gentrification as Global Urban Strategy', *Antipode*, 34(3), 427–50.

Smithey, L.A. (2009) 'Conflict Transformation, Cultural Innovation, and Loyalist Identity in Northern Ireland', in M. Ross (ed.) *Culture and Belonging in Divided Societies: Contestation and Symbolic Landscapes* (Philadelphia, PA: University of Pennsylvania Press), pp. 85–106.

Smyth, M. (1998) 'Remembering in Northern Ireland: Victims, Perpetrators and Hierarchies of Pain and Responsibility', in B. Hamber (ed.) *Past Imperfect: Dealing with the Past in Northern Ireland and Societies in Transition* (Derry: INCORE), pp. 31–49.

Socialist Environmental Alliance (2005) 'Election Flyer', socialistenvironmenta-lalliance.org/pdfs/westminsterleaflet.pdf, date accessed 25 October.

Stansfield, G. (2006) 'Divide and Heal', *Prospect*, 122, www.prospectmagazine. co.uk/2006/05/divideandheal/, date accessed 25 October 2009.

Strategic Investment Board (2009) www.sibni.org/, accessed 25 October 2009.

Sullivan, R. (1993) 'Eire Rally Link Claim', *Belfast Newsletter*, 10 August.

Swyngedouw, E. (1996) 'Reconstructing Citizenship, the Re-Scaling of the State and the New Authoritarianism: Closing the Belgian Mines', *Urban Studies*, 33(8), 1499–521.

Taylor, C. (1994) 'The Politics of Recognition', in C. Taylor (ed.) *Multiculturalism: Examining the Politics of Recognition* (Princeton, NJ: Princeton University Press), pp. 25–75.

Taylor, R. (1994) 'A Consociational Path to Peace in Northern Ireland and South Africa?', in A. Guelke (ed.) *New Perspectives on the Northern Ireland Conflict* (Aldershot: Avebury), pp. 161–74.

—— (2001) 'Consociation or Social Transformation?' in J. McGarry (ed.) *Northern Ireland and the Divided World: Post-Agreement Northern Ireland in Comparative Perspective* (Oxford: Oxford University Press), pp. 36–52.

—— (2006) 'The Belfast Agreement and the Politics of Consociationalism', *The Political Quarterly*, 77(2), 217–26.

—— (2008) 'The Belfast Agreement and the Limits of Consociationalism', in C. Farrington (ed.) *Global Change, Civil Society and the Northern Ireland Peace Process* (Basingstoke: Palgrave Macmillan), pp. 183–98.

—— (2009a) 'Introduction: The Promise of Consociational Theory', in R. Taylor (ed.) *Consociational Theory: McGarry and O'Leary and the Northern Ireland Conflict* (London: Routledge), pp. 1–12.

—— (2009b) 'The Injustice of a Consociational Solution to the Northern Ireland Problem', in R. Taylor (ed.) *Consociational Theory: McGarry and O'Leary and the Northern Ireland Conflict* (London: Routledge), pp. 309–30.

Thompson, J.L.P. (1989) 'Deprivation and Political Violence in Northern Ireland, 1922–85: A Time-Series Analysis', *Journal of Conflict Resolution*, 33(4), 376–99.

Tilly, C. (2004) *Social Movements, 1768–2004* (Boulder, CO: Paradigm Publishers).

Titanic Quarter (2009) 'About TQ', www.titanic-quarter.com/about.php?ID=3, accessed 25 October 2009.

Tonge, J. (2004) *The New Northern Irish Politics* (Basingstoke: Palgrave Macmillan).

—— (2006) 'Sinn Féin and the "New Republicanism"' in Belfast', *Space and Polity*, 10(2), 135–47.

—— (2009) 'From Conflict to Communal Politics: The Politics of Peace', in C. Coulter and M. Murray (eds) *Northern Ireland After the Troubles: A Society in Transition* (Manchester: Manchester University Press).

Trimble, D. (1989) 'David Trimble', in M. Crozier (ed.) *Cultural Traditions in Northern Ireland* (Belfast: Institute of Irish Studies), pp. 45.

Tully, J. (1995) *Strange Multiplicity: Constitutionalism in an Age of Diversity* (Cambridge: Cambridge University Press).

Ulster Nation (2007) 'Ulster Nation: A Third Way for Ulster', www.ulsternation.org.uk/, date accessed October 2009.

Van Den Berghe, P.L. (1981) *The Ethnic Phenomenon* (New York: Elsevier).

Van Evera, S. (2001) 'Primordialism Lives!', *APSA-CP: Newsletter of the Organized Section in Comparative Politics of the American Political Science Association*, 12(1), 20–22.

Varshney, A. (2002) *Ethnic Conflict and Civic Life* (New Haven, CT and London: Yale).

Vertovec, S. and R. Cohen (2002) 'Introduction: Conceiving Cosmopolitanism', in S. Vertovec and R. Cohen (eds) *Conceiving Cosmopolitanism: Theory, Context, and Practice* (Oxford: Oxford University Press), pp. 1–22.

Viggiani, E. (2006) 'Public Forms of Memorialisation to the Victims of the Northern Irish "Troubles" in the City of Belfast', *CAIN*, http://cain.ulst.ac.uk/viggiani/introduction.htm, date accessed 25 October.

Volkan, V. (1997) *Blood Lines: From Ethnic Pride to Ethnic Terrorism* (New York: Farrar, Straus and Giroux).

Walker, B. (1996) *Dancing to History's Tune: History, Myth and Politics in Ireland* (Belfast: Institute of Irish Studies).

Walter, B.F. (2002) *Committing to Peace: The Successful Settlement of Civil Wars* (Princeton, NJ: Princeton University Press).

Walzer, M. (1967) 'On the Role of Symbolism in Political Thought', *Political Science Quarterly*, 82(2), 191–205.

Weir, M. (2007) 'Private Members Business: Tax Varying Powers', *Northern Ireland Assembly*, 10 September.

West Tyrone Voice (2008) 'Submission to the Consultative Group on the Past' (West Tyrone: West Tyrone Voice).

Whitehouse, H. (2004) *Modes of Religiosity: A Cognitive Theory of Religious Transmission* (Walnut Creek, CA: Altamira).

Whyte, J. (1981) 'Why is the Northern Ireland Problem so Intractable?' *Parliamentary Affairs*, XXXIV, 422–35.

—— (1990) *Interpreting Northern Ireland* (Oxford: Clarendon Press).

Wilford, R. (1992) 'Inverting Consociationalism? Policy, Pluralism and the Post-Modern' in B. Hadfield (ed.) *Northern Ireland: Politics & the Constitution* (Buckingham: Open University Press), pp. 29–46.

Wilford, R. (2001) 'The Assembly', in R. Wilson (ed.) *Agreeing to Disagree? A Guide to the Northern Ireland Assembly* (Norwich: The Stationery Office), pp.156–65.

Wilford, R. and R. Wilson (2006) *The Trouble with Northern Ireland* (Belfast: Democratic Dialogue).

—— (2008) *Northern Ireland Devolution Monitoring Report: January 2008* (Belfast: Queen's University of Belfast).

Wilson, A. (1993) 'Which Equality? Toleration, Difference or Respect', in J. Bristow and A. Wilson (eds) *Activating Theory: Lesbian, Gay and Bisexual Politics* (London: Lawrence and Wishart), pp. 171–89.

Wilson, R. (2005) 'Northern Ireland's Peace by Peace', *openDemocracy*, www. opendemocracy.net/democracy-protest/ulster_2915.jsp, date accessed 25 October 2009.

—— (2009a) 'Politicians Still Lacking Policy that can Unite Divided Society', *Belfast Telegraph*, www.belfasttelegraph.co.uk/opinion/politicians-still-lacking-policy-that-can-unite-a-divided-society-14523219.html, date accessed 25 October 2009.

—— (2009b) 'From Consociationalism to Interculturalism', in R. Taylor (ed.) *Consociational Theory: McGarry and O'Leary and the Northern Ireland Conflict* (London: Routledge), pp. 221–36.

—— (2009c) 'Northern Ireland: Guns, Words and Publics', *openDemocracy*, www. opendemocracy.net/article/northern-ireland-guns-words-and-publics, date accessed 25 October 2009.

Wilson, R. and R. Wilford (2003) *Northern Ireland: A Route to Stability* (Swindon: ESRC).

Winter, J. (1995) *Sites of Memory, Sites of Mourning: The Great War in European Cultural History* (Cambridge University Press: Cambridge).

Winter, J. and E. Sivan (1999) 'Setting the Framework', in J. Winter and E. Sivan (eds) *War and Remembrance in the Twentieth Century* (Cambridge: Cambridge University Press), pp. 6–39.

Wolf, W. (2008) 'The limits of Liberalization', *Business Spectator*, 27 March, pp. 27–28.

Wolff, S. (2006) *Ethnic Conflict: A Global Perspective* (Oxford: Oxford University Press).

Wright, F. (1988) *Northern Ireland: A Comparative Analysis* (Dublin: Gill and Macmillan).

Yiftachel, O. and A. Ghanem (2004) 'Understanding "Ethnocratic" Regimes: The Politics of Seizing Contested Territories', *Political Geography*, 23(6), 647–76.

Young, A. (1995) *The Harmony of Illusions: Inventing Post-Traumatic Stress Disorder* (Princeton, NJ: Princeton University Press).

Younge, G. (2004) 'A Hierarchy of Suffering', *The Guardian*, 20 September.

Index